M000211624

Building Firewalls

with

OpenBSD and PF

Coming soon from devGuide.net

The OpenBSD Gazetteer by Jacek Artymiak
Building Virtual Private Networks with FreeBSD, NetBSD, OpenBSD,
Linux, Apple Mac OS X, and Microsoft Windows by Jacek Artymiak
The FreeBSD Gazetteer by Jacek Artymiak
The NetBSD Gazetteer by Jacek Artymiak
Scripting Caligari trueSpace with Python by Jacek Artymiak
Scripting Adobe Photoshop with JavaScript by Jacek Artymiak

You will find more information under this address:

http://www.devguide.net

Building Firewalls with OpenBSD and PF

Jacek Artymiak

Second Edition

Lublin

Building Firewalls with OpenBSD and PF, second edition
by Jacek Artymiak

Published by:
devGuide.net Jacek Artymiak

email: *openbsdpf-ed-02@devguide.net*
www: *http://www.devguide.net*

Copyright © 2003 Jacek Artymiak

All rights reserved. No part of this pubication may be reproduced, stored in a retrieval system, or transmitted, in any form or by any means, electronic, mechanical, photocopying, recording, or otherwise, without the prior consent of the publisher.

First edition 2003
Second edition 2003

Printed in the United States of America and the United Kingdom

03   10 9 8 7 6 5 4 3 2

ISBN: 83-916651-1-9

The author and the publisher disclaim any and all liability for the use of information and programs contained in this book.

All trademarks mentioned in this book are the sole property of their owners.

To Gosia

Table of Contents

Why I Wrote This Book

When I first started using OpenBSD sometime in 1999, it certainly wasn't because I wanted to write a book about it. All I needed was a stable server for my home network, something I could configure and forget about. I tried all obvious suspects: FreeBSD, NetBSD, OpenBSD, and four or five different Linux distributions, My choice was OpenBSD, because it installed without problems, was easy to configure, and did not have the infuriating problems with NFS that plagued me on Linux at that time. FreeBSD and NetBSD lost their race at the installation stage, after they failed to recognize some pieces of the hardware I was using. It wasn't a high-tech lab test, I just needed a stable server. OpenBSD behaved well, did not require much of my attention and was doing its job.

Then, sometime in 2000, I was asked to help secure a network, which was coming under an increasingly heavy barrage of attacks and was getting broken into approximately twice a month. The first thing we did was secure the hosts exposed to the outside world as much as the operating system allowed, but the rest of the job was going to be the responsibility of a firewall. I did some research and found out that many people recommended OpenBSD as the best solution for this job. Knowing it doesn't cost a penny to install, I quickly put OpenBSD on four firewall hosts guarding points of contact with the outside world and watched them in action. Attacks didn't stop, but none of them was successful. OpenBSD has earned its keep. And that's how it's been for the last three years.

Of course, OpenBSD is only one of many components of the security setup used at that site, but it is proving to be the most significant one. Over the last three years, that network has undergone significant changes in hardware and software, many security solutions were tried and discarded, yet Open-BSD is still running those four firewalls as well as some web servers, mail servers, DNS, DHCP, and NIDS.

One of my jobs is freelance technical writing, so it wasn't long before I got an idea that it might be useful to help promote the tools I use and like. I quickly wrote an article about installing and configuring OpenBSD and Daren Reed's *ipfilter*, the firewall that shipped with OpenBSD before May 2001. The article was published in February 2002 on the O'Reilly & Associates Network's ONLamp.com and became the first in the series now known under the name of *Securing Small Networks with OpenBSD*, available at:

http://www.onlamp.com/pub/ct/58

The word 'small' used in the title of that series is a little misleading, because OpenBSD is capable of meeting the demands of all kinds of networks, large and small. It was used because I wanted to help administrators of small and underfunded networks secure their installations with Open-BSD. Some of that material made its way into this book.

When I wrote my first article for ONLamp.com in late 2001, I only wanted to write a tutorial that would help others protect their networks with OpenBSD and *ipfilter*. It was meant to be something to help people get *ipfilter* working in a relatively short time. There were no plans for additional articles. I foolishly assumed that it would be all that was needed. Unfortunately for me, by the time that first article was published, the OpenBSD project abandoned *ipfilter* for Daniel Hartmeier's *pf*. I got a lot of mail telling me in more or less civilized ways that my article was a worthless bag of bits. So, I quickly wrote an update, which was promptly published on ONLamp.com.

After ONLamp.com published the second article, I received a lot of positive feedback, bug reports, and suggestions that I should write a book about OpenBSD. To tell the truth, I did not want to write a book on that subject, because I knew that the market was too small to be considered profitable by trade computer book publishers. But, as the number of requests for the book grew, I sat down and wrote a proposal, which I later submitted to a few good publishers. My proposal was turned down by everyone, which convinced me that a book on OpenBSD would not sell. Of course, the real reason could just as well be the weaknesses in my proposal. Either way, I was not interested in pursuing this further and put the whole thing on hold.

Then, in late 2002, I received an email message from a venerable academic publisher interested in publishing a book about OpenBSD. Unfortunately, we couldn't agree on the terms of the contract. By the time our talks broke down, I had a sizeable part of the manuscript ready for editing. I could forget it and move to other projects, but I felt it was too good to be trashed. I decided to risk it and announced *The OpenBSD Gazetteer*. As I was working towards the end of the manuscript, I could see that it was becoming too long for a single book. I had to split it into two books. *Building Firewalls with OpenBSD and PF* is the first book, *The OpenBSD Gazetteer* is the second. That way I can make sure that both books are not overly expensive, that they are delivered on time, and that they can be quickly updated.

The first edition of *Building Firewalls with OpenBSD and PF* was so popular that I had to quickly start work on the second edition, which would cover the changes made to the OpenBSD operating system and *pf* between releases 3.3 and 3.4. I also wanted to respond to the requests and suggestions made by the readers of the first edition. I hope that this new edition lives up to your expectations.

0.1 Acknowledgments

This book wouldn't exist if I had not met many great people who continue to support and encourage me along the way. First and foremost I wish to thank the OpenBSD user community for their support, and for challenging me with interesting questions, suggestions, and critique. Without them swamping me with requests to write a book about OpenBSD, this little tome would not be in your hands today. One of the most active members of the OpenBSD community supporting my efforts is Leonard Jacobs, who devoted a lot of his precious time to help me make this edition better than the first one. Thank you, Leonard!

Whenever I publish something on the Internet, I usually do it with the help of these great people: Chris Coleman (DaemonNews), chromatic (O'Reilly Networks), Tim O'Reilly (O'Reilly & Associates), Jose Nazario (OpenBSD Journal), and editors at various BSD news sites and forums. Thank you!

My special thanks must go to Theo de Raadt, Daniel Hartmeier, Artur Grabowski, Jason L. Wright, Miod Vallat, Dale Rahn, Nick Holland, Wim

Vandeputte (kd85.com), Austin Hook (The Computer Shop of Calgary), and other OpenBSD developers, evangelists and supporters, without whose hard work we wouldn't be able to enjoy OpenBSD, OpenSSH, and *pf*.

I also wish to thank doctors Joanna Markiewicz and Witalis Misiewicz who keep their watchful eyes on my health and make sure I don't dump core before my time.

Last, but not least I want to thank my dear wife, Malgosia, who patiently puts up with my non-standard working hours, deadlines that move everything else aside, and the growing farm of computer hardware. Without her support and understanding I'd never have written this book.

Jacek Artymiak
Lublin, Poland
October 2003

## Chapter 1

Introduction

What this book is about. What information you'll find on its pages. How to keep in touch with the author of this book, the developer of pf, *and the OpenBSD community.*

This book explains how to build, configure, and manage IP packet firewalls using commodity hardware, the OpenBSD operating system, and Daniel Hartmeier's *pf* packet filter. Its intended audience are network and security administration professionals and the users of the OpenBSD operating system. The material presented in this book requires basic knowledge of TCP/IP networking and Unix. Readers unfamiliar with either or both of these topics ought to consult [Stevens 1994], [Wright, Stevens 1994], [Stevens 1994a], and [Frisch 2002]. Links to online bookstores selling these and other titles mentioned in this book can be found at the following address:

http://www.devguide.net/books/openbsdfw-02-ed/

1.1 Why Do We Need to Secure Our Networks

The reasons for securing computers and networks against attacks are in many ways similar to the reasons for securing ourselves and our property in the real world. The likely suspects, the problems they cause, and the protection mechanisms we use to defend ourselves are often quite alike, it doesn't matter that we are dealing with 1s and 0s. In an ideal world, there would be no need for fences, gates, or locks, because the good side of the human nature and the laws of our society would be enough to protect ourselves, our privacy, and our property.

Unfortunately, we are not living in such a world nor we are likely to create one on this planet or anywhere else, at least not anytime soon. The fact that a small, but nevertheless noticeable through their actions, percentage of this world's population breaks laws, steals our belongings, trespasses on our property, and invades our privacy means that we must protect ourselves, our loved ones, and all that we hold valuable. And so we raise fences, buy padlocks, fit our homes and business premises with burglar alarms, and pay bodyguards to ensure our safety, or to at least make us feel a little safer.

Things are no different in the networked world. Just like the real world around us, the Internet gives people with malicious intent plenty of opportunities to perform their questionable activities. Even though a vast majority of the people and the companies connected to the Internet mean no harm to anyone and just want to get on with their business, there are people who take a certain kind of pride in wreaking havoc online, stealing information or disrupting network services. Some even turned it into a way to make a living. They can spy on our communications, break into computers and networks, block connections between machines, destroy data, falsify records, and bring whole systems to a halt. Their motives are almost always the same: money, the need to have something to brag about, the attraction of a difficult challenge, ideology, revenge, or plain curiosity.

Modern network technology gives attackers many ways to amplify the power of their actions by using numerous compromised low-profile hosts to launch attacks against selected high-profile sites. Equipped with automated cracking tools and access to hundreds of compromised hosts, a single person can potentially cause damage on a scale comparable to an attack on a nuclear power plant or an oil refinery. And just as attacks on oil refineries can create shortages of oil and raise costs of transport, attacks against certain hosts on the Internet can slow down or cut off large portions of the Internet damaging sales, communications or, in some cases, endangering human lives. Of course, not all attacks are visible and discussed on CNN. Instead of destroying things, someone may prefer to break into a network and listen to communications, copy classified files, or change essential records. Such covert operations can result in more damage than a mass-scale attack on the Internet infrastructure. They are also more profitable to an attacker than the 5 minutes of fame he (or she) gets on the global news networks.

Even though many corporate, university, or home networks can have little end value for an attacker, their sole ability to send packets on the Internet can be worth a lot to someone who wants to break into them and use compromised hosts to launch an escalated Distributed Denial of Service (DDoS) attack against other, more valuable hosts. Owners of computers and networks connected to the Internet have a responsibility to keep their network protected against external and internal attacks. If they don't take necessary precautions, they could be held responsible for damage done to somebody else's site. Taking all possible preventive steps is no longer an option, but an obligation, which quite likely will soon be enforced by laws declared by parliaments and governments around the world.

As usual, the best way to fight such attacks is through prevention. To avoid problems and to keep the bad guys out, many organizations invest large sums of money into security software, hardware, training, and auditing. This book shows how to save some of that cash using firewalls built with top quality free open source security software.

1.2 Why Do We Need Firewalls

Firewalls are one of the most essential tools in the security professionals' toolbox. Due to the nature of the work they perform, firewalls are the first line of defense against external attacks. They consist of a mixture of hardware and software placed at strategic points on the network, usually somewhere near the points of contact with other networks. Their basic purpose is to look at packets passing through them and letting those packets pass or blocking them according to the packet filtering policy implemented in the form of a list of packet filtering rules.

Over the last few years, firewalls acquired additional functionality and can perform much more than just plain packet filtering. Packet normalization, Network Address Translation (NAT), stateful filtering, packet logging, support for spam filters, dynamic rulesets, and other additional advanced functionality are now standard on many firewall products.

Although they are no silver bullet that magically fixes all problems, their ability to scrutinize, redirect, modify, and log packets make firewalls an ideal network security, audit, forensic, as well as management tool.

1.3 Why Open Source Software

Like almost all things in life, good security costs money. It has to be that way, because there are simply not enough skilled security specialists to look after all networks that need their attention. Organizations with deep pockets can afford to employ well-paid professional staff who provide better protection for their networks than organizations with tiny or non-existent IT security budgets. This is not always the case, but exceptions to this rule should not be used to justify cuts in spending on IT security.

An unfortunate result of low supply and high demand is the migration of highly skilled personnel to clients who can meet their salary requirements. This leaves a lot of small and underfunded networks in the hands of less experienced administrators, who might not know how to design, configure, and monitor these networks' safety mechanisms leaving them vulnerable to attacks from unscrupulous people looking for inside information, free warez storage, zombie hosts for DDoS attacks, or systems they can simply make inoperable for the sheer fun of doing it.

But even a fat wad of cash does not always solve all problems for large companies. Restricted by commercial licenses and limited by the size of their security budgets, even the giants of IT often cannot afford as high levels of protection as they would like to have. Fortunately, many good security products are now available for free and can be implemented using commodity hardware components and commodity free open source software (the word *free* is important here, as not all open source software is free of licensing traps).

Using free open source software makes more sense today than ever, not only because there are plenty of high-quality open source IT security tools, but because those who learn them now, will be sought after tomorrow. The world is entering the era of software commoditization. It will bring the cost of purchase of many tools to $0.00 and raise the salaries of people who know how to use these tools. The funds saved in that way can be moved to training, purchases of specialist books (like this one), and better hardware, which too can be built using commodity, off-the-shelf components, instead of expensive commercial black boxes that often run modified versions of free software anyway.

With so much high-quality free open source software available now and even more coming in the future, the race between commercial and free open source firewall software will soon be over, just as it happened in the fields of HTTP servers (Apache), electronic mail distribution (sendmail, postfix, qmail, and zmailer), server-side scripting (PHP, Perl, Python, Tcl), databases (MySQL, PostgreSQL), and many other segments of the market.

As Christopher Koch wrote in his recent CIO magazine article, 'Any CIO without an open source strategy in 2003 will be paying too much for IT in 2004.' The full text of his article is available at the following address:

http://www.cio.com/archive/031503/opensource.html

Open source has another advantage: it levels the playing field, because everybody is using the same tools, and in the case of security, it gives everyone the same high level of protection. Although it might seem to be against the interests of the big players, giving the same tools to the little guys is actually good for both sides. It makes sense when you think about it on a different level of selfishness. When the small guys can deploy top-quality software to better protect their networks they will be less likely used as launch pads for attacks against the rich guys' networks.

1.4 Why OpenBSD and pf

Why should you use OpenBSD and *pf* to protect your network? There are many reasons legal, financial, and technical.

As for the technical reasons, the first one is quite obvious; if you want to use Daniel Hartmeier's *pf* packet filter, you need to install OpenBSD, because it is closely integrated with that particular operating system. This will soon cease to be the only option, as ports to FreeBSD and NetBSD are already in the works, though it will be some time before they are fully integrated with those other operating systems.

The next technical reason is the maturity of the BSD code base. There's over 25 years of development stored in that code since BSD was born in 1976. That's a lot of experience in operating systems design stored in those CVS archive, all available for free. As the BSD source code matures, it becomes more stable thanks to the system development model, which for all free BSD systems is less dynamic than the development model of other free operating system like Linux. You always know who is responsible for what, and new code, although always welcome, is never accepted into the CVS tree without thorough review.

Then, there is the obsession with security that the OpenBSD team is famous for. Every new release of OpenBSD, published at regular 6-month interval, delivers important security enhancements, which later find their way into other operating systems. The source code undergoes periodic audits and the project constantly develops and integrates new security and cryptography tools, often well ahead of other free and commercial operating system developers. For example, the OpenBSD team was the first to ship a working implementation of IPSec. Recent additions of propolice, systrace, W^X, and a non-executable stack greatly improve the overall security of the system. The coming full PROT_ implementation will make it even more secure. If you are not sure OpenBSD is a good choice, just for the fun of watching their reactions, ask your operating system vendor's representatives about these features.

The OpenBSD project is also closely affiliated with the OpenSSH project, which develops a free and open source implementation of the SSH1 and SSH2 protocols that you may have already used. While many other free and commercial operating systems often include similar security tools, the ease of use, the compactness, and the close integration of every component make OpenBSD a much better choice for security applications than Free-BSD, NetBSD, or Linux.

As for the *pf* packet filter, it is a modern, solid piece of security software that grows in functionality every month. It offers many features unavailable on commercial firewalls. IPv4 and IPv6 packet filtering, NAT, stateful filtering, packet normalization, dynamic rulesets, bandwidth shaping (integrated ALTQ), load balancing, packet logging, spam filtering, and support for user authentication on the firewall are only a few items on the list of its standard features. If there is something one would want a firewall to do, it is probably already implemented in *pf*, or it will be there in the next release. Over the last two years, *pf* has earned excellent reputation for its ease of administration, richness of options, stability, and performance. And, since *pf* is running on top of a secure operating system, you can create your own custom solutions not possible with commercial hardware or software firewalls. You can be sure that the next months and years will bring many useful add-ons for *pf*.

Another good reason for choosing OpenBSD and *pf* is the freedom to configure them as you like. You are no longer restricted by limited functionality, complex licensing schemes, or fees. No less useful will be the availability of OpenBSD and *pf* for many hardware platforms, including i386, Sparc, Sparc Ultra, Alpha, and others. And, if you would like to have OpenBSD or *pf* ported to another hardware platform, all you have to do is download the code and get to work, or hire the OpenBSD developers to do it for you. (It's a win-win situation. You will get they tools you want, and the OpenBSD developers will get funds they need to keep on doing their great work for the world wide community.)

As for the legal reasons for using OpenBSD and *pf*, you should read the BSD license. Unlike 99.999% of licenses, this one is a pleasure to read. It makes OpenBSD truly free software, because it is not yet another GPL-style viral licensing, but a business-friendly set of rules that anyone can understand in 15 seconds. (This is not to say that GPL is useless, but some businesses cannot use software licensed under its terms.)

The following is not intended as a legal advice, but if you need to convince your boss or company lawyer to use OpenBSD, try to bring to their attention the fact that the BSD license lets anyone use the sources of the software licensed under its terms for any purpose, including making money with it. Such code can be merged with software licensed under any terms, free or commercial, as long as you acknowledge the copyright of the author(s) who created that code. It means that you can safely integrate OpenBSD and *pf* into your existing network without fear of violating some obscure licensing term. You can even package OpenBSD and *pf* and sell it or embed it in your expensive black box hardware. Also, because Open-BSD and *pf* are free (as in freedom *and* as in beer), you can install and use them on as many machines as you like. This will surely impress your accountants, lawyers, and bank managers.

1.5 Cryptography and Law

OpenBSD ships with strong free open source cryptographic software. Before you download or export it in any way, always check appropriate local and foreign cryptographic laws. You can start your search with the *Crypto Law Survey* page maintained by Bert Jaap-Koops:

http://rechten.kub.nl/koops/cryptolaw/   *(Crypto Law Survey)*

When in any doubt, *always* consult lawyers with expertise in crypto import/export laws. Some countries consider cryptography a weapon and punish people and companies using it as if they were smuggling weapons, when it is done without the approval of appropriate bodies.

1.6 How This Book Is Organized

The main text of this book is divided into sixteen chapters and four appendices.

Chapter 1, *Introduction* is this introduction, which tries to explain why we need to protect the computers and the networks we're in charge of, why we should use OpenBSD and *pf*, and how to keep in touch with the OpenBSD project, developers, and the author of this book.

Chapter 2, *Firewall Designs* presents popular firewall configurations and discusses their uses, pros and cons. Every design is illustrated with a diagram, and some less obvious designs are discussed as well.

Chapter 3, *Installing OpenBSD* discusses basic hardware and software requirements that must be met to let OpenBSD and *pf* do their job. Also discussed are factors that affect firewall performance and ways to improve it.

Chapter 4, *Configuring OpenBSD* explains how to configure IP networking, routing, kernel, and system startup scripts. The readers will also learn about user management, system hardening, patching, and installing additional software,

Chapter 5, */etc/pf.conf* introduces the reader to the structure of the *pf* configuration file, *pf.conf* and explains the use of macros in *pf* rules. Of additional interest are sections on tools for editing *pf.conf* and a short course in CVS.

Chapter 6, *Packet Normalization* explains why it is a good security practice to normalize fragmented packets, how it is done with *pf*, and how it helps improve the accuracy of reports generated by Network Intrusion Detection Systems (NIDS).

Chapter 7, *Packet Redirection* shows when and how packet redirection is used in Network Address Translation, Virtual Private Networks, network administration and some of the firewall designs discussed in Chapter 2, *Firewall Designs*.

Chapter 8, *Packet Filtering* dives deep into the subject of packet filtering.

Rules, options, flags, shortcuts, and everything else that has to do with packet filtering is covered there.

Chapter 9, *Dynamic Rulesets* discusses two important recent additions to *pf*: *tables* and *anchors*, and their use in creating dynamic rulesets.

Chapter 10, *Bandwidth Shaping and Load Balancing* walks the reader through the maze of the Alternative Queuing system (ALTQ), which was recently integrated with *pf*. You will find there tips for defining ALTQ queues and load balancing rules. Read this chapter if you want to keep MP3 downloaders at bay or when you need to implement load balancing on your servers or external connections to the Internet.

Chapter 11, *Logging and Log Analysis* is a description of various approaches to packet logging and analysis that can be implemented using *pf* and other free open source tools.

Chapter 12, *Using authpf* describes the *authpf* authenticating gateway user shell. This part of the *pf* package provides an additional level of security, especially handy when you are working with wireless networks.

Chapter 13, *Using spamd* explains how spamd can be used with *pf* to make spammers' ways less profitable.

Chapter 14, *Ruleset Optimization* explores various methods of ruleset optimization, from brute force to more streamlined rulesets.

Chapter 15, *Testing Your Firewall* walks the reader through the process of firewall testing and ruleset debugging.

Chapter 16, *Firewall Management* discusses the many facets of firewall management and tools that help.

Appendix A, *Manual Pages* contains a list of manual pages related to *pf* with short descriptions of their contents. Also included are tips on using the system manual.

Appendix B, *Rules for Popular (and Less Popular) Services*, a quick reference for ruleset writers.

Appendix C, *Rule Templates for Typical Firewall Configurations* is a starting point for constructing practical implementations of designs described in Chapter 2, *Firewall Designs*.

Appendix D, *Helping OpenBSD and PF* contains ideas for helping the good guys who gave us OpenBSD and *pf*.

1.7 Typographic Conventions Used in This Book

The right hand symbol (☞) is used to mark the beginning of a line that was too long and had to be broken into shorter pieces to fit on a printed page. For example:

http://www.devguide.net/
☞ *books/*
☞ *openbsdfw-02-ed/*

is the equivalent of:

http://www.devguide.net/books/openbsdfw-02-ed/

Another thing that you may notice often in this book are words ending with a number enclosed in a pair or parentheses. These are references to relevant OpenBSD manual pages and the sections they belong to. For example, when you see *pf(4)*, it is a reference to the manual page for *pf* from section 4 of the OpenBSD manual. If you wanted to display it, you'd use this command:

```
$ man 4 pf
```

> Appendix A, Manual Pages *contains essential tips on using the OpenBSD manual as well as a list of manual pages that you should start learning from.*

1.8 Staying in Touch with the OpenBSD Community

The OpenBSD community has several meeting places on the Web. The following list mentions a few of those that make good starting points.

http://www.openbsd.org   *(the official site of the project)*
http://www.openbsd.org/mail.html   *(mailing lists)*
http://www.benzedrine.cx   *(the home of pf)*
http://www.deadly.org   *(The OpenBSD Journal)*
http://www.kd85.com   *(all things OpenBSD in Europe)*
http://www.onlamp.com/bsd   *(BSD DevCenter on the O'Reilly Network)*
http://www.onlamp.com/pub/ct/58
                    (Securing Small Networks with OpenBSD by Jacek Artymiak)
http://www.bsdnewsletter.com   *(news from the world of BSD)*
http://www.daemonnews.org   *(news from the world of BSD)*
http://www.devguide.net
                    (publishers of books for the OpenBSD community)

1.9 Getting in Touch with the Author

Important updates, corrections, and announcements related to this book are
posted on the Web at the following address:

http://www.devguide.net/books/openbsdfw-02-ed/

If you would like to be kept updated on what Jacek's doing, be the first to
hear about updates or new editions of this book, subscribe to the *jacek-obsd*
mailing list:

http://www.artymiak.com/mailman/listinfo/jacek-obsd

Bug reports, questions, and comments about this book should be sent to:

openbsdpf-ed-02@devguide.net

If you like this book, let others know about it!

## Chapter 2

Firewall Designs

In this chapter we take a look at various firewall implementations and their applications in the real world. Also discussed are site security policies, as well as advantages and potential security risk of each firewall design.

There are literally dozens, if not hundreds, of ways to deploy firewalls on your network. Which one you choose depends on your site's security policy, network layout, usage patterns, and financial resources. But before you start assembling the firewall, define exactly what you want it to do.

2.1 Define Your Local Packet Filtering Policy

One of the elements of the written site security policy ought to be a chapter describing the local packet filtering policy. It can be as simple as saying "We do not allow any traffic from the outside, unless it is in response to the requests sent from hosts on our LAN," or it can be a thick book of rules detailing what kind of traffic goes in or out; or, it can be anything in between, depending on the local and international laws, your organization's needs, and the patterns of network usage, and many other factors that influence the process of establishing these rules. The only requirement is that you have it in writing, approved, stick to it, and revise it periodically as well as in response to new threats, attacks, and changes in network configuration. That way you'll be less likely to invent excuses to be lazy and not implement it. Another very important reason to have these rules in writing and approved by your superiors, or even audited by third parties, are the requirements of insurers who expect that such rules exist and are properly written, implemented, and audited. Also, if you are ever taken to court, an official piece of paper is a good thing to have. Of course, no matter what your site security policy says, your goal is always the same: achieving maximum protection from attacks originating from the outside *and* from the inside of your network while providing convenient access to various services.

Although it may not seem very polite to view your local users as potential attackers, and you might be right trusting them, at the same time you cannot be completely sure that someone, somehow hasn't broken into their computers in order to launch an attack against other sites or to spy on internal communications.

While you are planning various ways to keep intruders at bay, yet another important goal is to wisely use your security budget in order to save resources for handling emergencies and for the things that are not available for free like books, training, consulting, or hardware.

Once your site's security and firewall policies are stated in writing, you must implement them in practice, and review them periodically to accommodate changes in your network, your needs, and the threats that your network is facing.

> *Site security policies are a broad topic and we do not have enough space in this book to cover them in detail, but there are books that can help. For example, an excellent discussion of security policies and other network and system administration issues can be found in [Limoncelli, Hogan 2002].*

2.2 What Is a 'Firewall'?

Generally speaking, a *firewall* is a method of protecting hosts and networks connected to other hosts and networks against attacks (we define attacks as attempts to gain unauthorized access to your network, disruption of services, listening to or altering communications, stealing data or software, altering data or software) from the outside and from the inside. We use the word 'firewall' when we speak about various network configurations build for that purpose, although it is also used to describe software products and hardware devices also known as 'packet filters' that sit between two or more hosts or networks and filter packets according to a set of rules written by the person who oversees their operation.

What packet filters are good at is matching packets' headers and payload against a set of rules that establish packet filtering policies. Everything else that packet filters do builds on top of that basic functionality.

2.3 What Firewalls Are Not

The wrong way to think about firewalls is to assume that they are some sort of magic silver bullet that automatically provides full protection to any host or network that uses them. Of course, they can control who connects to what, but they cannot prevent information leakage if someone places classified documents on your company's web server or copies the latest sales figures to a disk and sells it to your competition. Having said that, firewalls can log traffic passing in and out of them, which makes it easy to find out just how that secret memo found its way to the competition, or which host was compromised by the attacker. An even more sophisticated packet filter could look at the payload of each packet (such solutions are already available) and silently inform appropriate law enforcement authorities when it detects certain keywords indicating that classified documents are being sent outside the company.

> *When you are implementing a firewall, you should also think of a larger picture: physical site and network security, user education, and proper hardening of all hosts protected with the firewall, as well as the firewall itself. (Host hardening involves turning off non-essential services, applying patches, enforcing the use of secure passwords, and using secure user authentication.)*

2.4 Hardware vs. Software Firewalls

Marketing people often talk about *software firewalls* and *hardware firewalls*, as if they were two different species. According to the glossy marketing literature published by various vendors, software firewalls are applications you install on top of an operating system, while hardware firewalls are these magic boxes that you plug between your router and your network. In reality, there is no such thing as a software or hardware firewall, because they all are packet filters implemented using a mixture of hardware and code. The software might be saved on an EPROM chip encased in a nice plastic box with little connectors sticking out of it, but the hardware alone won't work if there is no software to drive it. So, when someone speaks of a hardware firewall, they are talking about a piece of software sold together with a specialized piece of hardware that runs that particular packet filtering software.

2.5 Firewalls Great and Small

We will now discuss various popular firewall designs used in all kinds of network installations, large and small. Please note that there usually are many ways to implement these designs and there may be certain risks associated with these implementations. These differences are also discussed to help you decide what you need. Sample templates for each design are provided in Appendix C, *Rule Templates for Typical Firewall Configurations*.

2.5.1 Screened Host

A screened host is a machine protected from external attacks with a packet filter. It implements a very simple and secure firewall policy:

• No inbound packets pass through the packet filter unless they arrive in response to the requests sent from the screened host.

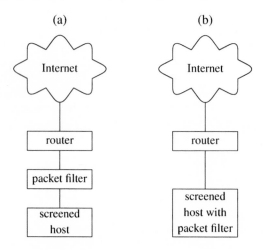

Figure 2.1: A screened host can be protected with a separate packet filter (a) or it can run packet filtering software itself (b).

Such hosts can be connected directly to the Internet or they can be a part of a Local Area Network (LAN). That way of limiting access from the outside is usually employed to protect workstations, desktop PCs, or laptops used at home, in a small office, or on the road. The packet filter can be (a) an external device plugged between the host and the rest of the network or (b) it can be implemented purely in software running on the screened host.

In design (a) the packet filter can be a special purpose device running packet filtering software, or it can be a separate computer running packet filtering software on top of some operating system, such as the OpenBSD/*pf* duo. Protecting laptops in that way can be a little problematic, because the weight and the size of a separate packet filter device make it too inconvenient to carry around, so design (b) is a good compromise. Design (a) can be further enhanced with the use of OpenBSD and *pf(4)* configured as an 'invisible' *filtering bridge* (discussed later in this chapter, and in Chapter 4, *Configuring OpenBSD*).

Design (b) requires the use of packet filtering software written specifically for the operating system running on the screened host. Therefore, if one wants to use design (b) *and* run *pf(4)*, there is no other choice but to run OpenBSD, or one of the systems that *pf(4)* has been ported to.

> *When a change of the operating system is not an option, design (a) with the packet filter as a separate piece of hardware ought to be used.*

Separating the packet filter from the protected host in the way it is done in design (a) is a more secure solution, because it prevents avoids the situation when a software failure in the packet filter or in the operating system of the screened host automatically gives the attacker access to that host.

Range	Network/Mask
10.0.0.0 to **10**.255.255.255	10/8
172.16.0.0 to **172.31**.255.255	172.16/12
192.168.0.0 to **192.168.255**.255	172.168/16

Table 2.1: Private IPv4 addresses as defined in [RFC 1918].

In both designs, the screened hosts must use *public* IP addresses unless they are on a LAN segment that uses *private* IP addresses. When the packet filter in design (a) is *not* configured as a filtering bridge, it will also need to have a routable public IP address unless the packet filter and the screened host are on a LAN segment that uses private IP addresses. If you are short of public IPv4 addresses, you will need to configure the packet filter as a filtering bridge or assign the public address to the packet filter and configure it to perform Network Address Translation (NAT) before it performs filtering. In that case, the screened host has a private IPv4 address from the range defined in [RFC 1918] and shown in Table 2.1. Of course, the problem of not enough IP addresses should not appear when you are using IPv6, which has a much wider address space. If you need to use NAT with IPv6, use site-local addresses FEC0/10 through FEFF/10 (see Chapter 5, */etc/pf.conf*).

> *When the screened host has more than one network interface, it will need to be protected with packet filters at all points of contact with the outside world, or it will be quickly broken into.*

2.5.2 Screened LAN or Screened LAN Segment

When your needs grow and you connect two or more computers together, you are starting to build a LAN. And when you want to connect your LAN to the Internet or other networks, you must decide how you are going to protect it. One popular design is a *screened LAN* or a *screened LAN segment*. A screened LAN is in many ways similar to the screened host described in the previous section. It even implements a similar firewall policy:

• All inbound packets are blocked unless they are sent in response to requests sent from the hosts on the screened LAN.

There are three possible implementation scenarios: the LAN can be protected with (a) a separate dedicated device (a boxed packet filter or a computer running packet filter software); (b) it can be a collection of screened hosts; or (c) it can be a mixture of (a) and (b).

Obviously, solution (a) is easier to manage, but it provides a single point of failure and does not provide as high a level of protection against attacks launched from the internal hosts against their neighbours on the same LAN. The internal security of design (a) can be increased a little bit, if you use an Ethernet switch instead of a hub to connect the hosts on the screened LAN. This will make it more difficult to spy on communications, but it does not solve all internal security problems associated with that design.

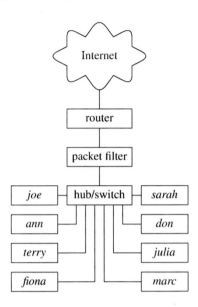

Figure 2.2: A screened LAN or a screened LAN segment protected with a separate packet filter.

Someone might say that an important advantage of design (a) is its lower cost, compared to design (b), but that argument may not be as strong when free software like OpenBSD and *pf(4)* is used to implement the firewall and when the company policy explicitly states that each host must be protected by a separate packet filter. This is not as unreasonable as it sounds, a failure of the packet filter in design (a) exposes all hosts on the LAN it protects, while a failure of a single packet firewall in design (b) compromises only one host, assuming that the other hosts on the same network do not trust each other and do not accept inbound connections without secure authentication and authorization.

> *When the screened LAN has more than one network inter-*
> *face connecting it to the outside world, it will need to be*
> *protected with packet filters at all points of contact with*
> *the outside world, or you will not be able to protect it at*
> *all. This policy must be strictly enforced and users*
> *cannot add any network interfaces on their own.*

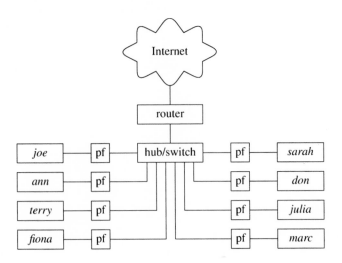

Figure 2.3: A screened LAN or a screened LAN segment can be a collection of screened hosts.

The IPv4 addressing issues for the screened LAN are similar to those for a screened host; every host must have a public IPv4 address unless the screened LAN is a part of a larger network that uses private IPv4 addresses or unless you choose design (a) and configure the packet filter to perform NAT. And don't forget to assign IPv4 addresses to the firewalls in design (b), unless you configure them as filtering bridges. NAT will help you make better use of your IPv4 address pool and rise the level of security of your LAN. Using it is not obligatory, but if it doesn't cost you a dime, why not use it? Again, IPv6 addressing makes the shortage of IPv4 addresses irrelevant, but it will still be a some time before everyone switches to IPv6.

2.5.3 Bastion Host

The design of a *bastion host* is similar to that of a screened host. The only differences between them are the configuration of the packet filter and the kind of services such host is running. Typical candidates for bastion hosts are all kinds of Internet and intranet servers: DNS, FTP, HTTP, NNTP, SMTP, etc. The packet filter protecting a bastion host implements a less secure policy than the packet filter protecting a screened host:

• Some inbound connections to selected services are permitted.

• Outbound connections can pass through the packet filter only when they are required to ensure proper functioning of the bastion host, or to serve incoming connections.

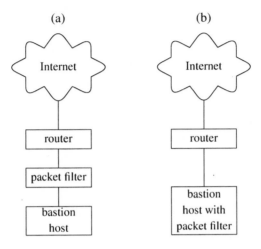

Figure 2.4: A bastion host can be protected with a separate packet filter (a) or it can run packet filtering software itself (b).

Since the bastion host is fully or partially exposed to the outside world, it is extremely important that it will be well-protected against attacks. The packet filter is only one half of the whole solution, the other half is proper configuration, hardening, and monitoring of the bastion host. In particular, it should not be running non-essential services that provide another way in for the unwanted visitors. Ideally, one bastion host should be running only one kind of publicly accessible service, i.e. DNS *or* HTTP *or* FTP, but not FTP *and* SMTP *and* NNTP. The simpler the overall configuration, the easier to manage and the more secure it will be.

The IPv4/IPv6 addressing issues for a bastion host are identical as those for the screened host.

2.5.4 Demilitarized Zone (DMZ)

It is quite common for a LAN connected to the Internet to start exposing some of its resources to the outside world, be it an HTTP server, and FTP store, or an NNTP site. This creates all kinds of security hazards that the network and the firewall have to cope with. If you have plans to offer external access to some services, isolate them in a *Demilitarized Zone (DMZ)*.

The DMZ design consists of at least one, more often two or more LAN segments, one screened and one with bastion hosts. The simplest DMZ design needs three network interfaces, one connecting the packet filter to the outside world, one connecting the packet filter to the screened LAN segment, and one connecting the packet filter to the DMZ segment.

The packet filter must have rules that implement the following policy:

- Hosts on the screened LAN have access to the outside world.
- Hosts on the screened LAN have limited access to the bastion hosts in the DMZ.
- External hosts have limited access to the bastion hosts in the DMZ.
- Bastion hosts in the DMZ do not have access to the screened LAN segment.
- Bastion hosts in the DMZ have limited access to the outside world.
- External hosts do not have access to the screened LAN segment.

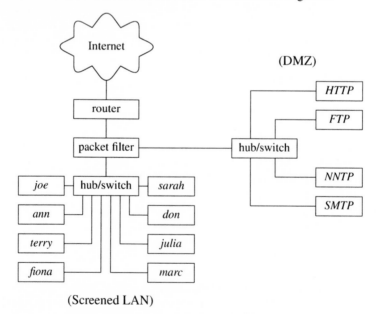

Figure 2.5: A screened LAN and a DMZ segment.

IPv4/IPv6 issues and the need to secure all external interfaces mentioned in previous designs also apply in the DMZ design. The filtering bridge and NAT configurations also have their place in this kind of design.

> *Although the DMZ design is slightly more complex, it is a bad idea to save money by placing publicly accessible servers in the screened LAN and configuring the packet firewall to let inbound traffic in. When one host becomes compromised, all other hosts on that LAN are also at risk. When someone breaks into an HTTP web server running in the DMZ LAN segment, it will only pose some danger to the bastion hosts in the DMZ, but not to the hosts in the screened LAN. You can protect hosts in the DMZ with separate packet filters, in order to raise the level of their security even higher. Such solutions may be required for high-profile sites.*

2.5.5 Large-Scale LANs

Large scale LANs are usually configured as a mixture of variations of all four designs mentioned in the earlier sections, connected to a high-speed backbone. Each host and LAN segment connected to the backbone must be protected with its own local firewall and these must be designed in such a way that they form a coherent large-scale firewall. It is a huge logistical problem and the trend to put everyone and everything on the Internet will only make it worse. For ideas on how to build, manage, and protect large-scale LANs refer to [Cheswick, Bellovin, Rubin 2003], [Dooley 2002], [Frish 2002], [Limoncelli, Hogan 2002], and [Yuan, Strayer 2001].

2.6 Invisible Hosts and Firewalls

The dramatic growth in the number of hosts connected to the Internet caused a shortage of IPv4 addresses. To solve that problem, researchers designed the next generation of IP called IPng or, more recently, IPv6. However, the simple expansion of the IP address space, although useful for network architects and administrators, does not change much from the point of view of security. (OK, this is only partially true, because IPv6 *does* include some handy security enhancements, but we cannot use them yet due to low proliferation of IPv6 networks.)

Two interesting solutions that lower the number of IP addresses needed to implement a firewall while providing additional security are: *filtering bridge* and *NAT*.

2.6.1 Filtering Bridge

An Ethernet *bridge* is a device that connects two network segments. It is a close relative of an Ethernet switch, which actually evolved from early Ethernet bridge designs. A nice feature of both of these devices is their lack of need for a separate IP address. This is handy from the point of view of security, because a device without an IP address is invisible to other hosts on the network and cannot become the target of an attack. Although you can buy a good hardware bridge or switch for a modest amount of money, it is beneficial in some situations to implement it using an ordinary PC equipped with a bunch of Ethernet cards or other types of network interfaces, running OpenBSD and *pf(4)*. Such machine will be able to do what bridges and switches do *as well as* packet filtering, packet logging, load balancing, bandwidth shaping and much more, in IPv4 and IPv6. Such setup is also call a *filtering bridge*.

The only tiny problem is the other side of the bridge's invisibility. It has no IP address, so how do you log on and manage it? Well, when the bridge is sitting in your office or server room, you could add a monitor and a keyboard, or a serial console to it, but that is not very convenient, although very safe, provided that the physical access to the console is well-secured. A better solution is to add another Ethernet card not used in the bridge setup and connect it to your network management workstation.

> *Be careful! By doing this you could be creating a back-door way to break into the bridge.*

However, if you design a separate network management LAN properly separated from the LAN you manage (a screened LAN with multiple connections to the main LAN, all protected from external access) it will be quite secure. Various designs are possible, Figure 2.6 shows one that could be an inspiration in your own search for security without sacrificing the ease of management. Information on how to configure a filtering bridge with OpenBSD and *pf(4)* is provided in Appendix C, *Rule Templates for Typical Firewall Configurations*.

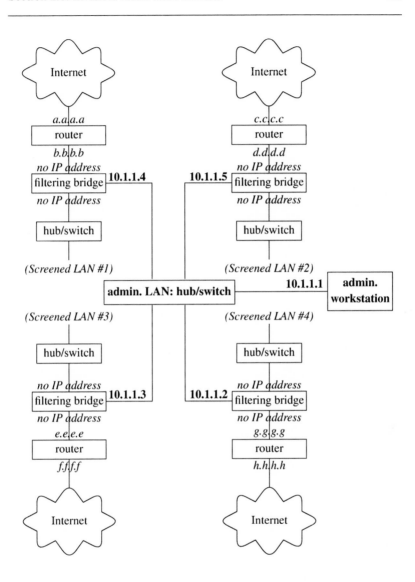

Figure 2.6: Four separate screened LANs protected with filtering bridges. The bridges are connected to an isolated administration LAN 10.1.1.0/24 (in bold).

2.6.2 Network Address Translation (NAT)

NAT is used to hide real IP addresses of hosts connected to a NAT device and to redirect packets to arbitrarily chosen addresses and/or ports. That simple functionality can be used in many creative ways in network security and administration.

Although NAT is often associated with firewalls, such as *pf(4)*, it is a totally independent mechanism. The fact that it is integrated with many packet filters is merely a proof of its good fit. You can learn more about NAT from Chapter 7, *Packet Redirection*.

2.7 Additional Functionality

Although all firewalls are based on packet filtering, often combined with NAT, this is not all that OpenBSD and *pf(4)* are capable of. The following list mentions many additional functions that OpenBSD and *pf(4)* can be configured to perform:

- *Proxy* — when you use OpenBSD and *pf(4)* in your firewall, it is also possible to run FTP, WWW (Squid), and other proxies, such as: *totd*, *tinyproxy*, *proxy-suite*, *jftpgw*, or *balance* on the same computer. (Try doing that with your 'hardware firewall'.) You'll find them in the Open-BSD packages and ports collections as well as on the Internet. Adding software to OpenBSD is described in Chapter 4, *Configuring OpenBSD*.
- *Packet logger* — as crackers increase their activities on the Internet and various intranets, the number of organizations that record all traffic passing in and out of their networks will grow. Military and many government agencies have been doing this for many years, as have large financial institutions, corporations, and other organizations storing and processing sensitive information. With OpenBSD and *pf(4)*, packet logging can be easily added to any of the firewall designs described earlier in this chapter. Apart from being able to perform packet filtering and redirection, *pf(4)* can be used as a packet logging and analysis station, either in conjunction with filtering and/or redirection or as a separate module. You can learn more about logging from Chapter 11, *Logging and Log Analysis*.
- *Network Intrusion Detection Systems (NIDS)* — a more advanced way to monitor traffic passing through the firewall is with some sort of a Network Intrusion Detection System (NIDS), such as *snort* (available in the

OpenBSD packages and ports collections). This book does not describe *snort* as this is a subject for another book, but the subject of *pf(4)* cooperation with NIDS returns on many of its pages.

- *Failover, load balancing, Quality of Service (QoS)* — with *pf(4)* configured to do NAT and ALTQ (recently integrated with *pf(4)*) it is possible to create custom failover, load balancing, and Quality of Service (QoS) configurations. This is something we discuss in Chapter 10, *Bandwidth Shaping and Load Balancing*.
- *User authentication* — an additional layer of security can be built into each of the firewall designs discussed in this chapter with the use of *authpf(8)*, the authenticating gateway user shell. This is particularly important for securing wireless networks. You can learn more about it from Chapter 12, *Using authpf(8)*.

## Chapter 3

Installing OpenBSD

*In this chapter we discuss various ways to obtain Open-
BSD, basic system hardware and software requirements,
and the process of installing OpenBSD on a typical PC-
compatible computer.*

Since *pf(4)* is closely integrated with the OpenBSD kernel, the easiest way
to obtain it is to install the OpenBSD operating system. Until recently it
was also the only choice, but that changed after *pf* had been ported to
FreeBSD and NetBSD. However, since these ports have yet to undergo
thorough testing in production environment, they are not described in this
chapter. Of course, as soon as they are accepted for wide use by the Free-
BSD and NetBSD user communities, the process of installing them will be
covered in future editions of this book. The rest of the information presented in this book applies to *pf(4)* running on FreeBSD, NetBSD, OpenBSD,
or any other system that *pf* is ported to in the meantime. Readers interested
in finding out more about the FreeBSD or the NetBSD port are invited to
visit these pages:

http://pf4freebsd.love2party.net/	*(FreeBSD port)*
http://foo.unix.se/joelw/pflkm.html	*(NetBSD port)*

3.1 Software Requirements

To begin your adventure with OpenBSD and *pf*, you will need a copy of the
OpenBSD operating system, version 3.4 or later. It can be obtained in sev-
eral ways. The recommended way is to purchase the *official* OpenBSD
CD-ROM set from the online store:

http://www.openbsd.org/orders.html	*(the offical OpenBSD online store)*
http;//www.kd85.com	*(kd85.com, the official European distributor)*

You can also download it from the project's official FTP server or one of its many mirrors scattered around the globe. If you decide to download the system, try to use the nearest mirror. That way you will put less strain on the official OpenBSD server. Using a mirror may be the only option around May 1 and November 1, when new releases of the system are being made available for download to the wild wide world and the official FTP server is swamped with requests.

ftp.openbsd.org   *(the official OpenBSD FTP server)*
http://www.openbsd.org/ftp.html   *(various mirrors)*

> *If you want to download OpenBSD, but don't know where to start, you will find step-by-step instructions later in this chapter.*

3.1.1 Buy Official OpenBSD CD-ROM Sets

Many users purchase original OpenBSD CD-ROM sets even when they download the same software for free from the Internet. This is no charity, but a smart investment in your own future, in the tools you use to make money. If you want the OpenBSD project to continue publishing two releases of their great software a year, then a small contribution in the form of a purchase of the official CD-ROM set is a good way to help it happen.

A purchase of the official CD-ROM set is also a good way to prove that the software you or your company use is legal. And, believe it or not, it may help in dealings with tax authorities. Users in various countries report that tax and software auditors grow suspicious, when you cannot show them the invoice, the license, the CD-ROMs, and the box that the software came in. As you can see a few dollars paid to the project can save you a lot of hassle. That's why businesses pay for official boxed releases of Linux, FreeBSD, and NetBSD even though the same software is available for free. Why not do the same with OpenBSD?

> *For more suggestions on how you can help the project see Appendix D,* Helping the OpenBSD Project *near the end of this book. The PDF version of that appendix is also available on this book's website. You are free to copy it or link to it.*

3.1.2 Additional Software Requirements

What other software, besides a copy of OpenBSD itself, you will need to install OpenBSD depends on the way you obtained it and the hardware you have at your disposal:

- *A copy of another operating system running on another computer.* If the machine that you will be installing OpenBSD on has a CD-ROM drive which it can boot from and you have a bootable OpenBSD CD-ROM (like the official OpenBSD CD-ROM set), then you need no other software. In some cases, you will need another computer that you can use to create a boot floppy disk. The boot disk will be needed in three cases: when you want to install the system from a non-bootable CD-ROM, when a bootable CD-ROM won't boot, or when you want to install OpenBSD over a network (another computer, LAN, or the Internet). Boot floppies can be created under Linux, OpenBSD, FreeBSD, NetBSD, or any other Unix; or you can use one of the recent versions of Microsoft Windows (95, 98, Me, NT, 2000, or XP). While it might be possible to create boot floppies under the old operating system before you replace it with Open-BSD, it should be your last resort, because it is difficult and often impossible to recover the old system once you get beyond the disk formatting stage during installation. You'll learn how to create them later in this chapter. If you decide to install the system over a network or from another computer (using two Ethernet cards and a crossover cable), you will need that other computer's operating system to run an FTP, HTTP, or NFS server, or the installation script will not be able to download it to the target machine. Again, this can be some flavor of Unix, Apple Mac OS X, Microsoft Windows, or something else, capable of serving FTP, HTTP, or NFS.
- *Hardware configuration utilities, drivers.* You should download all available configuration utilities for your computer, disks, controller cards, network interface cards, and the actual chips that these cards use. When the card manufacturer does not offer these on their web site, have a look at the chips' markings and go to the chip manufacturer's site.
- *A DOS boot disk.* (This applies to i386 machines.) You'll need it if you want to use the configuration utilities for network cards, RAID controllers, or other hardware. The procedure is simple: boot from the DOS disk and then run the configuration program (some floppy disk swapping will be required). When you do not have a copy of a DOS boot disk, you

can use the rescue disk for Microsoft Windows 95, 98, or Me. Since it is unclear what Microsoft thinks of using MS-DOS or Windows boot disks to configure computers in order to install other operating systems, the readers should either obtain a legitimate copy of MS-DOS or MS Windows that you will use for that purpose, or buy a copy of PC-DOS from IBM, or better still download FreeDOS, a free DOS clone:

http://www.ibm.com/software/os/dos/   *(IBM PC-DOS)*
http://www.freedos.org   *(FreeDOS)*

Once you have DOS in one form or another, make a boot disk, remove all unnecessary files from it, and replace them with the configuration utilities to avoid constant shuffling of the system and utility floppies.

3.2 Hardware Requirements

The computer that you will install OpenBSD on must be one of the architectures supported by OpenBSD and any devices that it is equipped with must also be supported by the system. Otherwise, some devices will not be visible to the system or, in rare cases, they may prevent OpenBSD from working at all (that can be cured with some kernel tweaking described in Chapter 4, *Configuring OpenBSD*). The list of hardware supported by each release of OpenBSD can be found in the *HARDWARE* file located in the root directory of that release, e.g. if you are downloading OpenBSD 3.4 from the official FTP server, you will find it in */pub/OpenBSD/3.4/HARD-WARE*. Note that this list is not exhaustive, because some companies license their hardware to others or make their products compatible with those that are widely accepted as *de facto* standards, like the famous Novell NE2000 Ethernet network card. Speaking of network cards (and other devices), you should always look for compatibility with the chipset on the card or on the mainboard, not necessarily with the name printed on the box that the component in question came in.

3.2.1 Which Hardware Platform Should You Choose?

The first hardware choice you need to make is about the hardware architecture you want to run OpenBSD on. As of release 3.4 there are ten to choose from, some more popular than others, but if it is the first time you are installing OpenBSD, then the obvious choice is *i386*, aka. the PC. It is recommended for first-time users of OpenBSD, because most people use it and there is much greater chance of finding a helping hand when things go wrong with the hardware/operating system interactions. Later, when you are comfortable with using OpenBSD in production environment, you should consider other hardware architectures, not because it is cool, but because it is highly advisable for security reasons.

> *That's right. Maintaining hardware platforms diversity is a good security practice, because the majority of rogue software that targets hardware is written with the i386 architecture in mind. This is less of an issue for a standalone, tightly secured firewall, but if you were running a DNS or web server on the same machine that you run your firewall on (not a good security practice, but unavoidable at times), then simply switching to another platform would make such server less vulnerable to those attacks that exploit the weaknesses in the i386 architecture. This is not to say that there are no weak points in other hardware architectures, but their lower popularity means that there are not so many people actively looking for them and writing software tools that exploit them. Security through diversity is a good practice.*

You should note though that not all hardware architectures may be suitable for your needs. Running OpenBSD on an ancient Apple Macintosh with a Motorola 680x0 CPU does have a certain 'geek' appeal, but using even the fastest of them as a packet filter on a high-speed link is not a good idea. Conversely, a decommissioned 300MHz Alpha workstation might be just the right thing. If you are interested in exploring this subject further, the latest list of supported architectures can be found on the *OpenBSD Platforms* page:

http://www.openbsd.org/plat.html   *(OpenBSD Platforms)*

Another good place to ask for help are the *misc* and *ports* mailing lists. To find out how to subscribe to them, visit the *Mailing Lists* page:

http://www.openbsd.org/mail.html   *(OpenBSD Mailing Lists)*

Architecture	Port	Location	INSTALL files
Digital Alpha	alpha	*3.4/alpha*	*INSTALL.alpha*
Hewlett-Packard HP 9000/300 and 400 workstations	hp300	*3.4/hp300*	*INSTALL.hp300*
Hewlett-Packard PA-RISC	hppa	*3.4/hppa*	*INSTALL.hppa*
Intel i386	i386	*3.4/i386*	*INSTALL.i386* *INSTALL.ata* *INSTALL.chs* *INSTALL.dbr* *INSTALL.linux* *INSTALL.mbr* *INSTALL.os2br* *INSTALL.pt*
Apple Macintosh (Motorola 680x0)	mac68k	*3.4/mac68k*	*INSTALL.mac86k*
Apple Macintosh (Power PC)	macppc	*3.4/macppc*	*INSTALL.macppc*
Motorola VME 680x0 motherboards	mve68k	*3.4/mve68k*	*INSTALL.mve68k*
Sun SPARC	sparc	*3.4/sparc*	*INSTALL.sparc*
Sun UltraSPARC	sparc64	*3.4/sparc64*	*INSTALL.sparc64*
Digital VAX	vax	*3.4/vax*	*INSTALL.vax*

Note that OpenBSD does not currently support Symmetric Multi-Processing (SMP). Only one processor is used on machines with more than one CPU.

Table 3.1: Hardware architectures supported by OpenBSD.

3.2.2 Motherboard

The motherboard in the machine you choose need not be an over-clocker's dream. Look for stable, server-grade products and avoid cheap all-in-one units with integrated sound, video, and other bells and whistles. If you want to use *pf* for logging packets, make sure the motherboard is equipped with a fast ATA interface, at least ATA/66. This will not be an issue if you decide to use a SCSI disk, as these will use separate PCI (not ISA, they are too slow) SCSI interface cards (although you can buy good motherboards with built-in SCSI interfaces). Another handy feature is dual BIOS or BIOS with write protection, just in case someone messes with this essential part of the system.

3.2.3 BIOS

Make sure that access to the BIOS can be protected with passwords and check if you can disable booting from external devices like the floppy disc after you install OpenBSD on the hard disk. A good BIOS ought to allow the administrator to protect access to its settings with a password. An even better BIOS design may use passwords to block **Ctrl+Alt+Del** keys, the reset key, or even the power switch.

3.2.4 Processor

Unlike 3D graphics, or other math-intensive tasks, bossing TCP packets around requires relatively little processor power. For example, a certain very famous manufacturer of packet filters and routers uses Motorola 680x0 CPUs running at 20MHz! They are plenty enough for a packet filter, because they run in an environment optimized for that particular task. Packet filters implemented on top of a general-purpose operating system require more power, though not as much as many other pieces of networking software.

Just how many CPU cycles your firewall machine will need depends on several factors:

- *The speed of the networks that the firewall is connected to.* The faster they are, the more packets they'll move per second. The speed of the firewall machine must be enough to keep up with the fastest of them, otherwise your firewall will be loosing you plenty of money in unused, but paid for, bandwidth. Assuming that the network interfaces you are using can handle the speed the networks work at, you can be certain that a 100MHz Pentium can cope with 10Mbps of traffic. This rule is not set in stone and will depend on several other factors, but it is a good starting point.
- *The length and the complexity of the firewall ruleset.* Every packet passing through the firewall is matched against all rules (except for NAT rules, where the first rule wins) and every additional rule increases the

total time it takes to check every packet. Although it may be only a few milliseconds per packet, it will quickly add up, when you multiply it by the number of packets passing through a busy link. You can decrease that time using the optimization techniques described in Chapter 14, *Ruleset Optimization*.

- *Running Network Intrusion Detection System (NIDS) software.* Intrusion detection is something that requires a lot of power because it is a huge database job that must be done very quickly. If you run an NIDS package like *snort* on the firewall machine, make sure you buy the fastest machine you can afford, because the signature database will grow very quickly as will the time it takes to match every packet. Solutions to this problem are: outsourcing the NIDS jobs to another machine (or a farm of machines, read about it in Chapter 10, *Bandwidth Shaping and Load Balancing*) on the network, signature database optimization, adding RAM, writing more generic signatures that can be matched more quickly.

- *Running additional software.* When you run a web server, or any other additional software, plan to use a faster CPU. This may not be such a huge problem, if you are running *pf* on your OpenBSD workstation for the sole purpose of protecting that single machine. It will be an issue if you are implementing a firewall running heavy proxy software, such as Squid.

- *Stateful filtering.* This is something that will make your firewall work faster, because once the initial packet passes through the firewall, all other packets that belong to the same connection can pass without going through the whole packet/ruleset matching procedure. Try to use stateful filtering whenever possible and safe to do so. For more information refer to Chapter 8, *Packet Filtering* and read the section that describes the `keep state` and `modulate state` keywords.

- `quick` *rules*. Proper use of the `quick` keyword can shorten the time it takes *pf* to perform packet matching. You will learn more about this keyword from Chapter 8, *Packet Filtering*.

- *Packet logging.* Writing and rotating logs takes time. Even though it is mostly the job of the I/O subsystem, the CPU is involved in it as well, and that takes time away from packet filtering. You can cure this by delegating packet logging to another machine whose sole purpose is packet logging. For more information refer to Chapter 11, *Logging and Log Analysis*.

- *Bandwidth shaping, Quality of Service (QoS), load balancing.* Prioritizing packets requires additional CPU time, so if you want to use it, plan for a faster CPU (and lots of RAM).

If all of the above seems to be vague, well, it is for a good reason. You must decide for yourself how much CPU power you'll need. A simple packet filter setup with NAT will happily handle 10Mbps of traffic with a 100MHz processor, 100Mbps of traffic will need a faster CPU, in the 200MHz range, although at that network speed other components like the system bus, the mainboard, and the network interfaces will play a more significant role.

A good rule of thumb is to bump the speed of the CPU up 100MHz every time one of the features mentioned on the list on the facing page is added. It is an extremely inaccurate rule, because some services like NIDS or proxy servers also need more memory, but it gives you a rough idea of what to expect.

Another important thing to remember is the lack of support for Symmetric MultiProcessor (SMP) architectures, which should be available in the near future, but for now OpenBSD cannot use more than one processor.

3.2.5 Memory

This one is easy. Choose the fastest memory you can buy and buy as much of it as you can afford. The minimum amount of RAM required to run OpenBSD is 24MB–32MB, which is quite enough for simple rulesets, but the more the better. For filtering and NAT alone, *pf* is unlikely to need more than 64MB. However, if you are planning to run some kind of proxy software like Squid, you should plan for at least 128MB or 64MB plus twice the amount of RAM that other software needs, just to be sure there is no need to swap RAM to disk. Swapping is always expensive and slows down the whole system, especially when the system is using ATA disks. Additional functionality like bandwidth shaping or running NIDS (or any other software beyond the basic system services) on the same machine, requires more RAM, and another 128MB is the minimum amount of memory required to avoid swapping.

In any case, you should plan for as much RAM as is necessary to avoid swapping, which has a negative effect on network performance. For example, if you notice that your network is periodically 'choking,' check if it could be because the firewall host is busy with some disk I/O operations, like swapping or rotating logs. Chapter 15, *Testing Your Firewall* contains help on monitoring system and network performance.

3.2.6 Disk Space

Modern operating systems occupy enormous amounts of space on disk and we've grown used to the idea that all systems need huge disks to run. This is not true in case of OpenBSD, which can function very well in limited disk space, well under 1GB, which will most likely remain unused unless you plan to save *pf* logs (see Chapter 11, *Logging and Log Analysis*).

Which disks should you use, ATA or SCSI? This is not such a huge issue with *pf*, because the only time you will need access to disks is when you load the system, load the *pf* ruleset, and write logs to disk. The only I/O intensive action is writing logs, and ATA/66 should be plenty enough for that, even if you are logging traffic on a 100Mbps link. Of course, the faster the better. If you decide to use SCSI disks, check if the motherboard has a built-in SCSI interface and if it is missing, buy a SCSI interface card. Make sure that the disks are compatible with the interface card. As for the drives themselves, ATA or SCSI, go for those with higher RPM ratings, lower seek times, and larger cache memories.

When you plan to run NIDS or WWW proxy, get SCSI drives rated 7,200RPM or faster. In this case, it may also be a good idea to run some sort of Redundant Array of Inexpensive Disks (RAID, discussed in Chapter 4, *Configuring OpenBSD*), which could be implemented in hardware, or software. Some server-grade motherboards come with simple RAID implementations on-board. These usually won't offer all of the features of a separate dedicated RAID setup, but may be good enough for your purposes, so it pays to investigate this option, because simplicity is better than top efficiency achieved at the cost of high complexity.

Large disk support. When the hard disk will not boot, even though the system installation went fine, you will need to make it bootable using the hard disk or computer manufacturer's configuration utilities. Sometimes, particularly when dealing with machines with old BIOS, your system might not correctly recognize the disk's size. That should not affect the OpenBSD installation, and you can simply make the disk bootable after you install OpenBSD on it, using utilities downloaded from the disk or computer manufacturer's Web site. These tools might only be available from the major companies' sites, so it pays to buy new and used hardware made by those that are still around, like Dell, Fujitsu, HP, IBM, Intel, Maxtor, Seagate, Samsung, or Toshiba. Start your search on their support sites.

If you are still having problems, read the *INSTALL* documents appropriate for your platform, where you will find detailed descriptions of various ways to solve problems with large disks. On the i386 platform, additional information about large disks can be found in *INSTALL.ata*, *INSTALL.chs*, *INSTALL.dbr*, *INSTALL.mbr*, *INSTALL.pt*, and *INSTALL.os2br*.

3.2.7 Network Interfaces

The computer you want to run *pf* on needs to have at least one (preferably, two) network interface, otherwise it will not be able to do much as a firewall. Although you could experiment with writing filtering rules for lo0 (the local interface, found in each Unix), it is not much fun and not that helpful. The interface connecting the computer running *pf* with the outside world can be an old dial-up modem, an ISDN terminal, a DSL box, an Ethernet card, a wireless transmitter, or anything else that can transmit and receive TCP/IP traffic.

While most of these devices are pretty standard, some may not be supported by OpenBSD. Wireless cards and the so-called 'winmodems' (modems with proprietary drivers written for the Microsoft Windows operating system) are the common culprits, because their manufacturers try to keep the technical details under wraps, to keep their secrets from the competition. Developers of free software like OpenBSD cannot get access to this information without signing some sort of a Non-Disclosure Agreement (NDA), which prevents public release of the source code written using the information they are given access to. And so this makes it impossible for developers working on free software to write drives for such devices. This is a fairly common behavior for manufacturers of any new kind of device that appears on the market. Things usually get more civilized after a year or two, when there is more competition on the market and the manufacturers decide to open their specification in order to gain more support for their products. Before that happens, the solution is to use those devices that are supported. The list of compatible hardware can be found in the *HARDWARE* file mentioned earlier in this chapter.

Apart from choosing a compatible network interface, you will also need to find one that matches the speed of your connection to other networks and the needs of the hosts or networks you are protecting. Another important factor will be your budget. Let's look at a few popular ways to connect computers.

Dial-up modems offer the lowest connection speeds and the least reliable service, but they are still in use at many homes and businesses. It is generally inadvisable to use them for connecting more than a couple of machines, but if there is no alternative, they're better than nothing, even with their maximum speeds of 56Kbps. A more reliable and faster, but often outrageously expensive type of network interface is an ISDN modem. They are still popular in Europe and the USA, especially in the creative services and publishing industry, but their days are numbered with the arrival of inexpensive DSL technology.

Various types of DSL modems work at much higher speeds (often under 10Mbps) and are generally more reliable than ordinary dial-up modems, although not as much as Ethernet cards nor are they as fast. DSL services are available in many speeds and at different prices, so it pays to shop around for the best price/performance deal. When you check the specifications, make sure you find out what are the *uplink* (transfers from your network to the outside world) and the *downlink* (transfers from the outside world to your network) speeds you are being offered. A low uplink speed may negatively affect availability of your in-house web server to the outside world. DSL uplink speeds are always lower than downlink speeds, which are important when you want to provide Internet access to a larger number of people on your LAN.

> *Another thing to check before you sign on the dotted line, are the clauses that forbid the user to connect more than one computer via a single DSL modem or forbid the use of NAT. If it is expressly forbidden, then you should probably forget about this provider and find someone who offers better terms, because there are no good reasons for such clauses.*

> *Yet another trap often found in DSL agreements are transfer limits, which are used to extract additional cash from subscribers who transfer large amounts of data. By using such clauses telecommunication companies admit that their networks do not have the capacity required to handle concurrent transfers at maximum speeds that the DSL modem they are selling are capable of. Much like banks, which cannot pay back all of your money when they go bankrupt.*

Ethernet cards are by far the most reliable and the fastest of network interfaces available today. They come in three speeds: 10Mbps, 100Mbps (Fast Ethernet), and 1000Mbps (Gigabit Ethernet). These interfaces are especially recommended for firewalls, because they are essentially a plug-and-forget type of device. Of course, not all Ethernet cards are created equal. There are some caveats that affect performance of the whole system and you should make sure that you do not create a bottleneck. First of all, forget the old ISA cards that you can buy a truckload for a dollar. They slow down the whole system and are not worth the trouble they cause. Always use PCI cards, and make sure that all cards you use work at 100Mbps. Older, 10Mbps cards can be used with 100Mbps equipment if it is marked 10/100Mpbs, but if you mix 10Mbps and 100Mbps cards on the same network segment you will slow down all devices on that segment to 10Mbps, unless you use a *switch* (some people use the name 'bridge') instead of a hub. Using switches is good for your network performance and security. Even though they are slightly more expensive than hubs, switches are almost always a better choice. The only time when a hub is more useful than a switch is when you want to monitor all traffic on a network segment using a single machine (hubs send packets to every host on the same network segment, switches only send packets to their destination hosts so others cannot see them). But remember, if you can use a hub to listen to communications, others can do it too so use it only as a temporary test tool and replace it with a switch as soon as you are done. Why make the bad guy's jobs easier?

Another good decision is to use cards and switches that perform advanced buffering of data. They are usually more expensive and come mostly from big-name manufacturers like Intel or 3Com, but they are well worth their price.

Also, it is well worth investing in cards that are faster than the networks you will be connecting your firewall to. So, if a network segment works at 10Mbps, use a 10/100Mpbs card, and if it works at 100Mbps, use a Gigabit Ethernet card. And yes, 10Gbps cards are in the works too.

Whatever speed your Ethernet cards are working at, always use twisted pair cables for 10BASE-T, 100BASE-TX, or 1000BASE-T Ethernet (with RJ-45 plugs). Make sure that the cables you use are Category 5 (Cat 5) products. Do not use thin coaxial cables (10BASE2), which are old, unreliable, and can waste many hours of your precious time when you are trying to debug

them. A single failure in a coaxial installation leaves all computers connected to the same cable without access to the network, while a failure of a
single twisted-pair cable disconnects only one machine. When you enter
the realm of Gigabit Ethernet, you may also need to use fiber cables to min-
imize signal loss and maximize bandwidth. This will no longer be a small
network, but *pf* can handle these without problems. These and other issues
faced by administrators of large networks are discussed in [Dooley 2002]
and [Limoncelli, Hogan 2002].

The latest incarnation of Ethernet devices—wireless cards and access points
work at lower speeds and are more susceptible to signal loss than copper or
fiber cables. Try to use them only at those points in your network where
there is absolutely no other way to connect hosts or network segments.
And yes, OpenBSD does support PCMCIA cards, so you can protect your
ad hoc WiFi network with *pf* just fine (remember to use *authpf(8)*, as
described in Chapter 12, *Using authpf*).

If you want to learn more about Ethernet, read [Spurgeon 2000]. For additional information about WiFi consult [Potter, Fleck 2002] and [Gast 2002].

3.2.8 Communicating with Your Computer During Installation

There are two ways to communicate with your computer during installation; you can use a keyboard and a monitor connected directly to the
computer or you can use a text terminal connected to the computer's serial
port.

If the machine you will be installing OpenBSD on has a DIN or PS/2
keyboard connector and a VGA or an SVGA video card, then all you need
to see what is happening during installation is a standard VGA or SVGA
monitor and a matching keyboard. This is the most convenient option on
i386 machines although there are exceptions like the PC/104 or
PC/104-*Plus* Single Board Computer (SBC) embedded systems, which may
be configured to do without keyboards or video cards:

http://www.pc104.org   (*PC/104 & PC/104*-Plus *information site*)

Other hardware platforms (e.g. Sun Sparc or Alpha workstations and
servers) usually let the operator control the machine via the serial port.
These machines offer full access to all settings, BIOS and hardware, and

don't need to be connected to keyboards or monitors, which is very convenient in data centers or everywhere else where space is at a premium. To install OpenBSD on such machines, you will have to find either a text terminal (they sell used for around $20 on eBay) or a laptop equipped with a serial interface (RS232) and a *text terminal emulator*, and connect one of these devices to the serial port on the target machine.

Access to BIOS or hardware settings via the serial port is less common on PC desktops or laptops, and not even all servers offer it as a standard feature. This can be fixed with cards like the PC Weasel or the PC Weasel 2000 available from Middle Digital, Inc., or the J1 card from Enidan Technologies, Ltd.

http://www.realweasel.com   *(Middle Digital, Inc.)*
http://www.enidan.com   *(Enidan Technologies, Ltd.)*

Before you connect to the serial port make, sure you have the right cable as not all manufacturers use the standard 9-pin RS232 connector (it may be marked as *COM1*, *COM2*, *serial*, *terminal*, or *console*). Also, make sure that the gender of the plugs on the cable matches the gender of the connectors on the target machine.

Another thing to look out for are the transmission settings, which should be listed in the target machine's manual, or somewhere on the outside of the machine's case. When you cannot find them, use the standard 9600 8N1 settings (that's 9600bps, 8 Data Bits, No Parity, 1 Stop Bit). If you are looking for a good terminal emulator (and an SSH client at the same time) for Microsoft Windows, try Simon Tatham's PuTTY:

http://www.chiark.greenend.org.uk/~sgtatham/putty/   *(PuTTY)*

> *The software is free, but watch out for crypto laws in your country. If you are unsure wether or not you are allowed to use it, follow the advice in Chapter 1,* Introduction.

If you are running Linux, BSD, or a commercial implementation Unix, you'll find plenty of free terminal emulators, all you have to do is search the relevant package and port repositories:

http://www.openbsd.org/ports.html   *(OpenBSD)*

http://www.netbsd.org/Documentation/software/	*(NetBSD)*
http://www.freebsd.org/ports/index.html	*(FreeBSD)*
http://rpmfind.net/Linux/RPM/	*(RPM-based Linux)*
http://www.debian.org/distrib/packages	*(Debian GNU/Linux)*
http://www.slackware.com/pb/	*(Slackware Linux)*
http://hpux.cs.utah.edu	*(Hewlett-Packard HP-UX)*
http://www.rge.com/pub/systems/aix/bull/	*(IBM AIX)*
http://freeware.sgi.com	*(SGI IRIX)*
http://www.sunfreeware.com (Sun Microsystems Solaris Operating System)	

3.2.9 How Are You Going to Install OpenBSD?

Another hardware issue to think about is just how OpenBSD will be loaded onto the target machine's hard disk. When you install OpenBSD for the first time, choose a computer with a storage device that will make system installation painless. A floppy disk drive will be sufficient, if you can plug your computer to local LAN, or to the Internet in order to download the system software; a CD-ROM drive will be enough when you want to install OpenBSD from a bootable CD-ROM disc (yet another reason to buy the official CD-ROM set); you will need both if you are installing from a non-bootable CD-ROM disc. The CD-ROM drive can be either an ATA or a SCSI device.

On some hardware platforms it may also be possible to boot from an attached external ZIP drive, tape or network, but it is less common and depends on the manufacturer or BIOS settings. Support for such installation procedures is typically found on PCs, workstations, or servers aimed at a higher-end market. Check your computer's manual to see if it possible. You will also have to take care of creating a bootable ZIP cartridge, or tape. The *INSTALL* files for each hardware platform contain useful hints, when such installation procedures are possible. When in doubt, ask on the *misc* or the *ports* mailing lists, or use your favorite web search engine to dig for clues. Useful answers to these problems can often be found in Linux *HOWTO* documents located at this address:

http://www.tldp.org   *(The Linux Documentation Project)*

Another good place to ask for help are mailing lists serving the NetBSD community, who are used to working with unusual configurations:

http://www.netbsd.org/MailingLists/   *(the NetBSD mailing lists)*

3.2.10 Tape Drives

If you plan to log all traffic passing through the firewall, you will have to store it externally so it doesn't fill all of the available disk space on the firewall host. It will be necessary to invest in a fast tape drive, preferably a SCSI unit. You will need to add it to the machine collecting logs, either the one that's running *pf* or a separate logging station. For more information about logging and the log storage space requirements refer to Chapter 11, *Logging and Log Analysis*.

3.2.11 Debugging Hardware

When hardware plays tricks, it is usually due to the problems with drivers, which can often be debugged in three ways: (a) using different hardware supported by OpenBSD, (b) editing the kernel (described in Chapter 4, *Configuring OpenBSD*), (c) fixing the driver for the offending piece of hardware (for advanced users only). Good sources of information are *INSTALL* files (see Table 3.1) for the platform you are using, Linux *HOWTO*s, the OpenBSD mailing lists, and the NetBSD mailing lists.

Sometimes a good book on hardware will be needed, such as [Rosenthal 2003]. Its author, Morris Rosenthal, provides a free boot sequence debugging flowchart, which might be worth investigating:

http://www.fonerbooks/poster.pdf   *(boot sequence debugging flowchart)*

3.2.12 Other Requirements

There are some other bits and pieces that should be considered, when you are building a firewall:

- *Connection to the Internet* — essential if you want to connect your network to the Internet, or when you want to install OpenBSD from the Internet; optional, if you have OpenBSD on CD-ROM, tape, ZIP, or on a server on your local network.
- *Uninterruptible Power Supply (UPS)* — for the firewall, internal hosts, and all network equipment (routers, switches, hubs, bridges, printers, etc.) OpenBSD has support for Advanced Power Management, see *apm(4)* and *apmd(8)*.
- *Optical links to external networks* — used to galvanically separate

networks. Use them, if you do not want a stray lightning to fry your LAN.

• *Cables* — network cables to connect the firewall to the outside world.

3.2.13 When in Trouble, Use the Manual

When you have a problem with a particular device, you should always check the OpenBSD manual page for that device. Of course, you will not have access to these pages before you install the system itself, but there is a solution in the form of the online access to the manual pages located at the following address:

http://www.openbsd.org/cgi-bin/man.cgi   *(OpenBSD Manual)*

The online help system can be used to access all manual pages from the past all the way to the latest incarnations of OpenBSD. If you are unsure what you are looking for, check the *Apropos* option and you will get a list of the closest matches. The system is simple, works, and there is no excuse for not using it. Once you have OpenBSD installed and working, use the manual pages that came with it. For hints on using the system manual available on the command line, refer to Appendix A: *Manual Pages*.

3.3 Downloading OpenBSD

The easiest way to download OpenBSD is with an FTP client that can copy whole directories such as *ncftp*, or with the good old *wget* (available for many popular operating systems):

http://www.ncftpd.com/ncftp/   *(ncftp)*
http://www.wget.org   *(wget)*

> *If you have trouble finding* wget *binaries for your system, use your favorite web search engine to locate them.*

You need to point your FTP client at */pub/OpenBSD/3.4* and copy the directory that contains the binaries for your hardware platform (see Table 3.1). If you use *wget*, use the following command to download OpenBSD 3.4 for *i386*:

```
$ wget --passive-ftp -r ftp://ftp.example.org/pub/
☞ OpenBSD/3.4/i386
```

Once you have the right binaries, download the *tools* directory that contains utilities for writing floppy disk images under MS-DOS and Microsoft Windows. They can be used to write any kind of floppy disk images, not just for the *i386* platform.

```
$ wget --passive-ftp -r ftp://ftp.example.org/pub/
☞ OpenBSD/3.4/tools
```

Note that you need to replace *ftp://ftp.example.org/...* with the URL pointing to the directory you wish to download from the chosen FTP server. The list of all currently available mirrors is published at the *OpenBSD FTP* page:

http://www.openbsd.org/ftp.html   *(OpenBSD Mirrors)*

3.4 Preparing Installation Media

When you are not using a bootable CD-ROM, you will have to use a boot floppy to start installation, the rest of the OS will be installed from a CD-ROM, tape, network, or however you choose to do it. The necessary utilities are located in the *tools* directory (see previous section). If you are using MS-DOS or Microsoft 95/98/Me write floppy images with *rawrite.exe*:

```
C:\openbsd> rawrite.exe floppy34.fs a:
```

On Microsoft Windows NT/2000/XP, use *ntrw.exe*:

```
C:\openbsd> ntrw floppy34.fs a:
```

On BSD, Linux, and Unix, use *dd(1)*:

```
$ dd if=floppy34.fs of=/dev/fd0 bs=36b
```

> *The location of the floppy disk device (/dev/fd0) may be different on your machine, check your system manual.*

If you are not having much luck with *floppy34.fs*, use *floppyB34.fs* (contains SCSI, Gigabit Ethernet, and RAID drivers), or *floppyC34.fs* (CardBus and PCMCIA drivers, particularly useful for installing OpenBSD on laptops).

3.5 Installing OpenBSD

Armed with a bootable CD-ROM, or a boot floppy disk, insert one of these devices into the appropriate drive and reboot the machine. This is what you should see on your screen (the actual messages may differ slightly):

```
reading boot.......
probing: pc0 com0 com1 pci mem[639K 31M a20=on]
disk: fd0 hd0
>> OpenBSD/i386 BOOT 1.29
boot>
```

The boot> prompt gives you a chance to type boot parameters, which you probably won't need in most cases. You can wait a few seconds for the next stage of the boot process to begin, or hit the **Enter/Return** key to start it right away:

```
booting fd0a:/bsd: 1339392+1871872+
```

A list of devices on blue background follows.

> *If something goes wrong here, you will have a few options: try other boot disks, remove the offending piece of hardware (check output to see which device was the culprit), or disable the offending device's driver in the kernel (see Chapter 4,* Configuring OpenBSD*). Also, if the computer won't boot from the floppy disk or the CD-ROM, you may have to go into the BIOS to change boot device settings. It is quite possible that your computer is set up to boot from the hard disk and skips the floppy and the CD-ROM drives. You can go into the BIOS if you press one of the special keys on the keyboard. To learn which key is that special one, reset the computer and the watch messages that show up on screen soon after the memory test. Typical choices are* **Ins**, **Del**, **F2**, **F10**, *etc.*

When all goes well, you should get to this point:

```
erase ^?, werase ^W, kill ^U, intr ^C, status ^T
(I)nstall, (U)pgrade, or (S)hell? i
```

Press the **I** key on the keyboard and then hit the **Enter/Return** key.
You should see a welcome message after which the system will ask you to
choose the terminal type used in the rest of the installation process. If you
have no specific preferences, different from the default vt220, just hit the
Enter/Return key:

```
Terminal type? [vt220] vt220
```

Next, you will have a chance to select your preferred keyboard encoding. If
you'd rather use the default US encoding, press the **N** key, then hit the **En-
ter/Return** key. Otherwise, press the **Y** key, hit the **Enter/Return**
key, and follow the instructions displayed on the screen:

```
Do you wish to select a keyboard encoding? [n] n
```

The next important message you see should be a warning about making
backup copies of data on the hard disk(s). This is the last chance to stop the
installation and make backups. No need to make them? Press the **Y** key,
then hit the **Enter/Return** key:

```
Proceed with install? [n] y
```

You should see a notice starting with the following message, ending with a
list of available hard disks:

```
Cool! Let's get to it...
  ...
Available disks are: wd0, wd1.
Which one is the root disk (or 'done') [wd0]
```

If you have only one hard disk, simply hit the **Enter/Return** key. Otherwise type the name of the disk you wish to boot OpenBSD from and hit
the **Enter/Return** key.

> *If you do not see all disks you have installed in your
> machine, you might need to try the floppy image with the
> SCSI disk drivers; for PCMCIA disks try the boot floppy
> with the PCMCIA drivers.*

Next, you will be given a chance to decide how much space on the chosen hard disk you wish to use for OpenBSD. We will not discuss sharing the same disk with other operating systems, because it is not a good practice to use such configurations on production firewall machines. Type yes and hit the **Enter/Return** key:

```
Do you want to use *all* of wd0 for OpenBSD? [no] yes
```

and you will enter the hard disk label editor (the OpenBSD version of MS-DOS *FDISK*, but much more powerful and useful). The disk label editor is not likely to win the best user interface category award, but it is functional. The first thing you need to do is display the current disk layout. To do that, type p and hit the **Enter/Return** key:

```
Initial label editor
> p
```

What you will see is a list of various parameters. The most important ones are:

```
  . . .
bytes/sector:
total sectors:
  . . .
```

With these, you can now find out the total capacity of the disk:

$$capacity(bytes) = bytes/sector \times total\ sectors$$

OpenBSD needs a minimum of two partitions: one for the / filesystem and one for swap. This is the easiest choice, but not the safest one. A much better way is to split your disks into more partitions, so you can implement more robust security controls over the filesystem. For example, some partitions like */home*, */tmp*, or */var* ought to be mounted in such way that they cannot be used to compromise the system by exploiting the set-user-ID (suid) and the set-group-ID (sgid) file options (see *chmod(1)*) or by filling the filesystem with garbage. The solution to the first problem are two handy *mount(8)* options: nodev and nosuid. The nodev option prevents the system from interpreting character or special device nodes (like the sensitive */dev/kmem*). Similarly, the nosuid options disables the set-user-ID and the set-group-ID file flags (see *chmod(1)*). These options are stored in */etc/fstab* (see *fstab(5)*), and you can display current settings with the *mount(8)* command once you install the system. If you start creating more than just a single / partition during the installation stage, the installer will add these options to */etc/fstab* automatically. It is possible to edit that file manually after you install the system.

You might wonder if it wouldn't be possible to just create a single / partition and set its options to `nodev` and `nosuid`. The answer is no, because some parts of the filesystem must have `dev` or `suid` options set. As for the problem of filling up the filesystem, dividing the disk into several partitions will automatically ensure that this is taken care of (partitions cannot grow without reformatting the drive).

Your disk could be divided into the following partitions (you will find instructions on how it's done on the following pages):

```
/
/home
/tmp
/usr
/usr/local
/var
/var/log
/var/mail
```

> *When you are setting up a logging firewall, you may also want to add another partition (or a separate disk) to store firewall logs. Storing them on a separate partition is good for security, because that way logs cannot fill the whole available space on the filesystem.*

The partition table printed on the screen may look similar to this one (when the disk is new and has never been formatted):

```
> p
  ...
16 partitions:
#      size    offset       fstype    [fsize   bsize    cpg]
  c: 3329424        0       unused    0        0
```

When you are reformatting a previously formatted disk, you could some-thing similar to the following output:

```
> p
  ...
16 partitions:
#       size   offset     fstype    [fsize   bsize   cpg]
 a: 3206956       63     4.2BSD     1024     8192    16
 b:   119381 3207019     swap
 c: 3329424        0     unused     0        0
```

When you see partitions other than c (you cannot delete it, because it rep-resents the whole disk), you will need to delete them before creating new ones. To delete a partition, type d and hit the **Enter/Return** key. You will be asked to type the letter representing the unwanted partition. Repeat this process for all existing partitions, except c.

Next, you will need to add at least two partitions (more if you want to use the nodev and nosuid options discussed earlier).

To add a new partition, type a and hit the **Enter/Return** key. You will then have to answer a few questions about the partition symbol (a through p, except *c*, start with a), partition offset, partition size, filesystem type, and mount point. A partition creation session looks like this:

```
> a
partition: [a]
offset: [63]
size: [3326337] 2000000
FS type: [4.2BSD]
mount point: [none] /
```

Partition offset. The number of the first free sector that can be a start of the next partition. For the first partition, it is usually 63. Accept it. For other partitions, the installer will suggest appropriate values based on the size of the previous partition. Simply accept these values, unless you have very important reasons to change them. (Note that this parameter is measured in *sectors*, not bytes.)

Partition size. This value must be lower than the total number of sectors available on disk in order to accommodate the swap partition and any other partitions you may want to create (on OpenBSD, just like on any other Unix, each directory, or filesystem, can be mounted on a different partition).

In the example on the facing page, the total number of free sectors on the disk is 3326337, out of which we cut 200000 for the / (root) filesystem.

The best way to start computing the size of partitions is to compute the size of the swap space, which should be at least twice the amount of RAM you have installed in your computer (in bytes). Then, divide that number by the number of bytes/sector for your disk and subtract the result from the total number of free sectors. (Note that this parameter too is measured in *sectors*, not bytes.)

The calculations required to change GB or MB values to bytes/sector are quite simple (suppose our machine has 128MB of RAM, and a 10GB hard disk):

$total\ capacity = 10GB = 10240MB$
$swap = 2 \times RAM = 2 \times 128MB = 256MB$
$/ = 1GB = 1024MB$
$/home = 512MB$
$/tmp = 2GB = 2048MB$
$/usr = 1GB = 1024MB$
$/usr/local = 1GB = 1024MB$
$/var = 1GB = 1024MB$
$/var/log = 3GB = 3072MB$
$/var/mail = 256MB$

Assuming that our disk has 1024 bytes per sector, the results (in sectors) are as follows:

$$swap = 256MB = \frac{256 \times 1024 \times 1024\ bytes}{1024\ bytes/sector} = 262144$$

$$/ = 1GB = 1024MB = \frac{1024 \times 1024 \times 1024\ bytes}{1024\ bytes/sector} = 1048576$$

$$/home = 512MB = \frac{512 \times 1024 \times 1024\ bytes}{1024\ bytes/sector} = 524288$$

$$/tmp = 2GB = 2048\,MB = \frac{2048 \times 1024 \times 1024\ bytes}{1024\ bytes/sector} = 2097152$$

$$/usr = 1GB = 1024\,MB = \frac{1024 \times 1024 \times 1024\ bytes}{1024\ bytes/sector} = 1048576$$

$$/usr/local = 1GB = 1024\,MB = \frac{1024 \times 1024 \times 1024\ bytes}{1024\ bytes/sector} = 1048576$$

$$/var = 1GB = 1024\,MB = \frac{1024 \times 1024 \times 1024\ bytes}{1024\ bytes/sector} = 1048576$$

$$/var/log = 1GB = 1024\,MB = \frac{1024 \times 1024 \times 1024\ bytes}{1024\ bytes/sector} = 1048576$$

$$/var/mail = 256\,MB = \frac{256 \times 1024 \times 1024\ bytes}{1024\ bytes/sector} = 262144$$

These values are not set in stone and, depending on your particular system configuration and needs, you may run out of space in one of these partitions or have plenty of free space lying unused. How can you find out just how big each partition ought to be? Start with the above template and install all software that you will use on the firewall. Use *du(8)* to find out how much space is left in each partition, e.g.: du -k /usr/local shows the number of *kilobytes* used in */usr/local*. When one of the partitions is filled above 75% of its total capacity, it might be a good idea to reinstall the system and adjust the size of that partition at the cost of another one that is filled well under its total capacity. If it is still too tight, you might consider moving the swap partition to another disk. Another good candidate for relocation is */var/log*. In either case, make sure that the second disk is plugged into a separate controller or the overall disk performance will decrease.

Partition filesystem type. For all non-swap partitions that value should be 4.2BSD. For swap partitions, use swap.

Mount point. The main (root) partition must be mounted under /, the swap partition does not have a mount point. When you plan to add additional partitions, their mount points are full paths that point to the directories that will be assigned to them. For example, if you are creating a separate partition for */usr/local*, its mount point will be */usr/local*.

You can check what partitions you created with the p command. When you are happy with your choices, use the q command. To prevent accidental damage, the installation script will ask you to confirm your choices:

```
> q
Write new label?: [y] y
The root filesystem will be mounted on wd0a.
wd0b will be used for swap space
Done - no available disks found.

You have configured the following partitions and mount points:

wd0a /
```

You can now start formatting the disk. The time it takes to finish this oper-ation is directly proportional to the disk's capacity. Type y and hit the **En-ter/Return** key. The disk starts spinning and you can make yourself a cup of tea and relax, you are getting close to having a fresh copy of Open-BSD to play with.

When all goes well, you should see the installation procedure ask you for the host name. Type it in and hit the **Enter/Return** key:

```
System hostname? (short form, e.g. 'foo') firewall
```

Next, you will be asked if you want to configure network services. You can skip that stage and do it later (see Chapter 4, *Configuring OpenBSD*), but if you do that you will not be able to install OpenBSD over the network and no FTP, HTTP, or NFS installation methods will be available.

If you decide to configure the network, type y and hit the **Enter/Return** key:

```
Configure the network? [y] y
```

The next piece of information that you see on screen should be the list of available interfaces:

```
Available interfaces are: rl0 rl1
```

The example on the previous page shows two interface cards, if you have more cards installed, but they are not recognized, you may need to configure them later on. Or, you could try alternative boot floppies with support for Gigabit Ethernet or PCMCIA cards, if that's what you are using.

Next, you need to tell the installation script which interface you wish to initialize. The order in which you initialize multiple interfaces does not matter as long as you configure them with proper settings that match the physical network layout:

```
Which one do you wish to initialize? (or 'done') [rl0] rl0
```

The next step is symbolic name assignment. The installation procedure suggest the host name you used earlier, but you can change it now or later (the information you enter here will be stored in */etc/hosts*, all you have to do is edit it:

```
Symbolic (host) name for rl0? [firewall] firewall
```

Next, you may set optional parameters for the interfaces. In the example below, the script is asking which type of media will be used to transmit packets (twisted pair, thin coaxial cable, or autoselect—the card will determine this automatically):

```
The default media for rl0 is
        media: Ethernet autoselect (none)
Do you want to change the default media? [n]
```

It is usually OK to accept the default values, but when you run into trouble and you don't know which parameters are applicable to your card or what they mean, check the online OpenBSD man pages (the URL was given earlier in this chapter). It is possible to change these parameters later, they are stored in the *hostname.** files, e.g. the *hostname* file for the rl0 interface is */etc/hostname.rl0*. For more information refer to Chapter 4, *Configuring OpenBSD*.

In the next step, you must assign a valid IP address to the interface, or you may type dhcp if you want the DHCP (see *dhcp(8)*) server on your network to assign the address automatically. It is not a good idea to assign the address of the firewall via DHCP, so either use a legal public IP address that you own, or use one of the private IP addresses (see Table 2.1). The address can be an IPv4 or an IPv6 number. After that, you will need to type in the netmask (see Chapter 5, *letc/pf.conf*):

```
IP address for rl0 (or 'dhcp') 192.168.255.10
  ...
Netmask? [255.255.255.0]
```

The information you enter here will be stored in *letc/hostname.** and *letc/hosts*, and can be changed afterwards.

After all interfaces have been configured, you should see these messages:

```
Done - no available interfaces found.
  ...
DNS domain name? (e.g. 'bar.com') [my.domain] example.com
```

You may now supply the DNS domain name for the firewall host (you can change it later, it is stored in *letc/hosts*). This part may be omitted, if you do not have your own domain, or when you plan to configure your firewall as a bridge, in which case it will not matter as such hosts are invisible. It is OK to just hit the **Enter/Return** key at this point or use any name you like as long as it doesn't clash with the host or domain names used on your network or on the external networks.

Next, you will be asked to supply the address of the DNS name server on your network. If the machine you are installing OpenBSD on will act as a basic firewall or a bridge, it will not need to use a DNS server, but there are exception: you need to use a DNS server, if you want to install OpenBSD over a network, but don't know the IP addresses of FTP, HTTP, or NFS servers you will use for that purpose. When OpenBSD is stored on your own internal servers, use the address of your local DNS server; when you install OpenBSD from an external server, like one of the public FTP mirrors, use the address of your ISP's DNS server.

```
DNS name server? (IP address or 'none') [none] 192.168.1.1
```

Whatever DNS information you supply here will be saved in *letc/re-solv.conf*. You can then enable access to the DNS server:

```
Use the nameserver now? [y] y
```

Once you are done with the DNS server configuration, you need to add the default route (the address of the default gateway that the firewall will send packets to). If you want that to be set up via DHCP, enter dhcp. Another option is to leave that information out, in which case you should type none. That last choice will not let you install OpenBSD over the network from external networks. You can later add the gateway's address to */etc/mygate*:

```
Default route? (IP address, 'dhcp' or 'none') 192.168.255.3
```

Once you are done, you'll be given a chance to edit network information with *ed(1)*. You probably don't want to do it, so hit the **Enter/Return** key and proceed with the installation leaving changes to the network configuration until later:

```
Edit hosts with ed? [n] n
 ...
Do you want to do any manual network configuration? [n] n
```

You are getting close to the start of the system installation stage, and now is time to set the superuser (root) account password:

```
Password for root account? (will not echo)
Password for root account? (again)
```

The password must be given twice. Once that is done, you can begin the installation of the operating system components. The installation program will give you several choices of software locations:

```
Sets can be located on a (m)ounted
filesystem, a (c)drom, (d)isk, or (t)ape device;
or a (f)tp, (n)fs or (h)ttp server.
Where are the install sets? (or 'done')
```

Choose the option that best matches your setup. The following discussion focuses on the installation over HTTP, which is a popular choice for machines without a CD-ROM drive. The FTP or NFS installation procedures are similar and will not be covered here to save space.

What you need to begin is an HTTP server that stores the following Open-BSD 3.4 files for your hardware platform:

```
bsd
bsd.rd
base34.tgz
etc34.tgz
comp34.tgz
man34.tgz
game34.tgz
```

The server itself does not need to be running OpenBSD, of course. All you need to make it work is place the files listed above in a publicly accessible directory and that that firewall host can connect to the server.

The first question that you will have to answer is the one about the address of the HTTP proxy. When there is no proxy to go through, type none and hit the **Enter/Return**:

```
HTTP/FTP proxy URL? (e.g. 'http://proxy:8080', or 'none')
[none] none
```

Then, you will be given a chance to see a list of HTTP servers on the Internet that you can use to install the system from. This will be a slow option, a local HTTP server is both more convenient and faster. If you want to see the list of available HTTP server that store OpenBSD binaries, type **y**, otherwise type **n** to use another, local or external HTTP server of your choice (you'll have to know its IP address):

```
Do you want to see a list of potential http servers? [n] n
```

Hit the **Enter/Return** key. Another parameter is the HTTP server's IP address:

```
Server IP address, or hostname? [192.168.255.1] 192.168.255.7
```

Finally, you need to supply the directory in which the files are residing, e.g.:

```
Server directory? [/] /openbsd/i386/
```

After you hit the **Enter/Return** key, you'll see a list of packages, some of which are optional, others essential. (This is the place where you will finally arrive at no matter which installation method you choose.) Selected packages are marked with x. To select/deselect a package type its name and hit the **Enter/Return** key. Only the most essential packages have been selected below, but if it is the first time you ar installing OpenBSD, you should add *man34.tgz*:

```
[x] bsd
[ ] bsd.rd
[x] base34.tgz
[x] etc34.tgz
[ ] comp34.tgz
[ ] man34.tgz
[ ] game34.tgz
```

After all is done, answer y to the following question:

```
Ready to install sets? [y] y
```

Answer n to the question about running the X Windows System. Running it on a firewall machine is *not* a good idea, unless you are planning to configure your OpenBSD workstation as a bastion host (see Chapter 2, *Firewall Designs*):

```
Do you expect to run the X Window System? [y] n
 ...
Saving configuration files...done.
 ...
Generating initial host.random file...done.
```

The last stage in the installation process is setting the local time zone:

```
What timezone are you in? ('?' for list) [US/Pacific]
 ...
Setting local time zone to 'NZ'...done.
 ...
Making all device nodes...done.
 ...
CONGRATULATIONS! ...
```

After all is done, you will be able to restart the system:

```
# halt
```

Then, restart the system with **Ctrl+Alt+Del** or a hardware reset button.

3.6 Securing Your Firewall Hardware

Remember that what is convenient during installation, is also yet another way for someone unauthorized to mess with your computer, so make sure you disable booting from all external storage devices except the hard disk.

Don't forget to protect access to BIOS settings with a password. If your computer's BIOS does not allow it, power your computer down after installing OpenBSD and disconnect or completely remove floppy disk drives, CD-ROMs and other devices that can be used to boot your computer using software other than what you installed.

## Chapter 4

Configuring OpenBSD

In this chapter we will discuss configuring OpenBSD for pf, performance, and security. Also discussed are user management and installing additional software from ports and packages.

Once OpenBSD completes its first reboot cycle, you will be able to log in as `root` using the password created during the system installation stage. There are a few things that you can do now—add ordinary user account, configure networking, *pf*, routing, add software, and patch the system.

4.1 User Management

Although you can do everything as `root`, it is never a good idea, because the system assumes that you know what you are doing and will not prevent you from doing stupid things like erasing the whole filesystem or over-writing */bsd* with garbage. You are the superuser after all, with all benefits and responsibilities it brings! The long history of stupid mistakes that required installing stuff from scratch convinces us that doing everything as `root` is dangerous and irresponsible. Let's see what you can do to help you save your system from your mistakes.

4.1.1 Adding Users

Every time you log on as `root` from the console, OpenBSD will remind you that it is not a good thing to do. (Another constant reminder is the # prompt, displayed in place of the $ prompt shown to ordinary users.) To avoid these reminders, create an ordinary user account that you will use to log on the firewall then 'become' `root`, if necessary. But the constant nagging is not the only reason to create an ordinary user account, without it you will not be able to log on your firewall via SSH (logging on as `root` over SSH is blocked by default and it should stay that way).

Logging as root is disabled, when the following entry is present /etc/ssh/sshd_config:

```
#PermitRootLogin yes
```

If you ever need to enable it (always a bad idea), remove the hash character (#) from that line and restart the sshd(8) *daemon with:*

```
# kill -HUP `cat /var/run/sshd.pid'
```

Adding a new user is simple, use *adduser(8)* and answer the questions you see on the screen. The first time you use it, the system will ask you a few questions related to the general settings that will be applied to all newly created accounts. Your answers are stored in */etc/adduser.conf* and can be changed at any time.

4.1.2 Letting Users Do As Root Does (su)

How does an ordinary user become root? With *su(1)*, but access to that command is limited to those users who belong to the wheel group. To add a user to wheel either type wheel when *adduser(8)* asks you about the groups you'd like to invite the newly created user to. Another way is to edit */etc/group*:

```
# vi /etc/group
```

and (assuming the name of the new user is joe) change:

```
wheel:*:0:root
```

to:

```
wheel:*:0:root,joe
```

To save changes, press the **Esc** key, then type :x, and hit the **Enter/Return** key. Afterwards, when you want to become root, type:

```
$ su
```

Hit the **Enter/Return** key and type in the root password you gave during installation. Congratulations! You are now the superuser root, with all of the powers and the responsibilities. To drop back to ordinary user status, type exit and hit the **Enter/Return** key. For more information, read the *su(1)* manual and remember not to give access to *su(1)* to anyone who asks. Ideally, you should only give it to the administrator that takes over the management of your machine. Junior administrators who are helping you, should only be given access to a few essential commands via *sudo(8)* discussed later in this chapter.

4.1.3 Changing the User Password

Users and administrators can change passwords with *passwd(1)*. You can only change your own password, unless you have root privileges, in which case you can change passwords for anyone on the system. The new password will need to be given twice:

```
# passwd joe
```

4.1.4 Giving Users Limited Access to Root Privileges (sudo)

Adding a user to wheel lets him or her become root, but that still doesn't prevent stupid mistakes. A better way to do it is through *sudo(8)*, which limits access to commands owned by root via settings stored in */etc/sudoers*. Unlike other system configuration files, */etc/sudoers* ought to be edited with a special tool, called *visudo(8)*. Only users with root privileges can use that command.

For example, to let joe run *pfctl(8)*, add the following line to */etc/sudoers*:

```
joe firewall = /sbin/pfctl
```

To save changes, press **Esc**, then type :x, and hit the **Enter/Return** key. Then, to use *pfctl(8)*, type something like this:

```
$ sudo pfctl -s rules
```

You will be asked to type your password (for user joe, not root).

> *Be careful with how much privileges you give to an ordinary user. Never, ever given anyone* `ALL : ALL,` `: /usr/bin/su,` *or* `: /usr/sbin/visudo` *rights.*

Access to *sudo(8)* and *su(1)* is independent of each other. For more information read the manual pages for *su(1)*, *sudo(8)*, *visudo(8)* and *sudoer(5)*.

4.1.5 Removing Users

Users can be removed with *rmuser(8)*, e.g.:

```
# rmuser joe
```

Again, you need to have `root` privileges to do that.

4.2 Hardening OpenBSD

Although OpenBSD is *very* secure in its default configuration, there are a few things that you can do to make it even safer, like disabling non-essential services or patching the system. Doing these things is essential before and after putting any system in production use regardless of its purpose and security track record.

4.2.1 Disabling Non-Essential Services

OpenBSD does not run many services enabled by default, but a few of these exists and should be disabled unless you really need them on a firewall. On OpenBSD 3.4 these services are: *ident(1)*, *comsat(8)*, *daytime*, and *time*. To disable them, open */etc/inetd.conf* in a text editor and put # at the beginning of these lines:

```
ident              stream  tcp    nowait  _identd
☞ /usr/libexec/identd      identd -el
ident              stream  tcp6   nowait  _identd
☞ /usr/libexec/identd      identd -el
127.0.0.1:comsat dgram   udp     wait    root
☞ /usr/libexec/comsat      comsat
[::1]:comsat     dgram   udp6    wait    root
☞ /usr/libexec/comsat      comsat
```

```
daytime          stream  tcp      nowait  root    internal
daytime          stream  tcp6     nowait  root    internal
time             stream  tcp      nowait  root    internal
time             stream  tcp6     nowait  root    internal
```

If you want to be 100% sure that the firewall exposes no unwanted services to the outside world, use the nmap(1) *port scanner (available in OpenBSD ports and packages) and aim it at your firewall host. Be careful with this tool and never install it on the firewall itself. Also, watch out who you are aiming it at. Port scanning can get you in trouble if you do it on hosts that you do not control, so don't try it outside of your network or you may encounter serious legal problems. Not every administrator has time to find out who is scanning her or his network.*

4.2.2 Patching

Patching the system is something that any OpenBSD administrator ought to do as soon as patches are available, because leaving your system unpatched is simply asking for trouble.

Applying patches to a firewall running OpenBSD is a bit different than doing the same on a workstation, because the firewall must not be loaded with the compiler toolbox (*comp34.tgz*) or the source code. There is just too much possible risk. The solution is to keep a separate machine for compiling modified binaries, which will later be transferred to the production machine. What is usually done be hand or by a custom script, may soon be automated by *debardage*, a very promising tool from *sysfive.com*:

http://debardage.sysfive.org   *(debardage home)*

Patch announcements are posted to *announce* and *security-announce* mailing lists. If you do not yet subscribe to these lists, do it now. Doing this will help you track patches released from the moment you subscribe, but you also need to check if there were any patches released before you subscribed. Also, the announcements are just that—announcements; you need to download the patches yourself. The list of patches for the current and previous releases of OpenBSD can be found on the *Errata* page:

http://www.openbsd.org/errata.html   *(OpenBSD Errata)*

*The OpenBSD team only supports the latest two releases
of the system. For example, after OpenBSD 3.4 was released, patches are only issued for OpenBSD 3.4 and 3.3,
but not for OpenBSD 3.2 or earlier releases. This policy
forces you to upgrade, which a good thing if you really
are serious about security.*

To apply patches, you will need to install the OpenBSD compiler tools
(*comp34.tgz*) and the OpenBSD sources for the same release as the one you
are running on the firewall, not the machine you are building patches on.
These are the same as the sources that have been used to build that particular release of OpenBSD, not the CURRENT sources held in CVS. For the
3.4 release, you need to to get the OPENBSD_3_4 branch of the source
code repository. Strictly speaking, the patches are in CVS, but extracting
them from there would take uninitiated users too much time and effort.

The official archives of sources for each release are available on the original
OpenBSD CD-ROMs or online from many OpenBSD FTP mirror servers
(see Chapter 3, *Installing OpenBSD*). If you are downloading them with
ftp(1), they are always available in the top directory for the release you are
using. For OpenBSD 3.4, descend into *pub/OpenBSD/3.4* and download
these files:

```
XF4.tar.gz
ports.tar.gz
src.tar.gz
sys.tar.gz
```

Next, move the source archives to the */usr/src* directory:

```
# mv XF4.tar.gz /usr/src
# mv ports.tar.gz /usr/src
# mv src.tar.gz /usr/src
# mv sys.tar.gz /usr/src
# cd /usr/src
```

and unpack them with:

```
# tar -zxvf *.tar.gz
```

Once you have the OpenBSD sources, you will need to download the patches. The latest set of patches is always available on the FTP mirror servers in the subdirectories of the *pub/OpenBSD/patches* directory. For example, if you are looking for patches for OpenBSD 3.4, you will find them in *pub/OpenBSD/patches/3.4*. Download the *3.4.tar.gz* archive into your home directory and unpack it:

```
# tar -zxvf 3.4.tar.gz
```

You will now have a directory named *3.4* with the following subdirectories:

```
alpha/
amiga/
common/
hp300/
i386/
m68k/
mac68k/
macppc/
mvme68k/
ports/
sparc/
sparc64/
vax/
```

Out of these subdirectories, only three are of interest to us: *common* (contains patches for all hardware platforms), *ports* (contains patches for the ports collection, applicable to all hardware platforms), and the subdirectory containing patches applicable to the hardware platform you use. For Intel x86 machines, you need the patches from *i386*.

As you can see, when you list them, they are numbered in the order they are released, and that's the order you should apply them in. This is important, because the same file may be patched more than once.

Every patch comes with detailed instructions on how you should apply it, so the first step is reading them:

> *Note that the author is using patches for OpenBSD 3.1 in*
> *this example, because there were no patches for Open-*

BSD 3.4 released at the time this book was sent to the printers. You should never patch sources of one release of OpenBSD with patches for another release.

```
# less /home/joe/3.1/common/004_sshbsdauth.patch
Fix a bug in the BSD_AUTH access control handling

Apply by doing:
        cd /usr/src
        patch -p0 < 004_sshbsdauth.patch
        cd usr.bin/ssh
        make obj
        make cleandir
        make depend
        make && make install
  ...
```

As you can see, we are told to change the present working directory to */usr/src* and apply this patch with:

```
# patch -p0 < /home/joe/3.1/common/004_sshbsdauth.patch

Hmm...  Looks like a unified diff to me...
The text leading up to this was:
--------------------------
|Fix a bug in the BSD_AUTH access control handling
|
|Apply by doing:
|        cd /usr/src
|        patch -p0 < 004_sshbsdauth.patch
|        cd usr.bin/ssh
|        make obj
|        make cleandir
|        make depend
|        make && make install
|
|Index: usr.bin/ssh/auth.c
|========================================================
|RCS file: /cvs/src/usr.bin/ssh/auth.c,v
|retrieving revision 1.41
```

```
|diff -u -r1.41 auth.c
|--- usr.bin/ssh/auth.c 19 Mar 2002 15:31:47 -0000        1.41
|+++ usr.bin/ssh/auth.c 22 May 2002 20:28:25 -0000
-------------------------
Patching file usr.bin/ssh/auth.c using Plan A...
Hunk #1 succeeded at 410.
done
$
```

What happens next depends on the commands listed in the *Apply by doing:* section. In case of *004_sshbsdauth.patch* for OpenBSD 3.1 shown above, we need to execute some additional commands to create new binaries from patched sources:

```
$ cd usr.bin/ssh
# make obj
# make cleandir
# make depend
# make && make install
```

Now you need to stop all related processes (*ssh/sshd* in this case) processes and restart them to make sure that the system and users use new binaries:

```
# kill -HUP `cat /var/run/sshd.pid'
```

Sometimes a full reboot will be required for the changes to have effect, in that case, restart the system with:

```
# reboot
```

Once you are happy that everything is working fine, you can copy new binaries to the production machine.

How do we know which binaries have been modified? The output from make install contains a list of binaries and other files changed during compilation. Make a list of their locations, ownership, and access rights. Use *scp(1)* to copy them to the production machine. Then, log on the production machine, become superuser with *su(1)*, replace old binaries with the new ones, and restart the relevant processes. (You must stop them first; merely restarting them with kill -HUP may not be enough.) A system reboot is not out of place in case of more extensive changes. Of course, it needs to be done at times when it will cause the least inconvenience to users. Use your own judgment to decide what needs to be done and when is the best time to do it.

> *You do not have to apply all patches. Patches issued for hardware platforms you do not use or for ports you do not install can be ignored. All others ought to be applied as soon as you learn about them.*

4.2.3 When a Patch Is Not Enough

There is another way to 'patch' the system, you can update the source of the system and ports via CVS and recompile everything. This will be necessary, if you are using binaries with statically-linked libraries (the library code and the actual program binary are glued together). When the same library is also available in dynamic form, you need to rebuild the library and the program that links it statically, even if the patch was issued for the library and not for the program. You will find the necessary information on these pages:

http://www.openbsd.org/anoncvs.html   (*OpenBSD AnonCVS*)
http://www.openbsd.org/faq/upgrade-minifaq.html   (*Upgrading OpenBSD*)

4.3 Configuring Networking

OpenBSD comes with most network services needed to run a firewall configured out of the box, all you have to do are some minor tweaks. Most of this is done during the installation stage, but may have to be fine-tuned before the machine is put into production use.

• *Hostname.* Stored in */etc/myname*, the hostname lets us use identifiers which are easier to remember that IP addresses. The contents of */etc/myname* is a short hostname, e.g. `firewall` instead of the full name, e.g. `firewall.example.com`. You can always check the full hostname and the short hostname with *hostname(1)*:

```
$ hostname
firewall.example.com
```

```
$ hostname -s
firewall
```

- *Host name database.* Stored in */etc/hosts.* A text file that stores host names, addresses, and aliases. Used when a *Domain Name System* (DNS) server is unavailable. Contains host names and addresses in the following format:

```
::1     localhost.prv.example.com     localhost
127.0.0.1    localhost.prv.example.com     localhost
# hostname and address on the private network
10.2.7.2    firewall.prv.example.com    firewall
# hostname and address on the DMZ network
10.3.8.2    dmzfw.dmz.example.com    dmzfw
# gateway
192.168.3.6    gateway.example.com    gate7
```

In the early days of the Internet, */etc/hosts* contained addresses and names of all hosts that existed at that time, nowadays it is used to store the names and addresses assigned to the host it is located on, or the hosts that are not in DNS, like some experimental machines that you do not want people to be able to find too easily. On a firewall, */etc/hosts* will usually contain the localhost address (127.0.0.1 for IPv4 or ::1 for IPv6) and one name/address/alias triple for each network it is connected to. In the example above, the firewall is connected to three networks, one private LAN segment, one DMZ LAN segment, and one external network.

- *Network name database.* Stored in */etc/networks.* That file is yet another remnant from the early days of Internet before DNS. It still comes in handy when you do not use DNS. If you decide to use */etc/networks*, add network addresses on separate lines, e.g.:

```
example.com    192.168.3    company
prv.example.com    10.2.7    private
dmz.example.com    10.3.8    dmz
```

Note that the network addresses are shorter than the host addresses. You can learn more about IP addresses from Chapter 3, */etc/pf.conf.* The format of information contained in this file is described in *networks(5).*

- *DNS Resolver.* Stored in */etc/resolv.conf.* If you want the firewall to make
  use of DNS (not run DNS, that's a different thing), add the addresses of
  the DNS servers you want the firewall to query to that file. The general
  format of */etc/resolv.conf* is shown below (for more information, read the
  man page for *resolv.conf(5)*):

```
lookup file bind
nameserver 10.5.3.8
nameserver 10.78.11.5
```

- *Interface configuration.* Stored in */etc/hostname.*.* Basic data required to
  configure network interfaces is stored in *hostname.** files whose names
  end with the name of the interface, e.g. if the firewall has three Realtek
  Ethernet cards, the address and configuration information (see the manual
  page for *ifconfig(8)*) for these cards will be stored in *hostname.rl0, host-
  name.rl1*, and *hostname.rl2.* These files are parsed by */etc/netstart*, when
  the system starts up. The file format for these files is described in *host-
  name.if(5)*, and additional information about configuring them can be
  found in *ifconfig(8)*.
- *Gateway.* Stored in */etc/mygate.* Every network segment has its own
  gateway to the world, the address where all packets not destined to hosts
  outside the same network segment are being sent to. It is a common mistake to confuse the gateway for the segment with the gateway for the
  firewall. When you are configuring firewalls using designs where Open-
  BSD and *pf* are also routing packets (Figures 2.1(a), 2.2, 2.3, 2.4(a), and
  2.5), the gateway address for local hosts behind *pf* is the local address of
  the machine that *pf* is running on, and the gateway address for the firewall
  is its external address.

In Figure 4.1, when the packet filter is not configured as an invisible filtering bridge, hosts on the private network are all configured with gateway
address *d.d.d.d* and the firewall is configured with gateway address *c.c.c.c.*
When the packet filter is configured as an invisible filtering bridge, hosts on
the private network are all configured with gateway address *b.b.b.b.*

4.3.1 More Than One Address on a Single Interface (Aliases)

Although not used very often on small networks, aliasing is quite common
on larger nets where a single machine acts as a firewall for more than one
host with a public IP address. In such cases, it is necessary to assign more

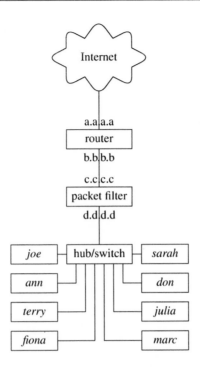

Figure 4.1: A screened LAN or a screened LAN segment protected with a separate packet filter.

than one IP address to a single interface. You can do it by hand with *ifconfig(8)*, e.g.:

```
# ifconfig rl1 alias 10.3.5.7
```

Such changes will not be permanent, so if you want them to survive the next reboot, you must add them to the interface configuration file:

```
# vi hostname.rl1
inet 192.168.255.11 255.255.255.0 NONE
inet 10.3.5.7 255.255.255.0 NONE
```

When you want to add an IPv6 address to *hostname.**, precede it with inet6 instead of inet.

To check the list of addresses assigned to an interface, use:

```
# ifconfig rl1
rl1: flags=8843<UP,BROADCAST,RUNNING,SIMPLEX,MULTICAST>
☞ mtu 1500
        address: 00:e0:4c:81:52:2f
        media: Ethernet autoselect (none)
        status: active
        inet 192.168.2.11 netmask 0xffffff00 broadcast
☞ 192.168.2.255
        inet 10.3.5.7 netmask 0xffffff00 broadcast
☞ 10.3.5.255
```

To check all interfaces, use:

```
# ifconfig -a
```

Aliasing is often used together with `binat` and `rdr` rules described in Chapter 7, *Packet Redirection*.

4.3.2 Pf Configuration Options

Once you finish configuring your firewall and you are ready to put it into production use, you should tell OpenBSD to run *pf* automatically at system startup. The startup scripts are already configured, and all you have to do is set two variables. Open */etc/rc.conf*, locate this line:

```
pf=NO
```

and change it to:

```
pf=YES
```

Another parameter found in */etc/rc.conf* and related to *pf* is the location of the *pf* ruleset that will be loaded at system startup:

```
pf_rules=/etc/pf.conf
```

If you feel you need to change it, replace */etc/pf.conf* with something else, but make sure it is owned by `root`, belongs to the `wheel` group and that only `root` has read/write privileges. This can be enforced with:

```
# chown root file
# chgrp wheel file
# chmod 0600 file
```

The last *pf* parameter found in */etc/rc.conf*, `pflogd_flags=`, is related to the *pflogd(8)* daemon and allows you to set some flags. You will find more information about it in Chapter 11, *Logging and Log Analysis*.

The changes you make to */etc/rc.conf* will not be put into use until the next system reboot. To enable *pf*, use the *pfctl(8)* utility as described in Chapter 16, *Firewall Management*.

4.3.3 Bridge Configuration Options

An OpenBSD bridge setup is a functional equivalent of an Ethernet learning switch (or an Ethernet bridge, for those who were around the time this name was more popular). As was already mentioned in Chapter 2, *Firewall Designs*, a bridge based on OpenBSD and mixed with *pf*, is a very practical and secure firewall solution because of its 'invisibility' to the outside world.

Bridge configuration is very simple and you should not have problems understanding it. From the point of view of the person configuring networking, a bridge is a group of interfaces known under a common name like *bridge0*. It is similar to a list of address aliases assigned to a single network interface. However, unlike those aliases, a bridge has no IP address.

> *This is a problem when you want to log on the bridge, which you can always do from the console, or over a separate interface with an IP address that you can connect to from another machine.*

Bridge configuration files are stored in */etc/bridgename.** files, e.g. the configuration for *babylon* will be stored in */etc/bridgename.babylon*.

Is it possible to configure more than one separate bridge on the same machine? Yes, but each interface can belong to at most one bridge. So, if you have a system with 6 network interfaces, you could configure it in the following ways:

- a single 6-point bridge
- a single 5-point bridge and a single 'visible' interface for logging on the bridge machine over a network
- two separate 3-point bridges
- three separate 2-point bridges
- one 2-point bridge, one 3-point bridge, and one 'visible' interface for logging on the bridge machine over a network
- an x-point bridge (where x is between 2 and 4) and two or more 'visible' interfaces or any other combination.

Of course, simple bridges only need two interfaces, and will be enough in many situations. If you decide to add another 'visible' interface to the bridge machine, make sure it is not accessible in any way from ordinary hosts. It should only be accessible from a separate administration network, ideally not connected to the outside world for maximum security. Figure 2.6 is a good example of how such configuration could look like.

A bridge can be created by hand with *brconfig(8)*, e.g. the following command creates and activates bridge *babylon* made from two interfaces: r10 and r11:

```
# brconfig babylon add rl0 add rl1 up
```

You can later add another interface to the bridge with:

```
# brconfig babylon add ne2
```

To remove an interface from the bridge, use:

```
# brconfig babylon delete rl0
```

To disable the bridge, use:

```
# brconfig babylon down
```

The changes you make to the bridge will only last for as long as the system's running. To make them permanent, write an */etc/bridgename.**

file, it will be automatically parsed by */etc/netstart*.

An */etc/bridgename.** file is a list of commands like these:

```
add rl0
add rl1
add ne2
up
```

There are six things you need to watch out for when you are using bridges:

- not all interfaces can be used to configure bridges. Some (very few) cards won't work.
- interfaces added to a bridge work in promiscuous mode, which puts additional load on the CPU. See Chapter 15, *Testing Your Firewall* for performance-related tips.
- when you are writing *pf* rules, you must remember that packets are matched on both interface, the one that packets arrive at and the one the packets leave from. This is not a problem for a 2-point bridge, simply write rules for one interface and pass all inbound and outbound traffic on another. But care must be taken when your bridge has more than two interfaces.
- remember that your bridge will forward all protocols, IP, IPX, Apple Talk, etc., so if you only want to process IPv4 and IPv6, add the `blocknoip` command to */etc/bridgename.** files for every interface, e.g.:

```
blocknoip rl0
blocknoip rl1
blocknoip ne2
```

- the 'visible' interface used for administration purposes will be seen not only on the administration segment, but also on other segments and you must write *pf* rules that disable access to it from all networks except the administration segment. For more information consult Chapter 8, *Packet Filtering*. Another way to protect it from unauthorized access would be to use *authpf(8)* to dynamically load rules that allow administrators access the bridge (see Chapter 12, *Using authpf*). Yet another way is to not use a visible interface, but log on the bridge via a serial console.
- bridge configuration is simple and it works almost out of the box, but when it doesn't there are a few things that you can do to make it work the

second time. First of all, edit */etc/hostname.** files for every interface
used in a bridge and remove all line that start with `inet`, `inet6`, or
`alias`. Next, reboot the system and check if everything is working.
When one of the hosts behind the bridge cannot communicate with the
rest of the world, ping it from another host and if you receive error messages, check the routing table on the target host with *route(8)*. You might
have forgotten to change the routes from the old gateway address to the
new one (the bridge has no IP address, hence the packets cannot be sent to
it). To check if everything is working, ping the broadcast address (form
the host you changed the routing table on), you'll find it with:

```
# ifconfig rl1 | grep broadcast
inet 10.1.1.1 netmask 0xffffff00 broadcast 10.1.1.255
# ping 10.1.1.255
```

To make the new route permanent, add it to */etc/netstart*.

Apart from letting *pf* to do the filtering of packets, bridges build with
OpenBSD can filter packets based on their *Ethernet addresses*, also known
as *hardware addresses* or *Medium Access Control (MAC) addresses*. This
topic is covered later in this chapter, when we discuss ARP requests. If you
are interested in logging packets passing through a bridge, read Chapter 11,
Logging and Log Analysis.

You can learn more about bridges from *bridge(4)*, *bridgename.if(5)*, and
brconfig(8).

4.3.4 IP Forwarding

When *pf* is supposed to do NAT or work as a filtering bridge, OpenBSD
must be configured to perform packet forwarding. You switch it on by
changing the value of the `net.inet.ip.forwarding` option:

```
# sysctl -w net.inet.ip.forwarding=1
net.inet.ip.forwarding: 0 -> 1
```

That change will not survive the next reboot, so you also need to edit
/etc/sysctl.conf and change:

```
#net.inet.ip.forwarding=1
```

to:

```
net.inet.ip.forwarding=1
```

When you want to do the same for IPv6 packets, repeat the above for `net.inet6.ip6.forwarding`.

4.3.5 Fixing FTP

One of the most common problems with firewalls is their handling of protocols that need to open more than one connection to communicate with another host. Such solutions are popular in peer-to-peer protocols, the H.323 multimedia communication protocol, and the good old File Transfer Protocol (FTP).

Multiple ports opened to serve the same connections are something that most firewalls can't handle properly on their own. Stateless firewalls don't work well with most of them (if at all); stateful firewalls (like *pf*) handle them a little better, but often break them. Both need additional help in the form of proxy software, available for free on the Internet or from the firewall manufacturer.

FTP is a good example of how protocols needing more than one connection can be made to work through firewalls, and how good proxy software can be used to control connections and fix problems that arise.

There are two modes that FTP clients and servers can work in: *active* and *passive*. The active mode, which is the default behavior of FTP, needs two connections, one for control (sending commands to the FTP serve) and one for data (file) transfers. The first connection is initiated by the client and can be traced by the firewall, but the second connection is initiated by the server and, from the point of view of the packet filter, looks like a connection attempt from the outside and will not be let through, because there is no information about its relation to the first connection. That's why we need proxy software. The idea behind proxies is simple, they capture connection attempts to external FTP servers and make the real connections on behalf of internal clients from the firewall host. The firewall accept connections initiated by external servers on a certain range of ports that the FTP proxy is listening to and the proxy passes those external connections to the internal client initiating the original connection. Both the FTP client and the FTP server communicate with the FTP proxy, without talking directly to each other. If all of this seems to be unnecessarily complicated, remember that it is the price that we pay for better security and convenience. Once configured, the proxy will work transparently and you will never need to worry about its presence. On top of that, a good proxy can limit access to external FTP servers, which helps prevent sensitive information leakage.

Fortunately for us, *pf* comes with its own *ftp-proxy(8)*, which looks like an ordinary FTP server to the FTP clients running on the private LAN segment and passes their requests through the firewall to external FTP servers that do the real work.

To enable *ftp-proxy(8)*, add the following line to */etc/inetd.conf*:

```
127.0.0.1:8021 stream tcp nowait root
☞ /usr/libexec/ftp-proxy ftp-proxy
```

The next step is the addition of a couple of rules to */etc/pf.conf*:

```
# Add this rule to the NAT section:
rdr on $prv_if proto tcp from any to any port 21 -> \
127.0.0.1 port 8021

# Add this rule to the packet filtering section:
pass in on $ext_if inet proto tcp from any to $ext_if \
port > 49151 keep state
```

The *$prv_if* and *$ext_if* codes are references to macros defining the names of the private and the external interfaces (see Chapter 5, */etc/pf.conf*). As you will notice, both the */etc/inetd.conf* and the `rdr` rules use the same port 8021, which may be changed to a different port when 8021 is not available, just make sure it is higher than 1023.

The default range of ports that *ftp-proxy(8)* will listen on for data connections is between 49152 and 65535, but you can change it with the −m and −M options. Additionally, you may have to add the rule that lets packets out of the internal network segment (*$prv_ad*) to the world. (You can skip this, if such rule is already present in */etc/pf.conf*):

```
pass out on $ext_if inet proto tcp from $prv_ad to any \
keep state
```

Then, restart *inetd(8)*:

```
# kill -HUP `cat /var/run/inetd.pid`
```

and reload *pf* rules:

```
# pfctl -F all
# pfctl -f /etc/pf.conf
```

The configuration of *ftp-proxy(8)* is described in its manual, so there is not much point rewriting it here. Default settings are good and can be safely used in most cases. When you run into problems with Network Address Translation (NAT), have a closer look at the description of the −n option. Another handy option is −A, which allows users to log on remote FTP servers as anonymous users, which usually means that they only get limited download privileges. This is enough for most non-technical users.

> *There is a way to connect to some servers without using* ftp-proxy(8). *Some FTP clients and servers can work in passive mode, which only needs one connection for data and control. A lot of FTP servers can detect problems with firewalls and switch to passive mode automatically. When automatic passive mode negotiation is not available, you can often do it by hand. Modern FTP clients and servers allow you to switch to passive mode with the* passive *command.*
>
> *Such solution, while usable, and better than nothing, is not perfect. You will still not be able to connect to many FTP servers, which is particularly noticeable when you try to browse FTP sites with a web browser—it will hang for a long time before returning an error message.*

Another problem with FTP are FTP servers sitting behind a firewall. They will most likely be located in a DMZ segment and will have a private IP. So, how does one reach an FTP server hidden so well? With *reverse ftp-proxy(8)* of course. You run it on the firewall host and make it wait for connections to port 21. When they arrive, they will be redirected to the FTP server in the DMZ and everything will work as if the server was directly accessible on the Internet.

Unfortunately, *ftp-proxy(8)* does not support it out of the box. You need to build your own version of *ftp-proxy(8)*. Don't worry it is not as scary as it sounds. You'll have to download OpenBSD sources (to another machine), update them to the latest version of OpenBSD (-rOPENBSD_3_4), apply the *ftp-proxy-reverse.diff* patch, and build a new *ftp-proxy(8)* binary. Scary? Only at the first sight. To begin, download *src.tar.gz* from */pub/Open-BSD/3.4* (you'll find the list of mirror servers in Chapter 3, *Installing OpenBSD*). Once you have it, download the *ftp-proxy-reverse.diff* patch from:

http://www.benzedrine.cx/ftp-proxy-reverse.diff   (reverse ftp-proxy patch)

Then, issue these commands:

```
$ su
# cd /usr
# tar -zxvf /home/joe/src.tar.gz
# setenv CVS_RSH ssh
# setenv CVSROOT the string that you put here is one of CVSROOT values
                 found on http://www.openbsd.org/anoncvs.html
# cvs -q get -rOPENBSD_3_4
# cd /usr/src/libexec/ftp-proxy
# patch < /home/joe/ftp-proxy-reverse.diff
# make
# cp /usr/libexec/ftp-proxy /usr/libexec/ftp-proxy.old
# cp /usr/obj/libexec/ftp-proxy/ftp-proxy
☞ /usr/libexec/ftp-proxy
```

What you will get is a new binary that can redirect FTP clients to FTP servers using private IP addresses hidden behind a firewall.

To enable *ftp-proxy(8)*, add the following line to */etc/inetd.conf*:

```
a.b.c.d:21 stream tcp nowait root
☞ /usr/libexec/ftp-proxy ftp-proxy -R 10.1.1.4:21
```

Let's explain a few things: a.b.c.d is the address of the external interface at which connection attempt from FTP clients will arrive; 21 is the standard FTP port number; 10.1.1.4 is the address of the internal host running the FTP server on port 21. When you want to run the FTP server on a higher port (> 1024), change the port number for the internal server, e.g.:

```
a.b.c.d:21 stream tcp nowait root
☞ /usr/libexec/ftp-proxy ftp-proxy -R 10.1.1.4:8021
```

If you want to learn more about FTP, consult [RFC 959] and [Stevens 1994].

4.3.6 Taking Control of ARP

Contrary to popular belief IP addresses are not enough for TCP/IP packets to reach their destinations. Another piece of information required to make it happen is the destination's *Ethernet Media Access Control (MAC) address*, sometimes called the *Ethernet address* or the *hardware address*. They are used by hosts, routers, and bridges to pass IP packets from one point on the network to another. Unlike IP addresses, which are assigned by the administrator, Ethernet addresses are assigned by the network interface card manufacturers. Every Ethernet network interface card in the world has a unique 6-byte number burned into its PROM chip and that number is its' Ethernet address. You can can find out what it is on your machine with *ifconfig(8)*:

```
# ifconfig rl0
rl0: flags=8843<UP,BROADCAST,RUNNING,SIMPLEX,MULTICAST>
☞ mtu 1500
        address: 00:00:1c:d7:4d:06
  ...
```

The Ethernet address is displayed as a string of six hex numbers separated with a colon(:).

Because Ethernet addresses cannot be used on the Internet (routing would be a nightmare), there must be a way to translate between the IP address space and the Ethernet address space. That is the job of the Address Resolution Protocol (ARP) [RFC 826]. The way it works is quite simple. Suppose that the gateway your internal network is connected to receives a packet whose destination address is 10.1.1.32. If requests for the same address have been received in the last few minutes, there is a chance that the IP/Ethernet address pair is still stored inside the ARP cache; when this is not a case, ARP will *broadcast* a message asking who has this address.

*A 'broadcast' is a message sent to all machines on the
same network segment.*

Such messages are being listened to by all machine on the same network
segment and the one that has an interface to which you assign the IP
address of 10.1.1.32 will send its IP/Ethernet address information to the
gateway who will store it in its cache. The machine answering
the gateway's call will store the gateway's IP/Ethernet information and both
will communicate with each other without sending ARP requests
unless there's been a long period of inactivity between them and one of
them removes the IP/Ethernet information from its cache. You can watch
ARP in action with *tcpdump(8)*:

```
# tcpdump -n -e arp
tcpdump: listening on rl0
16:55:11.548546 0:40:25:e3:40:af ff:ff:ff:ff:ff:ff 0806 60: arp
☞ who-has 10.1.1.32 tell 10.1.1.1
16:55:11.549173 0:41:26:e4:41:af 0:40:25:e3:40:af 0806 60: arp
☞ reply 10.1.1.32 is-at 0:41:26:e4:41:af
```

There might be a long time before you see anything, but eventually you
should start seeing output similar to the one shown above.

ARP essentially run on autopilot, which is why many young administrators
often do not know that it exists. Which is a pity, because there are a few
tricks that can make network management easier as well as making your
network more secure.

The first feature of ARP that can come handy in everyday network administration routine is the ability to change the MAC address of the interface.
Why would you want to do it? There are two popular cases: failover solutions (when one machine is taking over the responsibilities of another and
must have the other machine's IP and MAC addresses to cause the least
havoc on the network) and dealing with ISPs who filter MAC addresses and
are slow or unwilling to change their filter rules when you change the
network interface card that connects your network to their routers. The solution is to assign the old MAC to the new interface. Contrary to what
you'd expect, you cannot do it with *ifconfig(8)*, but must download and
build a separate tool called *sea*. Fortunately, it is quite easy to do. Download the *sea.c* source code:

```
$ lynx -dump
☞ http://www.devguide.net/books/openbsdfw-02-ed/sea.c > sea.c
```

build *sea*:

```
# gcc -Wall -o sea sea.c -lkvm
```

boot OpenBSD into single-user mode:

```
# reboot
boot> boot -s
```

run *sea*:

```
# ./sea rl0 00:00:00:00:00:01
```

> *Do not use the* `00:00:00:00:00:01` *address on your
> network. It is just an example. Use the old card's MAC
> address instead and do not use the old card on another
> host on the same network segment, unless you change it's
> MAC address as well. Two interfaces with the same MAC
> address is asking for trouble.*

Check that the interface is reconfigured properly:

```
# ifconfig rl0 | grep address
```

If all is working fine, add the *sea* command to */etc/netstart* to make sure
that the new MAC address is assigned automatically on every system
reboot. Next, restart the system:

```
# reboot
```

> *Not all cards allow you to change their MAC address, but
> they are in minority.*

What if you wanted to do as your ISP does and also filter packets based on
their MAC addresses? It is not possible with *pf*, but you can do it, if you
configure your host as a bridge (see earlier sections in this chapter), because
the MAC address filtering code is a part of the bridge code base, instead of

being a part of the *pf* code (this is no accident, there are good reasons for this).

There two kinds of rules for MAC address filtering: `block` or `pass`. Their syntax is simple: every rule starts with the `rule` keyword followed by:

- action keyword: `block` or `pass`
- direction keyword: `in` or `out`
- interface name: the `on` keyword followed by the name of the interface the rule will apply to.
- source MAC address: the `src` keyword followed by the MAC address of the interface the rule will apply to. This part is optional.
- destination MAC address: the `dst` keyword followed by the MAC address of the interface the rule will apply to. This part is optional.

> *The rules can be added with brconfig(8) or the can be listed in the appropriate /etc/bridgename.* file.*

For example, the following rule blocks all inbound traffic on `r10`:

```
rule block in on r10
```

This rule will pass all outbound traffic on `ne1`:

```
rule pass out on ne1
```

What if you wanted to block outbound traffic from just a few interfaces? Use the following rules (`ne1` is the external interface in this example):

```
rule block out on ne1
rule pass out on ne1 src 00:00:00:00:00:01
rule pass out on ne1 src 00:00:00:00:00:02
rule pass out on ne1 src 00:00:00:00:00:03
```

> *Please note that the last matching rule wins, hence the global* block *or* pass *rule should be listed* before *more specific rules. Also worth remembering is the fact that*

> *src and* dst *sections are optional and independent of each other; you can have either, or both, of them in your rules, if that's what you need.*

Another layer of defense is based on ARP is *static ARP*. As you might suspect, static ARP does not allow automatic ARP cache updates. How could it be useful? Suppose that someone takes over one of the hosts on your internal network, or plugs his laptop into a free connector on a hub or switch, to hijack the communications of another host on the same network segment. All he has to do is assign an IP number used by the target host to the host he is in control of (it is useful if the target other host is crashed or powered down, that can be arranged) and ping a few addresses on the same segment. Since all other hosts do not have the rouge machine's MAC address in their ARP caches, the hacker will ping a series of hosts, which will cause them to update their ARP caches. In a matter of seconds, the rouge machine is being recognized as the old host and can talk to other hosts as if nothing has happened. The attacker uses the very mechanism that makes ARP so useful—the automated discovery and learning of the Ethernet addresses. What can you do to prevent it?

First of all, you should be using a switch and not a hub. This makes network sniffing a lot more difficult. It isn't fool-proof (there are tools that turn switches into hubs by flooding them with requests that the switch cannot handle). Next, you supply the gateway machine with the static IP/Ethernet address information for all machines on the network segment in question and turn ARP off (the interface should have the NOARP flag turned on):

```
# ifconfig rl0 -arp
# ifconfig rl0
rl0: flags=88c3<UP,BROADCAST,RUNNING,NOARP,SIMPLEX,MULTICAST>
mtu 1500
# arp -d -a
# arp -s 10.1.1.32 0:41:26:e4:41:af permanent
# arp -s 10.1.1.33 0:41:26:e4:41:b0 permanent
# arp -s 10.1.1.34 0:41:26:e4:41:b1 permanent
# arp -s 10.1.1.35 0:41:26:e4:41:b2 permanent
```

> *Be careful! Disabling ARP and clearing the ARP cache is the best way to loose network connection. Do it from a*

script or from the console, where you have full control over the system.

You can use static ARP on every host on the same network segment as well. Their ARP caches only need to store the IP/Ethernet information for the gateway.

If you want the static ARP configuration to happen automatically at every system restart, place the `arp` commands in */etc/netstart* and add the `-arp` command to the appropriate */etc/hostname.** file.

The gateway will now only send and accept packets to/from the MAC addresses it has in its ARP cache, the cache will not be altered dynamically. It is a double-edged sword; when you change the network interface on one of the hosts, you will have to update the ARP caches entry for that host on the gateway, or the gateway will not be able to communicate with that host. You could also change the MAC address of the interface on that host to the address of the old interface.

On a related subject, when you are using OpenBSD configured as a bridge, you can prevent bridge table poisoning with the `-learn` and `discover` commands placed in the */etc/bridgename.** file for every interface that belongs to the bridge.

For example, to set up static entries in the bridge table for hosts connected to the bridge via `ne1`, `ne2`, and `ne3`, use:

```
flush
-learn ne1 static ne1 01:23:45:67:89:ab
-discover ne1
-learn ne2 static ne2 01:23:45:67:89:ac
-discover ne2
-learn ne3 static ne3 01:23:45:67:89:ad
-discover ne3
```

Is such protection strong? Not really, attackers can change their hosts' MAC addresses as easily as you can but, it does prevent stupid mistakes and makes it a little more difficult to break through your defenses. The best level of protection can be achieved when you combine pf, *MAC address filtering, authentication, encryption, and some kind of NIDS.*

4.4 Automated System Reboot

A system 'panic' is a an unforeseen event that causes system halt. The system drops to the debugger and waits for the operator to take care of the problem and reboot the machine, which is not always the desired behavior for a firewall, especially when the firewall is managed remotely. A better solution would be for the system to reboot itself. This can be done if you change ddb.panic to 0:

```
# systcl -w ddb.panic=0
```

Then, make this change permanents in */etc/sysctl.conf* and change:

```
#ddb.panic=0
```

to

```
ddb.panic=0
```

4.5 Swap Encryption

Another level of security, desired on workstation and servers, is swap encryption. This is less necessary on a firewall, but if you have some CPU cycles to spare, set vm.swapencrypt.enable to 1:

```
# systcl -w vm.swapencrypt.enable=1
```

Then, make this change permanents in */etc/sysctl.conf* and change:

```
#vm.swapencrypt.enable=1
```

to

```
vm.swapencrypt.enable=1
```

4.6 Working with Securelevels

Securelevels define different kernel security levels at which certain actions are permitted or not. There are four securelevels identified with numbers -1, 0, 1, and 2. The higher the securelevel of the kernel, the lower the privileges granted by the kernel.

To change a secure level, use *sysctl(8)*, e.g.:

```
# sysctl -w kern.securelevel=2
```

Permanent changes to that value should be recorded in */etc/rc.securelevel*:

```
securelevel=2
```

While you might be tempted to raise the default securelevel to 2 (the default value is 1) it is not always a good idea. Although you gain greater security, you also loose flexibility of administration, as some changes can only be undone if you put the operating system in single-user mode and you need to reboot the machine with:

```
boot> boot -s
```

Then, you can undo the changes that are forbidden under lower securelevels or in multi-user mode.

On a firewall, the most important securelevels are 1 and 2 and they:

- *Securelevel 1*. It is impossible to remove schg and sappnd flags (see *chflags(1)*) without booting into single-user mode. Imagine that you set schg on */etc/rc.conf*, */etc/pf.conf*, or */etc/rc.securelevel*—every change would require booting into single-user mode. Secure? Yes, but not convenient.
- *Securelevel 2*. It is not possible to make changes to NAT or filtering rules with *pfctl(8)*.

This is only a part of the things that change under different securelevels, but they are most often of concern to firewall administrators. For more information about securelevels, read *securelevel(7)*.

4.7 Setting Time and Date

It is an old joke that in Unix, when you want to check time, you use *date(1)*. But checking time and date is not the only thing you can do with this tool, it is also possible to set time and date. You must have `root` privileges to do it, though.

Read *date(1)* for more information. For more accurate time measurement, use NTP.

4.8 Configuring the Kernel to Solve Hardware Problems

When trying different configuration options doesn't help, there are four ways to solve hardware problems in OpenBSD:

1. replace the offending piece of hardware with one that is supported by OpenBSD
2. use the configuration utilities provided by the manufacturer to tweak hardware,
3. edit the OpenBSD kernel
4. build a new kernel.

When (1) and (2) fail, (3) and (4) are your last resorts. The last option is only possible when you already have OpenBSD installed on the target or backup machine. It is described in Section 5 of the *OpenBSD FAQ*, so we'll not dwell on it here.

http://www.openbsd.org/faq/index.html   *(OpenBSD F.A.Q.)*

Let's dwell on option (3). Although configuring the kernel is not difficult, it is one of the less-known procedures, often thought of a some kind of magic. In reality, there is no magic behind this, although editing the kernel may indeed seem like doing brain surgery while the patient is half-asleep. However, there may be times when you just have to edit the kernel no matter how much you fear it, simply to get the system to start at all. Not that it happens often, but when it does, you need to know what to do. The first thing you need to do when you are having problems with hardware, is removal of all non-essential hardware like sound, radio/TV, network, RAID, SCSI controller, and other cards. ISA cards are common culprits and if you are using any, chances are that they are causing problems. Try to remove them and boot OpenBSD in a bare configuration with an IDE hard disk, then if all goes well, add devices one at a time and watch messages displayed at boot time and in system logs (*/var/log/messages*).

```
rl0 at pci0 dev 6 function 0 "Realtek 8139" rev 0x10: irq 12
address 00:00:1c:d7:4d:06
```

Messages like the one above will tell you where you should look for problems, e.g. things like IRQ numbers and device names can later be used to find information related to the cause of the trouble.

4.8.1 Make a Copy of the Old Kernel

Before you start editing the kernel, you should make a copy of the old kernel file:

```
# cp /bsd /bsd.old
```

> *This may not always be possible (e.g. when you are installing OpenBSD), in which case you can be excused for not making a copy, but remember to be careful.*

4.8.2 User Kernel Config (UKC)

The User Kernel Config (UKC) is a tool for making changes to the OpenBSD kernel without rebuilding it from source. You can enter UKC in two ways:

1. at boot time, from the boot prompt:

    ```
    boot> boot -cs
    ```

2. while the system's running, as user `root` (the modified kernel will be written to */bsd.fix*):

    ```
    # config -e -o /bsd.fix /bsd
    ```

Once you enter the UKC, you should see the following message:

```
OpenBSD 3.4 (GENERIC) #44: Sat Mar 29 13:22:05 MST 2003
    deraadt@i386.openbsd.org:/usr/src/sys/arch/i386/com-
pile/GENERIC
Enter 'help' for information
ukc>
```

Out of many options available in UKC, the following are most important:

- list — shows the current kernel configuration. Displays many pages of information. Enter/Return scrolls pages forward. Most devices listed here have their own manual pages, where you can learn about them (just remember to remove the numeric suffix, when you try man *device-name* or apropos *devicename*).
- show — displays all device entries with the given attribute, e.g. if you are hunting down a troublesome ISA card, try looking for devices that use the same memory port or IRQ:

```
ukc> show irq 10
148 ne1 at isa0 port 0x300 size 0 iomem -1 iosiz 0 irq 10 drq
-1 drq2 -1 flags 0x0
151 we1 at isa0 port 0x300 size 0 iomem 0xcc000 iosiz 0 irq
10 drq -1 drq2 -1 flags 0x0
166 sp0 at pss0 port 0x530 size 0 iomem -1 iosiz 0 irq 10 drq
0 flags 0x0
167 wss0 at isa0 port 0x530 size 0 iomem -1 iosiz 0 irq 10
drq 0 drq2 -1 flags 0x0
ukc> show port 0x300
148 ne1 at isa0 port 0x300 size 0 iomem -1 iosiz 0 irq 10 drq
-1 drq2 -1 flags 0x0
151 we1 at isa0 port 0x300 size 0 iomem 0xcc000 iosiz 0 irq
10 drq -1 drq2 -1 flags 0x0
154 el0 at isa0 disable port 0x300 size 0 iomem -1 iosiz 0
irq 9 drq -1 drq2 -1 flags 0x0
162 mpu* at isa0 port 0x300 size 0 iomem -1 iosiz 0 irq -1
drq -1 drq2 -1 flags 0x0
```

When you find devices using the same memory port and/or IRQ, you will have to either change or disable one of them (see below) or run manufacturer's configuration utilities to change the memory port and/or IRQ settings in the device's BIOS.

- find — look for device. You can display whole families of devices, when you omit the number, e.g.:

```
ukc> find ne
 95 ne* at pci* dev -1 function -1 flags 0x0
 96 ne* at pcmcia* function -1 irq -1 flags 0x0
147 ne0 at isa0 port 0x240 size 0 iomem -1 iosiz 0 irq 9 drq
-1 drq2 -1 flags 0x0
148 ne1 at isa0 port 0x300 size 0 iomem -1 iosiz 0 irq 10 drq
-1 drq2 -1 flags 0x0
149 ne2 at isa0 port 0x280 size 0 iomem -1 iosiz 0 irq 9 drq
-1 drq2 -1 flags 0x0
212 ne* at isapnp0 port -1 size 0 iomem -1 iosiz 0 irq -1 drq
-1 flags 0x0
ukc> find ne2
149 ne2 at isa0 port 0x280 size 0 iomem -1 iosiz 0 irq 9 drq
-1 drq2 -1 flags 0x0
```

- add — adds a new device as a clone of another device. Simply follow the instructions you see on screen. When you want to add a driver for a device not included in the kernel, you will have to rebuild the kernel as instructed in *config(8)* and in section 5 of the *OpenBSD FAQ*:

  http://www.openbsd.org/faq/index.html

- change *device* — changes *device* parameters, like IRQ, memory port, or flags. Use this command after you change card settings to sync them with the kernel.
- disable *device* — disables *device*.
- enable *device* — enables *device*.

After you make changes to the kernel, you can save them with quit.

If you had to make changes to the kernel just to boot the system (and entered UKC with boot> **boot -cs**), remember to enter UKC again with:

```
# config -e -o /bsd.new /bsd
```

Then, repeat all the changes you made to the kernel, save them with quit, and run these commands:

```
# cp /bsd /bsd.old
# mv /bsd.new /bsd
# reboot
```

> *When you make a mistake or get lost, you can always abandon editing without making changes permanent with the* exit *command.*

4.8.3 Brain Transplants for OpenBSD

What if the hardware problems are so severe that your machine refuses to boot and you cannot enter UKC? When editing the kernel on the same machine is out of question, you can do it on another machine (it must use the same version of OpenBSD and the same hardware platform, unless you plan to cross compile for another platform).

Use the following command to edit the current kernel and write the modified version to */bsd.new*, leaving the original intact:

```
# config -e -o /bsd.new /bsd
```

Then, once you are done, you can transfer the kernel to another device. There are many ways to do it, you can boot the target from a floppy, mount the hard disk and copy the new image to the hard disk, or you can install the target's hard disk on another computer, mount it, and then copy the new kernel to it.

4.9 Adding and Compiling Software

There are two ways to add software to the basic OpenBSD system: ports and packages.

Ports are compiled from source while packages are pre-compiled binaries. Although ports are more advanced and more flexible, keeping source code and compiler tools on the firewall is not a good idea. You need another machine to build them and transfer finished binaries to the firewall. For additional information, see Section 5 of the *OpenBSD F.A.Q.*

If you decide to install a package, download it from the *packages* directory for your chosen hardware platform, e.g. */pub/OpenBSD/3.4/packages/i386*.

To install the packages, use *pkg_add(1)*, e.g. to install *nmap*:

```
# pkg_add nmap-x.xx.tgz
```

4.10 Configuring Disks

Hard disk configuration is done with *fdisk(8)*, *newfs(8)*, *disklabel(8)*, *mount(8)*, and *fsck(8)*.

The procedure required to add a new disk to the system, after the system is installed and running, is quite simple:

• put a new drive into the machine running OpenBSD.
• start the system.
• run *disklabel(8)* on the new disk drive, its device name is displayed in output generated with *dmesg(8)*.
• after you crate partitions with *disklabel(8)*, run *newfs(8)* to create file systems on the new disk.
• modify */etc/fstab* (read *fstab(5)* and *mount(8)*) so the system knows which point the new disk should be mounted at.
• reboot the system with *reboot(8)*.

When there are problems with disks, run *fsck(8)* on the problematic disk, that's what the system does automatically after crash.

4.10.1 RAID

The use of RAID on a firewall is not required unless you are planning to log all traffic passing through a very fast link. If you decide to do it, you will have two choices: implement it in hardware with a RAID controller supported by OpenBSD, or implement it in software, using OpenBSD tool. You will find all necessary information in *raid(4)* and *raidctl(8)*.

/etc/pf.conf

In this chapter we learn what /etc/pf.conf is, how it is structured, and what tools can be used to make writing and managing it a little easier. A short course in CVS is provided for those who may not know how to use it. Also discussed are syntax rules for macros, addresses, address families, ports, protocols, tables, and anchors.

Once you define your firewall policy and choose the firewall design that best matches it, you must describe what you want using the language that *pf(4)* understands. That description is called a *ruleset*. As you will no doubt notice, a lot of pages in this book are devoted to creating rulesets, so it is a good idea to learn some basics.

5.1 Inside pf.conf

Pf(4) rulesets are plain ASCII (see *ascii(7)*) text files. They are written according to the syntax rules described in *pf.conf(5)*. The default ruleset is located in */etc/pf.conf*, but it can be changed, if you wish so. Rulesets are managed with *pfctl(8)*, which checks their syntax before loading them into memory. When you are testing different rulesets, you can use the *pfctl(8)* −f option to load the chosen ruleset, e.g.:

```
# pfctl -f /home/joe/pf-test-2.conf
```

Once you are happy with one particular ruleset, you can either copy it to */etc/pf.conf* or configure your system to load that ruleset directly from its present location (see Chapter 4, *Configuring OpenBSD*). Just make sure that the ownership and the permissions for the new ruleset are set to:

```
# chown root:wheel /home/joe/pf-test-2.conf
# chmod 0600 /home/joe/pf-test-2.conf
```

Pfctl(8) is described in Chapter 16, *Firewall Management*.

> Although pf.conf *does not have to be stored in /etc, we'll refer to it using its default name and location to avoid confusion. If you want to choose a different name and/or location for this file, consult Chapter 4,* Configuring OpenBSD *for instructions on how to modify /etc/rc.conf.*

The *pf(4)* configuration file is divided into several sections, all of which are optional, but when they do appear in *pf.conf*, they must be listed in the expected order, with the exception of *macros* and *tables* that can be defined anywhere (but before they are used for the first time). The order of these sections in *pf.conf* is as follows:

- *Macro definitions* — the equivalent of global variables. Very handy when you are writing template ruleset that will use similar rules applied to different interfaces or address ranges. Macro definitions can appear anywhere in *pf.conf* as long as they are listed before they are used for the first time. More information on this subject is given later in this chapter.
- *Tables* — collections of host and network addresses used to construct dynamic rulesets and to speed up the process of packet/address matching. More information on this subject is given later in this chapter and in Chapter 9, *Dynamic Rulesets*.
- *Options* — global settings that affect all rules. There is no separate chapter devoted to them. Each option is discussed in connection with its behavior and the rules it affects.
- *Scrub rules* — packet normalization rules. Described in Chapter 6, *Packet Normalization*.
- *Packet queuing rules* — Alternative Queuing (ALTQ) rules. You need them when you want to implement bandwidth shaping, Quality of Service, or load balancing on your network. These rules are described in Chapter 10, *Bandwidth Shaping*.
- *Packet redirection rules* — implement Network Address Translation (NAT), redirection, masquerading, managing changes in network layout, and 'expanding' the shrinking IPv4 address space. Discussed in Chapter 7, *Packet Redirection*.
- *Packet filtering rules* — implement your packet filtering policy. Described in Chapter 8, *Packet Filtering*.

You will find an empty *pf.conf* template (*template-pf.conf*) on this book's companion web site:

http://www.devguide.net/books/openbsdfw-02-ed/index.html

5.1.1 Changing the pf.conf Section Order

The order of *pf.conf* sections (as well as correct rule syntax) is checked by *pfctl(8)* before loading the ruleset into memory. When errors are found, they are reported and the ruleset is not loaded into memory. It is possible to override the section order if you really want to, but there seems to be little advantage in doing so. If you really want to try it, add the `set require-order no` option to your ruleset in the options section.

5.1.2 Breaking Long Lines into Smaller Pieces

When *pf(4)* rules grow longer than the width of the text editor window, they become difficult to read. You can fix that by breaking them into shorter pieces, if you end each line with a backslash (\), as in:

```
block in on $ext_if from any to \
                        $ext_ad
```

which is the equivalent of:

```
block in on $ext_if from any to $ext_ad
```

5.1.3 Grouping Rule Elements into Lists ({})

It is possible to compact several rules into one if you group several elements in braces, e.g. the following three lines:

```
block in on rl0 all
block in on rl1 all
block in on ne0 all
```

can be replaced with one line:

```
block in on {rl0, rl1, ne0} all
```

5.2 Macros

Pf(4) rulesets can quickly become complex and difficult to debug. One way to shorten the time you spend hunting for errors is to use macros in place of real names of network interfaces, addresses, protocols, ports, and other repetitive information found in filter rules.

Life is much simpler with macros; they not only help avoid stupid mistakes, but also make it easier to adapt existing rulesets to changes in hardware configuration. For example, if you use macros in place of interface names, the only change you will need to make to the ruleset after changing a network card in your firewall is a simple edit of the macro definition.

Macro names must start with a letter from the $a-zA-Z$ range of the lower part of the ASCII set and may contain letters (from the same range), digits ($0-9$), and underscores (_). Macro names may not be keywords used in *pf(4)* rules. The string that the macro expands to must be enclosed in a pair of double quotes ("). When you're referring to a macro, precede its name with a dollar sign ($), as in:

```
###########################################################
# macro definitions
#---------------------------------------------------------
# ext_if: the name of the external interface
ext_if = "ne2"
# ext_ad: the address of the external interface
ext_ad = "e.e.e.e/32"
# www_ad: the address of the HTTP server residing in
#         the DMZ
www_ad = "w.w.w.w/32"


###########################################################
# NAT rules: "rdr", "nat", "binat"
#---------------------------------------------------------
# packets arriving on the external interface ($ext_if)
# arriving from any source (from any) and sent to the
# external address ($ext_ad) to port 80 (port 80) will
# be redirected to the the HTTP server residing in
# the DMZ and listening for connections on port 8080
# (-> $dmz_ad port 8080)
```

```
rdr on $ext_if proto tcp from any to $ext_ad port 80 \
                               -> $dmz_ad port 8080
```

For simplicity and security, macros are not expanded recursively, so the following notation is not legal:

```
ext_if = "ne0"
dmz_if = "ne1"
prv_if = "ne3"
all_if = "{$ext_if, $dmz_if, $prv_if}"
```

A proper definition of all_if would be:

```
all_if = "{ne0, ne1, ne2}"
```

It is possible to redefine a macro while *pf(4)* is running, without reloading the whole ruleset, as it is explained in Chapter 16, *Firewall Management.*

5.3 Tables (table)

Tables are collections of IP addresses. They are similar to groups of host and network addresses listed in braces, but more efficient. Another difference is the fact that you can add or remove addresses to and from a table at will. Also, macros can store other information or names, while tables are used solely for addresses. Their syntax is simple, each table definition starts with the table keyword followed by table name (in <>), table options (optional), and a list of addresses in braces:

```
table <DMZ> persist {192.168.34.10/24}
table <myLANs> persist {10.0.200.1/24, 10.0.12.2/24}
```

References to tables use their names, e.g.:

```
block in on ne0 from any to <myLANs> port 25
pass in on ne0 from any to <DMZ> port 25
```

It is OK to group tables in braces:

```
block in on ne0 from any to {<DMZ>, <myLANs>} port 25
```

It is also OK to define an empty table:

```
table <spammers> persist
```

Why define an empty table? Because it is possible to load, remove and modify tables with *pfctl(8)* while *pf(4)* is running, without the need to reload the whole ruleset, and without flushing the ruleset. This feature is used in dynamic rulesets described in Chapter 9, *Dynamic Rulesets*.

Table options have the following meaning:

* const — once the table has been created, it cannot be modified or re-moved, you will need to boot OpenBSD into single-user mode and do the changes by hand (see Chapter 4, *Configuring OpenBSD* for explanation of securelevels). This option is handy when you want another layer of pro-tection, but makes table management a pain.
* persist — table won't be removed when there are no rules that refer to it. This prevents automatic removal of tables after rules that refer to them are flushed from memory and lets you define an empty table that you will populate later on. You can still modify that table with *pfctl(8)* (see Chap-ter 16, *Firewall Management*).

Tables can be used in place of lists of addresses and macros defining lists of addresses. For example, the following constructs are similar in effect, but tables are evaluated faster (the gains in speed will be more noticeable for longer lists of addresses):

```
# address group, and ...
myLANs = "{10.0.200.1/24, 10.0.12.2/24}"
pass out on ne1 from $myLANs to any
# ... the equivalent table
table <myLANs> persist {10.0.200.1/24, 10.0.12.2/24}
pass out on ne1 from <myLANs> to any
```

If, instead of listing addresses in brackets, you'd like to have them automat-ically loaded by *pf(4)* from one or more files, use the file keyword:

```
table <myLANs> persist file "/etc/spammers" \
                   file "/etc/openrelays" \
                     file "/root/scanners" \
                       file "/root/idiots"
```

Addresses in these files must be given one per line, e.g.:

```
192.168.255.1
192.168.255.2
192.168.255.3
```

Any line that begin with # will be ignored. It is OK to use hostnames, their names will be resolved into IP addresses when *pfctl(8)* loads them into memory, e.g (it is possible that a single hostname will be resolved into more than one IP address, if that's what DNS reports):

```
192.168.255.1
www.example.com
mail.example.com
```

Tables cannot be used in `rdr` rule's redirect target addresses (except for `round-robin` pools), although you can still use them as source or destination addresses in these rules (see Chapter 7, *Packet Redirection*). Also, they cannot be used in the routing options of filtering rules (see Chapter 8, *Packet Filtering*).

5.4 Anchors (anchor, nat-anchor, rdr-anchor, binat-anchor)

Anchors are used to mark points at which you can inject additional rules into the main ruleset that's already loaded into memory. Like tables, these rulesets can be modified while *pf(4)* is running. Each anchor can contain several separate sections, each with it's own name, independent of others. The names of these sections do not have to be pre-defined in the main ruleset. When you define more than one section in a single anchor, they are evaluated in the alphabetic order.

Only the main ruleset can contain anchors. The names of anchors ought to be unique and cannot be reserved names used in *pf(4)* rules. There are four types of anchors, used to load four different kinds of rules:

* `nat-anchor` *abc* — used to mark the place that you can add more `nat` rules to. The name of the anchor is *abc*.
* `rdr-anchor` *abc* — used to mark the place that you can add more `rdr` rules to. The name of the anchor is *abc*.
* `binat-anchor` *abc* — used to mark the place that you can add more `binat` rules to. The name of the anchor is *abc*.

- anchor   *abc* — used to mark the place that you can add more filter
rules to. The name of the anchor is *abc*.

You will find more information about anchors in Chapter 9, *Dynamic
Rulesets*; Chapter 12, *Using authpf*, and Chapter 16, *Firewall Management*.

5.5 Common Components Found in pf Rules

Every *pf(4)* rule is made of several parts, some obligatory and some optional. We will now discuss common parts found in many *pf(4)* rules. Those
parts that are more specific parts are discussed in other chapters, where it is
appropriate.

5.5.1 Directions (in, out)

The direction keywords (in, out) match inbound (in) and outbound
(out) packets. Users new to *pf(4)* often get this wrong and we'll be
returning to this subject in the following chapters.

The key to proper use of these keywords is remembering that the direction
the packets are traveling in is relative to the firewall machine. Imagine that
you are sitting inside the firewall and you should have no problem deciding
which packets are inbound and which ones are outbound. It is not OK to
group both keyword on the same line, as in:

```
block in all
block out all
```

cannot be replaced with:

```
block {in, out} all
```

5.5.2 Interfaces (on)

Every *pf(4)* rule needs to be assigned to a specific interface. The name of
the interface should be listed after the on keyword, as in:

```
block in on rl0 all
```

It is OK to group several interface names on the same line, as in:

```
block in on {rl0, rl1, ne0} all
```

If you are unsure what interfaces are available on your machine use the following commands:

```
$ dmesg
$ ifconfig -a
```

When *dmesg(8)* shows interfaces missing from the *ifconfig(8)* output, you need to configure those that are missing. To do that, consult Chapter 4, *Configuring OpenBSD*. If *pfctl(8)* complains about the interface name, check the spelling, then check if that interface is properly configured, when you run *ifconfig(8)*, as in:

```
$ ifconfig rl0
```

And if you do not see UP in the flags field, then the interface is not initiated at system startup. It may be missing its */etc/hostname.** file or there may be a problem with the hardware or kernel configuration. See if Chapter 4, *Configuring OpenBSD* will help. When the status field is not active, you need to check if the cables are connected. You will find additional help on that subject in Chapter 3, *Installing OpenBSD* and Chapter 4, *Configuring OpenBSD*.

5.5.3 Address Families (inet, inet6)

Pf(4) can match packets with IPv4 and IPv6 addresses. When you want to match either of these address families, use one (or both) of these keywords: inet (IPv4), inet6 (IPv6). The use of these keywords is optional. A lot of the area covered by the address families is also covered by constructs used to define addresses of hosts and networks (address notation, tables). Not all rules apply to both address families, but that's something that will be brought to your attention later in this book.

5.5.4 Protocols (proto)

It is often necessary to block or pass certain protocols. This can be achieved with the proto keyword followed by the protocol name or the number of the chosen protocol. The list of protocol names and numbers is stored in */etc/protocols*. For example, to block UDP packets on the external interface, you'd use:

```
block in on ne0 proto udp all
```

It is also OK to group protocols:

```
block in on ne0 proto {udp, tcp} all
```

Note that you cannot use protocol `ip` (number 0), *pfctl(8)* won't allow it. The latest list of protocols and their numbers can be found at:

http://www.iana.org/assignments/protocol-numbers   *(IANA protocols)*

5.5.5 Addresses (from, to, any, all, no-route)

One of the most important sections in every *pf(4)* rule are addresses. Therefore, it is a good idea to spend now some time discussing address notation:

• *IPv4 addresses* — Every IPv4 address has a length of 32 bits. It is written as a group of four integers joined with dots, e.g. 10.0.3.1 to make it more convenient to remember and write. Every address is divided into two parts: network and host. The relationship between these two parts is inversely proportional: the shorter the network address the more hosts on the same network can be connected without routing, or the more subnets it can be divided into. How do you know which bits in the address belong to the network part and which belong to the host part? Use a *netmask*. For example, if you see something like 10.0.3.7/24 it is a notation describing a network whose address is 10.0.3 and which has 256 unique host IPv4 addresses. This notation is often called Classless Inter-Domain Routing (CIDR). The /24 suffix is the netmask and contains the number of bits in the address that describe its network part, so in this example we know that the network part of 10.0.3.7 is made of the first 24 bits and the host addresses are created using the remaining 8 bits. The first 24 bits in the example address do not change, so there is another way to think of netmasks as numbers that define how many initial bits in an IPv4 address remain unmodified.

The number of hosts that can have addresses on a given network is calculated using the following formula:

$$hosts = 2^{32-netmask} - 2$$

For our example network address, the result is:

$$hosts = 2^{32-24} - 2 = 254$$

The netmask can be any integer between 0 and 32, although some of its values have a special meaning: 0 is a shortcut for all networks, not very useful in practical applications; 31 is a funny network, because it has only two addresses, but cannot contain any real hosts, because two addresses on each network are always reserved; finally, 32 is an address of a single host. Hosts with addresses on the network with the same netmask are said to belong to the same: *subnet, network segment,* or *broadcast domain* (because packets sent to the broadcast address are received by all of these hosts).

- *IPv6 addresses* — The IPv6 addresses have a length of 128 bits and use a slightly different notation. First of all, because the addresses are longer, they use hex notation instead of decimal notation and are divided into 8 pairs separated with colons instead of dots, e.g.:

```
FEC0:A702:0000:0000:0000:448A:0000:0005
```

As you can see, even with this notation, an IPv6 address is quite long. However, there is a trick that makes it possible to compress parts with 0s, as in:

```
FEC0:A702::448A:0000:0005
```

The : : symbol that replaces 0s may only be use once to avoid ambiguity. Other than that, IPv6 addresses work just like IPv4 addresses, and they too use netmasks e.g.:

```
FEC0:A702::448A:0000:0005/64
```

The formula used to compute the number of hosts on a network is a bit different for IPv6 addresses, because the netmask can be longer (0–128 bits).

$$hosts = 2^{128-netmask} - 2$$

The above information about IPv6 addresses ought to be enough to get you started, but if you crave more, refer to [RFC 2373].

Both types of addresses can be grouped in braces or listed in tables (both constructs are described in this chapter). Because *pf(4)* can check the source and the destination addresses of packets it looks at, there are special keywords that you put in front of addresses to tell *pf(4)* which ones are source (`from`) and which ones are destination (`to`), e.g.:

```
# match packets with source address 10.0.1.3/24 and
#                destination address 192.168.23.4/18
  ... from 10.0.1.3/24 to 192.168.23.4/18 ...
```

There are also two shortcuts for telling *pf(4)* to match all addresses:

```
# match packets with any source address and destination
#                    address 192.168.23.4/18
  ... from any to 192.168.23.4/18 ...
# match packets with source address 10.0.1.3/24 and any
#                          destination address
  ... from 10.0.1.3/24 to any ...
# match packets with and source and any destination
#                          addresses
  ... from any to any ...
```

The last example can be written in an even shorter form:

```
  ... all ...
```

Another shortcut is the `no-route` keyword, which matches addresses, which have no routes defined at the time they are matched. This particular keyword won't be of much use if your firewall has a default route defined (it won't match any packets). Its usefulness will be visible on finely-tuned filtering bridges that control packet flow between network segments that do not need to communicate with the outside world directly and don't need a catch-all default route. A sample rule using `no-route` could look like this:

```
# block all outbound packets with destination IP addresses for
# which no routes exist.
block out on ne1 from any to no-route
```

It doesn't matter if you are using IPv4 or IPv6 addresses, the syntax stays the same.

5.5.6 Dynamic Assignment of Addresses (hostname, (if), :broadcast, :network)

When you use a PPP device like the good old analog or DSL modem, the IP address of the interface this device is connected to will be assigned via DHCP in a more or less random way. Since there is no way of knowing which address will be assigned when you log on, this creates an interesting problem. Unless OpenBSD is configured as an invisible filtering bridge (see Chapter 4, *Configuring OpenBSD*, *pf(4)* must know the address of each interface mentioned in its ruleset. If it is missing, the ruleset won't load. Fortunately, there is a way out of this with the *(interface)* notation which tells *pf(4)* to adjust the address in parentheses whenever the address of the interface changes. So, instead of writing:

```
# redirect all packets sent to port 80 on the external
# interface to the internal HTTP server listening on port 8080
ext_if = "tun0"
ext_ad = "10.3.4.6"
rdr on $ext_if from any to $ext_ad port 80 \
 -> 192.168.55.13 port 8080
```

you could write:

```
# redirect all packets sent to port 80 on the external
# interface to the internal HTTP server listening on port 8080
ext_if = "tun0"
rdr on $ext_if from any to ($ext_if) port 80 \
 -> 192.168.55.13 port 8080
```

You could also write the name of the interface without parentheses, e.g.:

```
rdr on $ext_if from any to $ext_if port 80 \
 -> 192.168.55.13 port 8080
```

OpenBSD 3.4 introduced an interesting extension to this notation in the form of the :broadcast and :network keywords, which expand into the broadcast addresses assigned to the given interface, or the addresses of networks assigned to the given interface:

```
block out on ne1 from any to ne1:broadcast
pass in on ne1 from ne1:network to any
```

Note that if you use the expanded interface notation, you should not put interface name and modifiers inside parentheses. For example, the following rule is not correct:

```
pass in on ne1 from (ne1:network) to any
```

Always check what these rules will expand into with:

```
# sudo pfctl -f testfile ; sudo pfctl -s rules
```

Another trick of similar nature is to use the name of the host. For example, if your firewall host's name is fw0, you could write the following rule blocking access to the host via interface ne1:

```
block in on ne1 from any to fw0
```

Interface names and hostname are not interchangeable. To see that they can result in different sets of rules consider the following rules:

```
# (replace ne1 and fw0 with the name of the interface and host
# used in your machine)
# rule 1:
pass in on ne1 from any to fw0
# rule 2
pass in on ne1 from any to ne1
```

Load rule 1 and check how it was translated with:

```
# sudo pfctl -f testfile ; sudo pfctl -s rules
```

Then, replace rule 1 with rule 2 and do the same. If you see rules that you did not expect (like IPv6 rules), write rules that block them. To make the ruleset more efficient, use the quick keyword in those blocking rules, see Chapter 8, *Packet Filtering*.

5.5.7 Ports (port)

An even finer degree of control than source or destination address matching can be achieved with port matching. Ports are used to connect to various services, for example, when you are sending mail to someone, your mail is delivered to port 25 (smtp) on the recipient's mail server.

Ports can be specified in NAT and filtering rules, in numeric or mnemonic form. The list of ports and service found at those ports is stored in */etc/services*.

Port names and numbers are listed after the port keyword, e.g.:

```
... port 25 ...
```

When you use ports in your rules, list them after the port keyword, and use the proto keyword to specify protocols matched by these rules, otherwise *pfctl(8)* will complain when you try to load them, e.g.:

```
... proto tcp from any to 192.168.12.63/32 port \
                              {25, 80} ...
... proto {tcp, udp} from 10.0.0.5/12 port 20001 \
                        to any port domain ...
```

Ports can be listed in groups as shown in the section on macro writing, but you can also define numeric ranges of ports with the following operators:

- = *x* — *equal to x*, port number must be equal to *x*.
- != *x* — *not equal to x*, port number must *not* be equal to *x*.
- < *x* — *less than x*, port number must be lower than *x*.
- <= *x* — *less than or equal to x*, port number must be lower or equal to *x*.
- > *x* — *greater than x*, port number must be higher than *x*.
- >= *x* — *greater than or equal to x*, port number must be higher or equal to *x*.
- *x* >< *y* — *greater than x and less than y*, port number must be between *x* and *y*.
- *x* <> *y* — *less than x and greater than y*, reverse of *x* >< *y*.

If you don't find the information you are looking for in */etc/services*, try this:

http://www.iana.org/assignments/port-numbers   *(IANA port numbers)*

5.5.8 Tags (tag, tagged)

One of the latest additions to the *pf(4)* box of tricks is its ability to mark packets with 'tags' that inform other rules that certain packets have been matched by the previous rule. This introduces yet another level of protection in addition to addresses, ports, protocols, interface names, and direction specifications.

How would you use it? Why would you use it? To double check that the packets passing through the firewall have been sent by trusted clients and to make sure that packets by a certain rule have been processed by an earlier rule. Think of the following rules, which passe all outbound packets that enter the firewall on its internal interface through the external interface to the wide world:

```
pass  in on $int_if from any to any
pass out on $ext_if from any to any
```

These rules do not take into account the possibility of someone who has access to the firewall host sending packets (spoofed or legitimate) from the firewall itself. If you wanted to ensure that only those packets that enter the firewall through the internal interface can pass through its external interface, you'd change your rules to:

```
block in on $int_if all
pass in on $int_if from $int_if:network to any tag PRVNET \
 keep state
block out on $ext_if all
pass out on $ext_if tagged PRVNET keep state
```

Note that the `tag` keyword is used to mark packets, while the `tagged` keyword is used to check packets for tags. The tags themselves are text strings. It is possible to do a negative match with the ! modifier. For example, the following rule will *not* match packets marked with tags:

```
pass out on $ext_if tagged ! PRVNET keep state
```

There are a few things to remember when using tags:

- tags are used internally, i.e. you cannot tag packets on one host and write `tagged` rules for them on another host.
- tags are used in packet redirection and filtering rules.

- rules that use `tag` or `tagged` keywords must also use `keep state`.
- any packet can have only one tag assigned to it at any given time.
- once a packet is marked with a tag, it will retain it even if it matches other rules without the `tag` keyword.
- when a tagged packet matches another rule that uses the `tag` keyword, its tag will change to that of the new matching rule.

5.6 Tools for Writing and Editing pf.conf

In the long-time Unix tradition of keeping things simple, the only tool needed to create or edit *pf.conf* is a plain text editor. Which one should you choose? The choice is yours, and as long as it can read and save plain ASCII, it will do just fine. For example, the author of this book uses *vi(1)*. Granted, it is not the most intuitive of text editors, but like it or not, *vi(1)* is available on all default OpenBSD installations, and you will need to learn it sooner or later. Those who want to make learning *vi(1)* less painful are well advised to buy a copy of [Lamb, Robbins 1998].

What if you can't stand *vi(1)*? OpenBSD comes with another default editor, *mg(1)*, a simple clone of Emacs. But *mg(1)* is not that much more intuitive than *vi(1)*. Is there something else you could use to edit *pf.conf*?

Sure, other alternatives exist, but they must be installed from the packages collection. Some of them are *vi(1)* or Emacs clones, but if you are looking for something different, try *ee*, *jed*, *joe*, *nano*, *pico*, or *wily*. Have fun, experiment, and see which one you like most. Fortunately, they are all free software, so you can try them and switch from one to another without spending a dime. Instructions on how to install software from the packages collection are given in Chapter 4, *Configuring OpenBSD*.

5.6.1 Why Not Edit pf.conf on Another Machine?

Of course, nobody's saying that you must edit *pf.conf* on the firewall. If you really cannot stand editing in text mode, then by all means use whatever text editor you like on your desktop or laptop, and transfer your ruleset to the firewall machine using *scp(1)* afterwards.

5.6.2 Syntax Highlighting

If you use a text editor with syntax highlighting, like *vim* of XEmacs search the Web for *pf.conf* syntax modes. Files for other editors may also be available.

5.6.3 GUI Tools for Writing Rulesets with a Mouse

Recently, some brave developers wrote 'clickable' GUI applications for easy ruleset creation. They look promising and may evolve into some very interesting tools. To have a wider appeal, GUI *pf.conf* configurators must provide additional value to the administrators. For example, a GUI-based ruleset tester/simulator and an integration with CVS would be nice to have. Knowing the worldwide open source software community, it won't be long before such tools are available.

5.6.4 Scripting pf.conf

When you have to manage more than one firewall, or when you need to dynamically adjust firewall rulesets, it pays to learn scripting tools like shell, AWK, Perl, Tcl, or Python. You will find plenty of free information available online. If you prefer to learn from books, Addison-Wesley, Prentice-Hall, and O'Reilly & Associates publish very good general-purpose programming books as well as more specialist titles targeted specifically to system administrators.

5.7 Managing pf.conf Versions with CVS

Pf(4) rules change quite often when you are fine-tuning the firewall and it is a good idea to keep a track of the changes you make with *cvs(1)*. While many people think of it as a programmer's tool, CVS is not limited to storing source code of programs and scripts. Any kind of file, text or binary can be stored in CVS.

Working with CVS is quite easy. The CVS repository can reside anywhere you choose. You could create a CVS repository of *pf.conf* files in */root* on the firewall machine, but a more secure solution would be to keep it on the computer you usually work on. When the repository is kept up to date and well-commented, you will quickly create a collection of rules that you will be able to go back to when you need to add a new firewall, or change the existing network configuration. If you are managing more than one firewall, create separate repositories for each machine's *pf.conf*.

To create a repository, first create a directory where all your firewall repositories will be held, e.g.:

```
$ mkdir ~/cvs
```

Next, create a temporary directory into which you'll import the initial version of *pf.conf* from host `fw0`:

```
$ mkdir ~/tmppfconf
```

This could be anywhere, but it's probably most convenient to create it in your home directory. Just in case you asked, the name of the repository and the name of the directory where CVS keeps repositories are two different things.

Then, change the present working directory to this new directory you've just created, export the `CVSROOT` environment variable (used by all CVS commands; must contain the path to the CVS repository), and initialize your new CVS repository:

```
$ cd ~/tmppfconf
$ export CVSROOT=/usr/joe/cvsdir
$ cvs init
```

Before you copy */etc/pf.conf* to the machine that you will keep its CVS history on, copy it to the ordinary user's home directory and change its privileges (the following procedure assumes that you are logged as an ordinary user on the firewall host and that user `joe` belongs to group `wheel`, see Chapter 4, *Configuring OpenBSD* for more information):

```
$ su
# cp ./etc/pf.conf /home/joe/
# chmod 0660 /home/joe/pf.conf
# exit
```

You can now log off the firewall host and copy *pf.conf* from the firewall with scp to *~/tmppfconf* and commit (add) it to the repository:

```
$ cd ~/tmppfconf
$ scp joe@fw0.example.com:/home/joe/pf.conf ~/tmppfconf/
$ cvs import -m 'Initial configuration of fw0.' fw0 joe start
```

The *pf.conf* that you have just imported into the CVS repository will be stored in the `fw0` module (when you download configuration files from other hosts, place them in the temporary directory and import with a module name that's different from `fw0`). To begin working with it, do the following:

```
$ cd ..
$ cvs co fw0
$ cd fw0
```

Every time you make changes to *pf.conf*, use the following command to store them in the CVS repository, so you will have a trace of the changes you've done and will be able to go back to earlier versions of *pf.conf*:

```
$ cvs ci -m 'Added NAT rules for the DMZ.' ./pf.conf
```

In the future, when you want to checkout the last revision from the repository, use:

```
$ cvs co pf.conf
```

What if you want to checkout one of the revisions committed to the repository before the last one? Use the `-r` option followed by the number of the revision, as in:

```
$ cvs co -r 1.17 pf.conf
```

If you want to see the repository log for a file, use this command:

```
$ cvs log pf.conf
```

When you want to transfer a modified version of *pf.conf* to the firewall host, do the following:

```
$ scp ./pf.conf joe@fw0.example.com:/home/joe/pf.conf
```

Then, log on the firewall and:

```
$ cd /home/joe
$ su
# cp ./pf.conf /etc/pf.conf
```

```
# chmod 0600 ./etc/pf.conf
```

And reload the ruleset with *pfctl(8)*.

This is only a short intro to CVS, you can learn more from *cvs(1)*. And if you really want to get into CVS (as you should) read [Vesperman 2003]. A very good (and free) CVS manual can be found at:

http://www.cvshome.org   *(CVS home)*

## Chapter 6

Packet Normalization

In this chapter you will learn how pf(4) *can help you normalize malformed packets that may be sent with malicious intent to or from your network.*

Not all packets sent over the Internet are well-formed, which may cause problems to hosts or routers running TCP/IP stacks that cannot properly handle fragmentation. This can happen by accident, or it may be done on purpose. When you network receives or sends malformed packets, they are more than likely to be sent by someone trying to compromise your network. It may not always be the case, somewhere on the Internet someone might have just misconfigured a router, but if you have no way of getting in touch with the administrator, you will have to take preventive action anyway.

Why would someone want to use packet fragmentation? One reason is to exploit errors in TCP/IP implementations, another is to bypass or slow down your Network Intrusion Detection System (NIDS). Yet another reason could be an attempt at launching a Denial of Service (DoS) attack. Crackers using packet fragmentation send multiple copies of rogue packets fragmented in different ways, hoping that your NIDS will not be able to match them against its signature database.

The solution to weak TCP/IP stack implementations and NIDS flooding is capturing rogue packets before they reach their destination and reassembling them into well-formed packets. These have a much higher chance of being properly handled by the destination host's TCP/IP code and of being quickly matched against your NIDS signature database. Then, assuming that you keep the signature database current, your NIDS ought to catch most attack attempts before they succeed.

6.1 Implementing Packet Normalization (scrub)

The process of packet reassembly and normalization performed by *pf(4)* is called *scrubbing*. It is performed for all packets matching *scrub rules*. These rules are evaluated by *pf(4) before* packet queuing, redirection, and filtering rules (see Chapter 10, *Bandwidth Shaping*; Chapter 7, *Packet Redirection*; Chapter 8, *Packet Filtering*).

You can scrub incoming or outgoing packets, but which ones should *you* scrub? There are two schools of thought. One claims that it is enough to scrub only inbound packets (i.e. those arriving at the external interface from the outside of your network). The other claims that all packets that match `in` rules on all interfaces (inbound packets sent from the outside and outbound packets sent from your network) ought to be scrubbed. While the paranoid mind eagerly gravitates toward the second solution, remember that each rule carries an additional cost in CPU cycles and memory usage. Not that these are some enormous burdens, but they might add up rather quickly on a busy corporate network, even if OpenBSD and *pf(4)* are running on a very fast machine. On the other hand, even though you trust your users, how can you be sure that their computers have not been compromised? There is no one-size-fits-all solution, and you must determine what you need. Whatever you choose, *pf(4)* is there to help you.

6.1.1 Scrub Rule Syntax

Scrub rules have a very simple syntax. Each rule starts with the `scrub` keyword followed by:

- *The direction keyword (`in` or `out`).* Specifies if the rule matches inbound or outbound packets. These keywords are also discussed in Chapter 5, */etc/pf.conf.*
- *The packet logging switch (`log`).* This part of a scrub rule is optional. You can read more about it in Chapter 11, *Logging and Log Analysis.*
- *The name of the interface(s) to which it applies (`on` followed by the interface name).* This part is optional and may be omitted, if the rule applies to all interfaces.
- *Address family specification (`inet` or `inet6`).* Currently, *pf(4)* reassembles *only* IPv4 packets. IPv6 fragments are discarded, so it makes little sense to include these in your rules, even though *pfctl(8)* parses them without complaining.

• *Addresses of source/destination hosts (or* all, *if the rule applies to pack-ets sent from or to any address, which is a handy shortcut).* Host address notation is discussed in Chapter 5, */etc/pf.conf.* (Note that scrub rules do not use the port keyword).
• *Scrub options.* Described later in this chapter.

The following examples show a few rules without scrub options:

```
########################################################
# macro definitions
#------------------------------------------------------
# ext_if -- the name of the firewall's external
#           interface
ext_if = "ne1"
# dmz_ad -- the DMZ network address
dmz_ad = "192.168.255.1/24"


########################################################
# scrub rules: "scrub"
#------------------------------------------------------
# example 1: scrub all incoming packets on all
#            interfaces
scrub in all

# example 2: scrub all packets on all interfaces
scrub in all
scrub out all

# example 3: scrub all incoming packets on the external
#            interface sent from any address to the DMZ
#            segment
scrub in on $ext_if from any to $dmz_ad
```

6.2 Fine-Tuning Scrub Rules

The are two ways to fine-tune scrub rules, with *pf(4)* options and with scrub rule options. The former appear in the options section, while the latter are listed as a part of the scrub rule you want them to modify. You could think of them as global and local variables.

6.2.1 Pf Options (limit frags, timeout frags)

The `limit frags` *n* option sets hard limits on the number of memory pools used by the packet filter for packet reassembly. It tells *pf(4)* how much memory it can use to store packet fragments. The default value is 5000, but you can adjust it up or down. Lower values of `limit frags` result in more dropped connections, but use less memory. Administrators use this option to avoid performance hits and to prevent attacks aimed at overwhelming the firewall's resources. The rule setting the `limit frags` option must be listed in the options section of */etc/pf.conf*, like in this example:

```
#########################################################
# options: "set"
#-------------------------------------------------------
# limit the number of fragments kept in memory to 30000
set limit frags 30000
```

You can check the current limits with the following command:

```
$ sudo pfctl -s memory
states       hard limit    10000
frags        hard limit     5000
```

Another important general option is `timeout frag`, which tells *pf(4)* how long it should store unassembled fragments, before they are flushed from memory.

6.2.2 Scrub Rule Options

The process of packet normalization can be further refined with the following scrub rule options:

• `fragment reassemble` — reassemble fragmented packets. This is the default behavior and this option can be omitted. Fragments are held in memory until all pieces of the original packet have been collected. You can set a limit on the number of fragments kept in memory with the `limit frags` option. Use this option when you use Network Address Translation (NAT). This is the recommended way to scrub packets, use it together with `reassemble tcp`.

- `fragment crop` — track and pass fragments without reassembling packets, drop duplicate fragments and crop overlaps. This algorithm uses a lot less memory than `fragment reassemble`, but does not work with NAT.
- `fragment drop-ovl` — drop all duplicate and overlapping fragments and their further corresponding fragments. This approach is more aggressive than `fragment crop`, and may result in more terminated connection, but it is also more secure. If you are not running an NIDS, then this algorithm could be used instead of `fragment reassemble`. It too does not work with NAT.
- `max-mss` *m* — set the Maximum Segment Size for packets matching the rule to *m* bytes. Packets scrubbed with the rule where this option is used will have a MSS less or equal to the give value. The size of the resulting IP packet will be longer by 40 bytes, so check that the MSS you set is less than MTU for the network that packet will travel through or fragmentation will occur again. Typical values of MSS and MTU for Ethernet are 1460 and 1500. If you want to adjust MTU for a chosen interface, you can do it with *ifconfig(8)*. Although conventional wisdom suggests that the larger the MMS the better the network performance, this is not always the case. [Stevens 1994] and [Wright, Stevens 1994] explain the link between MSS and network performance.
- `min-ttl` *n* — set the minimum Time-To-Live for the matching packets to *n* hops. TTL is an integer value (0–255) decremented by each router that IP packets pass through. The longer the TTL, the longer the packet will circulate inside the network. This modifier is only useful for fine-tuning your network's performance. And then only when you know what you are doing. In most cases, you will want to increase the TTL of packets, when some of them are not reaching their targets. You could also use it to limit the number of hops they do on the network so they do not leave it, for example. TTL will not be a problem for small installations, but may be an issue in large corporate, government, or educational networks. For more information about TTL, read [Stevens 1994] and [Wright, Stevens 1994].
- `no-df` — clear the *don't-fragment* (DF) bit in the IP flags field. Packets with DF unset can be fragmented along their way by other routers. You will need this option, if the packets your network is sending to other networks need to pass though routers that cannot handle large packets, or when routers on your network have the same problem with the packets sent from the outside. Use this option when you want to successfully scrub NFS and other packets that have the DF bit set. When this options

is used, it also advisable to use the `random-id` options.

- `random-id` — replace IP identification fields with random values. Makes it more difficult to count hosts hidden behind a NAT box. This is done increasingly often by DSL providers who do not want their customers to use more than one computer per one DSL modem. Of course, the same technique is used by people interested in finding out the real layout of the network hidden behind NAT. This options is good for security, but remember that it only works with outbound packets (`out` rules).

- `reassemble tcp` — normalize TCP connections in the following way: neither side of a TCP connection can reduce the TTL of IP packets (TTL will be raised automatically); TCP packets' timeout values will be modulated in a random fashion to avoid detection. Unlike other scrub rules, rules that use this option may be written without the direction keywords (`in`, `out`), in which case they apply to both directions.

The above options, with the exception of `random-id`, are mostly of interest to administrators of large networks. Their use and the way they affect performance of networks is best described in [Stevens 1994] and [Wright, Stevens 1994], which should be required reading for all administrators of TCP/IP networks.

The following examples illustrate the use of scrub options:

```
#########################################################
# macro definitions
#-------------------------------------------------------
# ext_if -- the name of the firewall's external
#            interface
ext_if = "ne1"
# src_ad -- the address of the firewall's external
#            interface
src_ad = "s.s.s.s/32"
dmz_ad = "d.d.d.d/24"


#########################################################
# options: "set"
#-------------------------------------------------------
# limit the number of fragments kept in memory to 30000
set limit frags 10000
```

```
##########################################################
# scrub rules: "scrub"
#--------------------------------------------------------
# example 1: scrub all outbound packets departing from
#            the external interface and replace their
#            IP identification numbers with random
#            values
scrub out on $ext_if all random-id

# example 2: scrub all inbound packets arriving on the
#            external interface, clear their DF flags,
#            set TTL to 100, set MSS to 1460, use
#            fragment reassemble
scrub in on $ext_if all \
    no-df min-ttl 100 max-mss 1460 fragment reassemble

# example 3: scrub all outbound packets departing from
#            the external interface, clear their DF
#            flags, set TTL to 10, set MSS to 1460, use
#            fragment crop
scrub out on $ext_if all \
         no-df min-ttl 10 max-mss 1460 fragment crop

# example 4: scrub all inbound packets arriving on the
#            external interface trying to reach hosts
#            in the DMZ segment, clear their DF flags,
#            set TTL to 10, set MSS to 1460, use
#            fragment drop-ovl
scrub in on $ext_if from $src_ad to $dmz_ad \
        no-df min-ttl 100 max-mss 1460 fragment drop-ovl
```

6.3 Who's Sending All Those Malformed Packets?

To find out where all those malformed packets could be coming from, log packets matching scrub rules and then use *traceroute(8)* or *traceroute6(8)* (for IPv6 traffic) to locate the possible source of malformed packets. Be careful and do not blame the source host for sending malformed packets on the basis of the content of the source IP address field alone. It may have nothing to do with this. Packets may be getting mangled somewhere between the source host and your network, when they are passing through one of the many routers. The results displayed by *traceroute(8)* or *traceroute6(8)* will help you locate points at which this could be happening. Your next step could be a polite email to the administrators overseeing those routers asking them to look into the matter.

For more information about *pf(4)* logs, read Chapter 11, *Logging ang Log Analysis*.

Additional sources of information on the subject of packet fragmentation are [RFC 815], [Wright, Stevens 1994], [Handley, Paxson, Kreibich 2001], and [Malan, Watson, Jahanian, Howell 2000].

## Chapter 7

Packet Redirection

In this chapter you will learn how Network Address Translation (NAT) works, what it is useful for, and how to write pf(4) *NAT rules.*

Network Address Translation (NAT) is a method of redirecting (forwarding) packets between addresses and ports. NAT's main applications are security and network management. As implemented in *pf(4)*, NAT works for both IPv4 and IPv6 addresses, even though IPv6 removes some need for using NAT.

This technique, also known as *masquerading* (for those who speak Linux) is implemented in the form of a set of packet redirection rules that *pf(4)* checks for every packet it receives.

7.1 Security Applications

The numeric addressing of hosts on IP networks is both a benefit and a danger. Obviously, without some form of addressing, hosts would never find themselves on the Internet. But the same address can also be used to detect the layout of the network of an organization that someone is interested in spying on, breaking into, or disabling its communications. It is just like a street address. When someone knows where you live, they can find you, break in, make noise to distract you, or spy on you.

NAT provides the equivalent of a P.O. Box for IP networks. For example, instead of exposing a DNS or an HTTP server to the world under a public IP address, we can give its public address to the NAT device and configure it to redirect packets to the real server with a private IP address sitting behind NAT. How does this increase the security of servers hidden behind NAT? Well, many popular network services like DNS, SMTP, or HTTP are using lower TCP/UDP ports (0–1023), which servers like *sendmail*, or *apache* can bind to when they run with `root` privileges. Since the user

root is a superuser with full access to all resources, when someone finds a
way to break into the system via an exploit in one of the servers listening on
lower ports, they can take control of the whole system. But what if the
server was listening on a higher port (1024–65535) and running as an ordinary user with severely limited privileges? Sure, that would help, but your
web browser won't know which port the HTTP server is listening on, because it always expects to find it at port 80. You can re-configure your own
web browser, but how will you convince the rest of the world to do the
same? That's where NAT helps. Simply give your NAT device the public
address of your HTTP server and configure it to redirect all packets sent to
port 80 on that address to a higher port (e.g. 8080) on the HTTP server
hidden behind NAT. The HTTP server may have a private IP address and if
you put it inside a DMZ, it will be quite secure. Just remember to configure
the HTTP server to listen for connections on port 8080.

Configuring servers to run in a *chroot(2)* jail will also help, although the
chroot(2) environment is often difficult to configure. In the event of a
break-in the intruder will have very little space to play his/her tricks. As
chance would have it, OpenBSD comes with *apache* configured in *chroot*
by default.

Another use of NAT in security is hiding the real number and addresses of
hosts on your LAN behind a single address. Although there are techniques
for discovering that information, it is difficult without access to the link that
your network connects to the outside world. So far, the main users of host
counting techniques are telecom companies trying to prevent users from
connecting more hosts to their DSL boxes than is permitted by their user
agreements.

> *If you would like to make host counting more difficult for
> those who are too nosy, read about the* random-id
> *option in Chapter 6,* Packet Normalization.

7.2 Expanding the IPv4 Address Space

The IPv4 address space is limited to 2^{32} unique numbers. It used to be
plenty enough in the early days of the Internet, but the IPv4 address space
quickly became a scarce resource after the Internet boom that started
around 1994. Facing a real threat of running out of IP addresses many
people thought of the same thing and decided that the IP address space

ought to be expanded to give every possible device connected to the Internet its own unique number. What sounded simple in theory, became difficult to implement in practice, because it would require changes to all devices using TCP/IP. Not a problem for your PC running OpenBSD, but an impossible task when your device is traveling though space or when it is buried under the sea bed. In a way, it is similar to changing engines in all cars in the world at the same time, while they are cruising at 60mph. This and other reasons account for slow adoption of IPv6 (formerly known as IPng).

> *The good news is that IPv6 is no longer light years away.*
> *Far from it. The recent decisions of the US government*
> *and military requiring a move to IPv6 look like the boost*
> *that is needed to finally convince people to switch to IPv6.*
> *And, yes, OpenBSD and* pf(4) *work with IPv6 just fine.*

NAT comes to the rescue, when you are running out of public IPv4 addresses by allowing you to use private IPv4 addresses [RFC 1918] on your LAN while you expose only a single public address to the outside world.

The idea is very simple: assign a single public IPv4 address to the NAT box and then assign private IPv4 to the hosts behind it. All packets sent from those hosts have their source address rewritten and appear to be coming from the NAT host, which stores information required to pass responses from the external hosts back to the internal ones. Since the hosts behind NAT have no public IP addresses, they cannot be reached from the outside, which is a good thing from the point of view of security.

A variation of this technique is *bi-directional NAT*. It works just like ordinary NAT, but each host behind NAT with a private IPv4 address is bound to a single public IPv4 address assigned to the external interface on the NAT device (this is possible with *ifconfig(8)* aliases described in Chapter 4, *Configuring OpenBSD*). This technique is used in Virtual Private Network (VPN) designs, which do not cooperate too well with NAT [Yuan, Strayer 2001], [Cheswick, Bellovin, Rubin 2003].

> *Both NAT configurations can be used with IPv6 ad-*
> *dressing. Hosts behind NAT should use FEC0/10 through*
> *FEFF/10 (site-local) addresses as defined in [RFC 2373].*
> *If you are using OpenBSD and pf, you can redirect IPv4*

and IPv6 traffic on the same machine, together or independently of each other.

Another thing worth remembering is that the use of public IP addresses on the NAT's external interface and the use of private IP addresses for hosts behind NAT are not obligatory and you may configure your NAT using any mixture of private and public addresses you need.

Also, some hosts behind NAT configured with OpenBSD and pf(4) *can use regular NAT while others use bi-directional NAT. It is all up to you.*

7.2.1 Does IPv6 Make NAT redundant?

This is one of the questions people are often asking when they hear that NAT was an in-flight fix to the problem of IPv4 running out of address space. 'Surely, if IPv6 gives every device on Earth and in the Universe their own address, we will no longer need NAT. Right?' they say. Yes and no. NAT will still have its place and will be used for packet redirection although it may find a new niche as an elegant solution to load balancing problems, such as those discussed in Chapter 10, *Bandwidth Shaping and Load Balancing.*

7.2.2 What Problems Does NAT Cause?

Handy as it is, NAT often breaks VPN and there is not much you can do about it, because all VPN solutions that check the integrity of packets will immediately drop connections after they discover that the source or the target address has changed. There are workarounds for this problem, but none of them can really be recommended for use with VPNs. However, considering the dynamics of Open Source, someone will come up with a solution to this problem soon.

Another problem is bad cooperation of NAT with bridge configurations, such as those described in Chapter 4, *Configuring OpenBSD*. This is caused by the fact that the bridge makes changes to packets before they are seen *pf(4)* and this confuses *pf(4)*. The solution to this problem is very simple—use two separate machines, one doing NAT, another configured as a bridge.

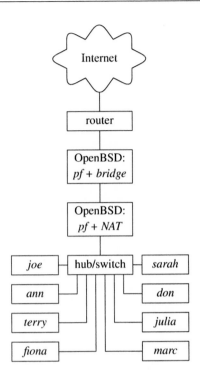

Figure 7.1: A solution to the bridge/NAT incompatibility problem.

7.3 NAT Rules

There are three kinds of NAT rules:

1. nat — translation between groups of internal addresses and a single external address.
2. rdr — address and port redirection.
3. binat — bidirectional translation between one internal address and one external address.

If you plan to use NAT, you must first enable IP forwarding in the Open-BSD kernel. You can learn how to do it from Chapter 4 *Configuring OpenBSD*.

Unlike packet filtering rules, packet redirection rules are matched using the 'first matching rule wins' algorithm, which means that you must always put

more specific rules before more general ones. For example, consider these
two rules: (1) redirect all traffic sent to port 80 from the outside to port
8080 on your HTTP server sitting in the DMZ, (2) redirect all traffic sent to
port 80 from your boss' home machine to port 8888 on your HTTP server
sitting in the DMZ. Unless rule (2) is placed before rule (1), it will never be
matched and all traffic will be redirected as per rule (1).

7.3.1 Hiding Hosts Behind a Single Address with nat Rules

NAT rules perform network address translation for groups of internal hosts,
with private addresses hidden behind a firewall, which access the outside
world through a single interface with one public IP. (The external interface
could have more IP addresses assigned to it.) This not only solves the
problem of connecting more than one host through a single interface, but it
also hides the details of your internal network's layout, the number of hosts,
and other information that the intruder may find useful. Hosts with private
IP addresses hidden behind NAT are not reachable from the outside, all the
outside world sees is a single public IP address (*e.e.e.e* in Figure 7.2).

The magic is possible because the firewall keeps a record of who sent what
and where, so it can send replies to the right host. To do that it must keep a
table of sorts and mark packets it sends to the Internet. This marking
allows attackers to deduct how many hosts are hidden behind the firewall
and gives them an idea of what might be going on behind it, provided they
can capture that traffic. It is also used by companies selling DSL access to
the Internet to find out who's breaching their contracts. (Some DSL access
providers forbid their customers to use NAT, and impose penalties on those
who use it. If your provider does this, consider switching to another.) The
latest versions of *pf(4)* can fool these detection systems, as described in
Chapter 6, *Packet Normalization*.

NAT rules have the following syntax:

- *The* no switch. Tells *pf(4)* to not perform network address translation. It
  is used to selectively turn redirection off for certain users or types of connections. This part is optional.
- *The* nat keyword. This part is required.
- *The* pass keyword. This part is optional. When you use it, the packet is
  sent to the destination host without matching it against the packet filtering
  rules.

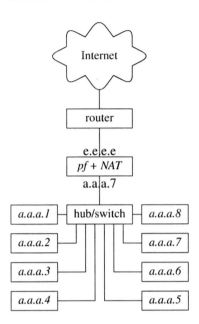

Figure 7.2: All connections to the outside world sent from a.a.a.a/24 hosts appear to be originating from e.e.e.e/32.

- *The name of the interface or the list of interfaces.* Starts with the on keyword. You need to tell *pf(4)* which interface each nat rule applies to, so this part is required.
- *The name of the IP address family.* Possible values are inet (for IPv4 addresses) or inet6 (for IPv6 addresses). This part is required if the target address (listed after ->) expands to more than one address family; this happens when you use the hostname or the interfae name in place of a single IPv4 or IPv6 address.
- *Protocol specification.* Discussed in Chapter 5, */etc/pf.conf.*
- *Source host(s) addresses and ports.* These are addresses and ports you want to do NAT for. Addresses are discussed in Chapter 5, */etc/pf.conf.*
- *Tag marker.* You can mark packets translated with nat for a double-check filtering with the tag keyword followed by the identifier string. Such packets can later be matched with the tagged keyword. This part is optional. For more information on this subject, consult Chapter 5, */etc/pf.conf.*
- *Target host(s) addresses and ports.* These are addresses and ports that

packets are sent to by source hosts. This syntax is used very rarely. Addresses are discussed in Chapter 5, */etc/pf.conf.*

• *External address used to perform NAT on.*

• *Pool options.* Discussed in Chapter 10, *Bandwidth Shaping and Load Balancing.*

• The `static-port` option. This is optional, when you use it, NAT does not modify the source port of translated packets. It may help you with VPN setups and those connections that somehow break when you pipe them through `nat` rules. This part is optional.

How do you connect your private network to the outside world? It's quite simple, actually:

```
########################################################
# macro definitions
#------------------------------------------------------
# ext_if -- the name of the firewalls's external
#           interface
ext_if = "ne1"
# ext_ad -- the public IPv4 address assigned to the
#           firewall's external interface
ext_ad = "e.e.e.e/32"
# prv_ad -- the range of private IPv4 addresses
#           assigned to hosts on the screened LAN
prv_ad = "p.p.p.p/24"
# nat_proto -- NAT-ed protocols
nat_proto = "{tcp, udp, icmp}"


########################################################
# NAT rules: "rdr", "nat", "binat"
#------------------------------------------------------


nat on $ext_if inet proto $nat_proto \
    from $prv_ad to any -> $ext_ad
```

When it is time to add a new network segment, modify the macros:

```
########################################################
# macro definitions
#------------------------------------------------------
```

```
# ext_if -- the name of the firewalls's external
#          interface
ext_if = "ne1"
# ext_ad -- the public IPv4 address assigned to the
#          firewall's external interface
ext_ad = "e.e.e.e/32"
# prv1_ad -- the range of private IPv4 addresses
#           assigned to hosts on the screened LAN #1
prv1_ad = "p.p.1.p/24"
# prv2_ad -- the range of private IPv4 addresses
#           assigned to hosts on the screened LAN #2
prv2_ad = "p.p.2.p/24"
# nat_proto -- NAT-ed protocols
nat_proto = "{tcp, udp, icmp}"


#######################################################
# NAT rules: "rdr", "nat", "binat"
#-----------------------------------------------------
```

**nat on $ext_if inet proto $nat_proto from \
  {$prv1_ad, $prv2_ad} to any -> $ext_ad**

Shouldn't we use the names of the interfaces that connect our private networks to the firewall? No, we want the outside world to see all connections originating from the firewall's external IP address and that address is assigned to the firewall's external interface. Those two pieces of information must match.

Just like rdr rules, nat rules allow us to use the no and ! modifiers before interface names and private host addresses. These operators have many useful applications. For example, when you translate addresses on two or more network segments, as shown above, the hosts from different segments cannot communicate with each other. To solve that, you must add another two rules before the main NAT rule:

```
#######################################################
# macro definitions
#-----------------------------------------------------
# ext_if -- the name of the firewalls's external
#          interface
ext_if = "ne1"
```

```
# ext_ad -- the public IPv4 address assigned to the
#             firewall's external interface
ext_ad = "e.e.e.e/32"
# prv1_ad -- the range of private IPv4 addresses
#             assigned to hosts on the screened LAN #1
prv1_ad = "p.p.1.p/24"
# prv2_ad -- the range of private IPv4 addresses
#             assigned to hosts on the screened LAN #2
prv2_ad = "p.p.2.p/24"
# nat_proto -- NAT-ed protocols
nat_proto = "{tcp, udp, icmp}"


#########################################################
# NAT rules: "rdr", "nat", "binat"
#-------------------------------------------------------


no nat on $ext_if inet proto $nat_proto \
            from $prv1_ad to $prv2_ad
no nat on $ext_if inet proto $nat_proto \
            from $prv2_ad to $prv1_ad
nat on $ext_if inet proto $nat_proto \
    from {$prv1_ad, $prv2_ad} to any -> $ext_ad
```

The no nat rules match packets before they are matched by the nat rule and so communication between the two local network segments is enabled.

It is also possible to limit their scope to IPv4 or IPv6 packets (inet and inet6, respectively).

Not all is rosy with NAT, of course. It changes the source ports in IP packets, which some applications complain about, although this is not such a huge problem. A more serious danger is a real possibility of running out of ports on the external address. While 65535 ports is enough for a single host, there is a real possibility that it will run out when the same number of ports is shared among several dozens of hosts behind NAT as they will all use ports associated with the firewall's external IP address.

The solution is to assign two or more public IP addresses to the external interface using the *ifconfig(8)* alias option or, to make changes permanent,

store that information in the appropriate */etc/hostname.** file. You'll find
the necessary instructions in Chapter 4, *Configuring OpenBSD*. Then, you
can write two separate NAT rules that translate addresses of two different
network segments on two different external addresses, even though these
addresses are assigned to the same external interface on the firewall:

```
#########################################################
# macro definitions
#--------------------------------------------------------
# ext_if -- the name of the firewalls's external
#           interface
ext_if = "ne1"
# ext1_ad -- the first public IPv4 address assigned to
#            the firewall's external interface
ext1_ad = "e.e.e.e/32"
# ext2_ad -- the second public IPv4 address assigned to
#            the firewall's external interface
ext2_ad = "e.e.e.f/32"
# prv1_ad -- the range of private IPv4 addresses
#            assigned to hosts on the screened LAN #1
prv1_ad = "p.p.1.p/24"
# prv2_ad -- the range of private IPv4 addresses
#            assigned to hosts on the screened LAN #2
prv2_ad = "p.p.2.p/24"
# nat_proto -- NAT-ed protocols
nat_proto = "{tcp, udp, icmp}"


#########################################################
# NAT rules: "rdr", "nat", "binat"
#--------------------------------------------------------


no nat $ext_if inet proto $nat_proto \
        from $prv1_ad to $prv2_ad
no nat $ext_if inet proto $nat_proto \
        from $prv2_ad to $prv1_ad
nat on $ext_if inet proto $nat_proto \
    from $prv1_ad to any -> $ext1_ad
nat on $ext_if inet proto $nat_proto \
    from $prv2_ad to any -> $ext2_ad
```

What if you cannot get another public IP address? There is not much you can do about that, but you can try to divide the available port space between competing LAN segments:

```
nat on $ext_if inet proto $nat_proto from $prv1_ad to any \
                    -> $ext1_ad port 10000:20000
nat on $ext_if inet proto $nat_proto from $prv2_ad to any \
                    -> $ext2_ad port 20001:30000
```

Another issue that is sometimes problematic is the assignment of source ports. *Pf(4)* does it in a random way, which not all applications like. You can solve that with a NAT proxy rule that looks like this:

```
nat on $ext_if inet proto $nat_proto from $prv1_ad port 22 \
                    to any -> $ext1_ad port 8022
```

What if you wanted to map ports in a one-to-one fashion, 1024 to 1024, 30000 to 30000, etc.? Use the asterisk notation:

```
nat on $ext_if inet proto $nat_proto \
 from $prv1_ad port 1024:65535 to any -> $ext1_ad port 1024:*
```

Such specific rules go between no nat and nat rules.

It is also possible to turn off source port modifications in nat *rules with the* static-port option placed at the very end of such rule:

```
nat on $ext_if inet proto $nat_proto from $prv1_ad port 22 \
                    to any -> $ext1_ad static-port
```

or:

```
nat on $ext_if inet proto $nat_proto from $prv1_ad \
                    to any -> $ext1_ad static-port
```

NAT rules are often used together with matching packet filtering that either block or pass packets after they are redirected with nat, e.g.:

```
# NAT internal hosts on the external interface ext_if
nat on $ext_if inet proto tcp from $prv_ad to any -> ($ext_if)
```

```
# block connections to port 25 on any external host
block out on $ext_if inet proto tcp \
     from ($ext_if) to any port 25
```

You could replace these rules with a single NAT/pass rule (use the `pass` keyword):

```
nat pass on $ext_if inet proto tcp \
    from $prv_ad to any port != 25 -> ($ext_if)
```

Another important tool that binds NAT rules with filter rules are tags. You can read more about them in Chapter 5, */etc/pf.conf*. Please note that the `pass` and `tag` keywords don't mix. If you use the `pass` keyword in a `nat` rule and tag packets, then the packet filtering section will be skipped and the `tagged` keyword will be redundant. Keep this in mind when you wonder why some rules don't match packets or when you get lost and feel overwhelemed by the complexity of your ruleset (a clear sign that you overengineered your ruleset).

Additional information about the NAT/filtering interactions can be found in Chapter 8, *Packet Filtering*.

The `nat` rules can be replaced with other `nat` rules from an external source while *pf(4)* is running. To use that feature, you'll have to use anchors. They are especially useful in authorization with *authpf(8)* and you can read more about them in Chapter 9, *Dynamic Rulesets*, and Chapter 12, *Using authpf*.

7.3.2 Redirecting Packets to Other Addresses and Ports (rdr)

The `rdr` rules are written using the following syntax:

* *The* no *switch.* Tells *pf(4)* to not perform packet redirection. It is used to selectively turn redirection off for certain users or types of connections. This part is optional.
* *The* rdr *keyword.* This part is required.
* *The* pass *keyword.* This part is optional. When you use it, the packet is sent to the destination host without matching it against the packet filtering rules.
* *The name of the interface or a list of interfaces.* Starts with the on

keyword. You need to tell *pf(4)* which interface each `rdr` rule applies to, so this part is required.

- *The name of the IP address family.* Possible values are `inet` (for IPv4 addresses) or `inet6` (for IPv6 addresses). This part is required if the target address (listed after `->`) expands to more than one address family; this happens when you use the hostname or the interface name in place of a single IPv4 or IPv6 address.
- *Protocol specification.* Discussed in Chapter 5, */etc/pf.conf.*
- *Redirected host(s) addresses and ports.* These are addresses and ports you want to redirect. Addresses are discussed in Chapter 5, */etc/pf.conf.*
- *Tag marker.* You can mark packets translated with `rdr` for a double-check filtering with the `tag` keyword followed by the identifier string. Such packets can later be matched with the `tagged` keyword. This part is optional. For more information on this subject, consult Chapter 5, */etc/pf.conf.*
- *Target host(s) addresses and ports.* These are addresses and ports that packets will be redirected to. Addresses are discussed in Chapter 5, */etc/pf.conf.*
- *Pool options.* Discussed in Chapter 10, *Bandwidth Shaping and Load Balancing.*

The `rdr` rules redirect packets from one port to another. A classic example of using traffic redirection is an HTTP server sitting in a DMZ, yet accessible to hosts outside your network as shown in Figure 7.3. Ordinarily, such server must listen on port 80, and the machine it runs on must be directly accessible to external hosts. This setup is not very safe, so you might consider moving the server behind a firewall, into a DMZ network segment.

However, if you do that, the HTTP server is inaccessible, because it has no public IP address and it's the firewall that receives requests sent to the that server instead.

The firewall must redirect these packets to the HTTP server residing inside the DMZ network segment. This is accomplished with the following NAT rule:

```
##########################################################
# macro definitions
#-------------------------------------------------------
# ext_if -- the name of the firewall's external
#           interface
ext_if = "ne1"
```

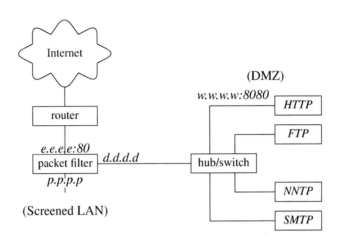

Figure 7.3: Rdr rules divert packets received by the firewall to the hosts hidden in
the DMZ segment

```
# ext_ad -- the public IPv4 address assigned to the
#           firewall's external interface
ext_ad = "e.e.e.e/32"
# www_ad -- the private IPv4 address assigned to the
#           HTTP server in the DMZ
www_ad = "w.w.w.w/32"


#######################################################
# NAT rules: "rdr", "nat", "binat"
#-----------------------------------------------------


rdr on $ext_if inet proto tcp \
    from any to $ext_ad port 80 -> $www_ad port 8080
```

The above rule redirects all TCP (proto tcp) packets arriving at the
firewall's external address e.e.e.e/32 (on $ext_if), originating
from any source address (from any) and destined to the HTTP server listening on port 80 (to $ext_ad port 80) to the address of the real
HTTP server located in the DMZ at w.w.w.w/32 (-> $www_ad). The
server listens on port 8080 (port 8080). That port is unprivileged, and
the attacker has less chance of breaking things, should the server be compromised. As you will soon discover, when you try this rule in practice, it

works for connections made from the outside to your web server, but not from your private screened LAN. This obstacle is easily removed by adding another rule:

```
##########################################################
# macro definitions
#---------------------------------------------------------
# ext_if -- the name of the firewalls's external
#           interface
ext_if = "ne1"
# prv_if -- the name of the firewalls's screened LAN
#           interface
prv_if = "ne2"
# ext_ad -- the public IPv4 address assigned to the
#           firewall's external interface
ext_ad = "e.e.e.e/32"
# prv_ad -- the range of private IPv4 addresses
#           assigned to hosts on the screened LAN
prv_ad = "p.p.p.p/24"
# www_ad -- the private IPv4 address assigned to the
#           HTTP server in the DMZ
www_ad = "w.w.w.w/32"


##########################################################
# NAT rules: "rdr", "nat", "binat"
#---------------------------------------------------------

rdr on $ext_if inet proto tcp \
    from any to $ext_ad port 80 -> $www_ad port 8080
rdr on $prv_if inet proto tcp \
    from $prv_ad to $ext_ad port 80 -> $www_ad port 8080
```

The second rule sets up redirection for packets sent from the screened LAN to the HTTP server residing in the DMZ. You can rewrite the above ruleset in the following way (notice that the interface names are now in curly braces):

```
##########################################################
# macro definitions
#---------------------------------------------------------
```

```
# ext_if -- the name of the firewalls's external
#           interface
ext_if = "ne1"
# prv_if -- the name of the firewalls's screened LAN
#           interface
prv_if = "ne2"
# ext_ad -- the public IPv4 address assigned to the
#           firewall's external interface
ext_ad = "e.e.e.e/32"
# prv_ad -- the range of private IPv4 addresses
#           assigned to hosts on the screened LAN
prv_ad = "p.p.p.p/24"
# www_ad -- the private IPv4 address assigned to the
#           HTTP server in the DMZ
www_ad = "w.w.w.w/32"


########################################################
# NAT rules: "rdr", "nat", "binat"
#------------------------------------------------------
```

**rdr on {$ext_if, $prv_if} inet proto tcp **
    from any to $ext_ad port 80 -> $www_ad port 8080

The last rule will be expanded into two, and when you check it with
pfctl(8), you will see the following output:

```
$ sudo pfctl -s nat
rdr on ne1 inet proto tcp from any to e.e.e.e port www ->
☞ w.w.w.w port 8080
rdr on ne2 inet proto tcp from any to e.e.e.e port www ->
☞ w.w.w.w port 8080
```

The rdr rules can use the pass keyword to skip the packet filtering stage
and send the redirected packets straight to the target host. Note that the
pass and tag keywords don't mix. If you use the pass keyword in an
rdr rule and tag packets, then the packet filtering section will be skipped
and the tagged keyword will be redundant.

7.3.3 Forcing Everyone to Use a Web Cache

What if you wanted to redirect all queries to port 80 on all addresses to a web cache? Return to an earlier setup with two separate rules and change the second rule:

```
###########################################################
# macro definitions
#----------------------------------------------------------
# ext_if -- the name of the firewalls's external
#           interface
ext_if = "ne1"
# prv_if -- the name of the firewalls's screened LAN
#           interface
prv_if = "ne2"
# prv_ad -- the range of private IPv4 addresses
#           assigned to hosts on the screened LAN
prv_ad = "p.p.p.p/24"
# ch_ad -- the private IPv4 address assigned to the
#          HTTP cache server
ch_ad = "w.w.w.w/32"


###########################################################
# NAT rules: "rdr", "nat", "binat"
#----------------------------------------------------------
```

```
rdr on $prv_if inet proto tcp \
    from $prv_ad to any port 80 -> $ch_ad port 1080
```

In the example above, the web cache listens on port 1080. Note that this technique of forcing everyone on the internal network to connect to the Web through the cache server is controversial, and you must not impose it on your users without careful thought. For more information consult [Wessels 2001].

What if you want to bypass the cache yourself? Use the no modifier, as in:

```
###########################################################
# macro definitions
#----------------------------------------------------------
  ...
```

```
# boss_ad -- the address of the privileged user who can
             bypass the HTTP cache.
boss_ad = "p.p.p.b/24"

#########################################################
# NAT rules: "rdr", "nat", "binat"
#-------------------------------------------------------

no rdr on $prv_if inet proto tcp \
    from $boss_ad to any port 80
rdr on $prv_if inet proto tcp \
    from $prv_ad to any port 80 -> $ch_ad port 1080
```

As you can see, the no modifier makes the -> . . . part of the rule unnecessary (and such rules do not parse, as they do not make sense). Always list exceptions to general NAT rules *before* these rules, or the exceptions won't be matched.

Another useful modifier is !, which negates the values (interface names, source and target addresses) it precedes:

```
rdr on ! ne1 inet proto tcp from ! s.s.s.s/32 to \
    ! e.e.e.e/32 port 80 -> d.d.d.d/32 port 8080
```

The above rule redirects all IPv4 TCP packets arriving on any interface except ne1 from any address except s.s.s.s/32 and destined to any address except e.e.e.e/32.

7.3.4 Other Uses of rdr Rules

The rdr rules are very handy because they can be used to configure proxies, redirect traffic from a dead host to a backup host, and so on. For example, the FTP proxy setup described in Chapter 4, *Configuring OpenBSD* uses them, as does *spamd(8)* described in Chapter 12, *Using spamd*.

7.3.5 binat

The last of the three NAT rules are binat rules, which bind an external public address to an internal private address. VPN setups often use this bidirectional translation, and it can provide additional security for hosts exposing public services. Their syntax follows these rules:

- *The* no switch. Tells *pf(4)* to not perform packet redirection between two addresses bound by the binat rule it begins. It is used to selectively turn redirection off for certain source or target addresses (ports have no meaning in binat rules). This part is optional.
- *The* binat *keyword.* This part is required.
- *The* pass keyword. This part is optional. When you use it, the packet is sent to the destination host without matching it against the packet filtering rules.
- *The name of the interface on which binding occurs.* Starts with the on keyword. You need to tell *pf(4)* which interface each binat rule applies to, so this part is required.
- *The name of the IP address family.* Possible values are inet (for IPv4 addresses) or inet6 (for IPv6 addresses). This part is required if the target address (listed after ->) expands to more than one address family; this happens when you use the hostname or the interface name in place of a single IPv4 or IPv6 address.
- *Protocol specification.* Discussed in Chapter 5, */etc/pf.conf.*
- *Internal address.* This is the address of the internal host you want to do bidirectional mapping for. Addresses are discussed in Chapter 5, */etc/pf.conf.*
- *Tag marker.* You can mark packets translated with binat for a double-check filtering with the tag keyword followed by the identifier string. Such packets can later be matched with the tagged keyword. This part is optional. For more information on this subject, consult Chapter 5, */etc/pf.conf.*
- *External address.* This is the external address bound to the matching internal address with the given binat rule. Addresses are discussed in Chapter 5, */etc/pf.conf.*

These rules are similar to rdr rule, but they do not allow such fine degree of control, in particular it is not possible to redirect ports. While the following rule set works with rdr rules, it is not possible with binat rules.

```
rdr on $ext_if inet proto tcp from any to $ext_ad port 22 \
                         -> 192.168.1.1 port 1022
rdr on $ext_if inet proto tcp from any to $ext_ad port 25 \
                         -> 192.168.1.2 port 1025
rdr on $ext_if inet proto tcp from any to $ext_ad port 53 \
                         -> 192.168.1.3 port 1053
rdr on $ext_if inet proto tcp from any to $ext_ad port 80 \
                         -> 192.168.1.4 port 8080
```

Compare it with `binat` rules:

```
binat on $ext_if inet proto tcp from 192.168.1.37 to any \
                                   -> $ext_ad_1
binat on $ext_if inet proto tcp from 192.168.1.38 to any \
                                   -> $ext_ad_2
binat on $ext_if inet proto tcp from 192.168.1.54 to any \
                                   -> $ext_ad_3
```

As you can see, every internal address must have its own equivalent external address. They can all be bound to the same external interface, though. If you want to know more, consult the *ifconfig(8)* man page (look for information about aliases).

Again, `no` and `!` modifiers are allowed, as are address class modifiers (`inet` and `inet6`), and `pass` or `tag` keywords (the interactions between them are similar to those in `nat` and `rdr` rules).

> *Binat rules can bite you when you least expect it. They are bi-directional. Packets sent from internal hosts appear to be sent from the public external IP address and the packets arriving from the external hosts appear on the inside to be coming from the internal hosts, which can get messy. A combination of* `rdr` *and* `nat` *are a better choice in a vast majority of cases.*

Whatever NAT rules you write, remember two things:

- do not try to redirect packets to the same interface they arrive on, it will not work (routing options for filter rules may help you here, see Chapter 8, *Packet Filtering*);
- do not redirect to the local interface on the firewall (127.0.0.1), because it creates a potential security risk (we break this rule with *spamd*, but such decisions should not be taken lightly).

7.4 Proxy ARP

Proxy ARP is sometimes thought of as an equivalent of NAT, but it is not an exact match. You can use it to connect two network segments and the proxy ARP host will answer requests for the host hiding behind it, but there will not be true NAT happening and packets sent from private addresses will not have their IP source address or port numbers changed.

Enabling proxy ARP is easy, the intermediate host that acts as a proxy has static ARP entries in its ARP cache that inform it that the address of the host hiding behind it (the internal host) is bound to the proxy host's external interface. No enable two-way communication, the administrator sets up routes that tell the proxy host where it should send the packets it receives. Static ARP and routing are discussed in Chapter 4, *Configuring OpenBSD*.

Packet Filtering

Packet filtering is something pf(4) *does exceptionally well. No matter what configuration of OpenBSD and* pf(4) *you use, there is always a bit of packet filtering to be done.*

Packet filtering rules, if present in *pf.conf* are examined after scrub rules (see Chapter 6, *Packet Normalization*) and NAT rules (see Chapter 7, *Packet Redirection*). There are three kinds of packet filtering rules:

- `block` — block matching packets.
- `pass` — let matching packets through.
- `antispoof` — a special case of `block` rules.

8.1 The Anatomy of a Filtering Rule

Packet filtering rules, just like other *pf(4)* rules, are written using specialized grammar, similar to that of NAT rules, but capable of describing much finer detail:

- *The action (`block or pass`) keyword.* Indicates what action will be taken when a matching packet is found. This part is required.
- *The direction (`in or out`) keyword.* Decides which packets are matched, inbound or outbound. This part is required.
- *The log (`log or log-all`) keyword.* Tells *pf(4)* to log matching packets. This part is optional.
- *The `quick` keyword.* Tells *pf(4)* to not evaluate other filtering rules once a matching packet is found. This part is optional.
- *The interface name(s).* This part is optional, but rarely omitted. When it is missing, the rules apply to all interfaces, which is rarely desired.
- *Routing options.* These options can be use to fine-tune routing of packets, logging, etc. This part is optional.
- *Address family (IPv4 and/or IPv6).* This part is optional.

- *Protocol name(s)*. This part is optional.
- *Source host address and port number (optional)*. This part is optional.
- *Target host address and port number (optional)*. This part is optional.
- *Options*. This part is optional.

The large number of keywords and their possible configurations make them a bit overwhelming for a beginner, but there is a method behind this madness. The following guide should make them easier to digest.

8.1.1 What Is pf Supposed to Do (block, pass)?

The `block` or `pass` keywords tell *pf(4)* what to do with the packet that matches all conditions listed after either `block` or `pass` (we are leaving the `antispoof` keyword aside until the end of this chapter, but think of it as a special case of `block` rules). These keywords are *required* and either of them must be used at the beginning of every filtering rule. To block all inbound and outbound packets, use:

```
block in  all
block out all
```

The opposite would be `pass` rules that let all traffic in and out of the firewall:

```
pass in  all
pass out all
```

With such rules in place, all traffic can move freely in or out of the firewall. Both policies are too general for practical use, but they are handy for explaining the basics.

As a general rule, the more conditions you list after `pass` or `block` the more specific the rule will be. Conversely the less conditions you use, the more general the rule will be. As you will see later on, it is always a good idea to start your packet filtering section with a set of:

```
block in all
block out all
```

It is safer to block all traffic first and only open those routes that are absolutely necessary later. Apart from being a safer way to write *pf(4)* rulesets, such an approach greatly simplifies the ruleset, which is good, because simple rulesets are easier to debug and put less stress on the firewall. Therefore, the shorter the ruleset, the shorted the time it takes to evaluate it.

Unlike NAT rules, where the first matching rule wins and the packet is translated according to that particular rule, filtering rules are evaluated until there are no more matching rules, and the last matching rule wins. Suppose you have four hosts and you wanted to do NAT just for three of them, you'd need to use the `no nat` rule excluding one of these hosts form NAT *before* the `nat` rule that applies to the other three hosts. Things are different with filtering rules, if you wanted to block outbound packets sent from one of hosts on your LAN, you'd need to list the `block` rule after the `pass` rule.

8.1.2 Return to Sender (drop, return-icmp, return-icmp6, return-rst, return)

A plain `block` rule drops all matching packets without sending any kind of notification back to the host that tried to initiate the connection. Silently dropping all unwanted packets is a good security practice, because the firewall does not have to waste its own resources on sending redundant information, and because 'silent' firewalls are harder to scan and fingerprint. (Broadly speaking, *scanning* is the process of looking for open ports that the attacker could use to break into your firewall or network, while *fingerprinting* is the process of identifying the operating system or other software running on the scanned host.)

However, as with all general rules, there are exceptions. One of these is sending the ICMP `destination-unreachable` message to hosts trying to connect to port 113 (`auth`). It is quite safe to do so and is considered to be good net citizenship. Returning that message helps some services, such as `sendmail`, complete connections faster, without waiting for connections to port 113 to time out.

This can be achieved with a rule that begins with:

```
#######################################################
# macro definitions
#-----------------------------------------------------
```

```
# ext_if -- the name of the firewall's external
#           interface
ext_if = "ne1"
# ext_ad -- the address of the firewall's external
#           interface
ext_ad = "e.e.e.e/32"


##########################################################
# packet filtering rules: "antispoof", "block", "pass"
#--------------------------------------------------------
# block all inbound connections
block in all
# block all inbound connections to port 113 (auth)
# and return ICMP destination-unreachable
block return-icmp in quick on $ext_if proto tcp \
     from any to $ext_ad port auth
# allow inbound connections to port 25 (smtp)
pass in quick on $ext_if \
     from any to $ext_ad port smtp
```

You can add the ICMP message number or name after the `return-icmp` keyword, although it is optional and only required in special cases. Note that `return-icmp` works for IPv4 packets, IPv6 ICMP messages will be send when you use the `return-icmp6` keyword. ICMP and ICMP6 are documented on the *icmp(4)* and *icmp6(4)* pages of the OpenBSD manual. For more information about ICMP, read [RFC 792]; if you want to learn how it works in practice, and how it is implemented, especially on BSD systems, consult [Wright, Stevens 1994].

Another possibility is to answer unwanted packets with the TCP RST reply. This is achieved with the `return-rst` keyword, which can be followed by an integer number defining the TTL (time to live) value for the returned packet as in (note that TTL value is enclosed in parentheses and must be listed after the `ttl` keyword):

```
##########################################################
# macro definitions
#--------------------------------------------------------
# ext_if -- the name of the firewall's external
#           interface
ext_if = "ne1"
```

```
# ext_ad -- the address of the firewall's external
#            interface
ext_ad = "e.e.e.e/32"


############################################################
# packet filtering rules: "antispoof", "block", "pass"
#----------------------------------------------------------
block return-rst in quick on $ext_if proto tcp \
      from any to $ext_ad port auth
```

or:

```
block return-rst (ttl 100) quick in on $ext_if proto tcp \
      from any to $ext_ad port auth
```

Note the use of the `proto` keyword, which limits the scope of the rules shown in this section to TCP; you could also use `proto udp` to limit these rules to UDP packets; or, you could combine them with `proto {tcp, udp}`. You must specify these protocols (one of them or both, as needed) when you also specify ports (`port`).

The `return-rst` keyword applies to TCP packets. Should you want something more, use the `return` keyword, which returns TCP RST for TCP packets and ICMP `destination-unreachable` for UDP and other packets:

```
block return quick in on $ext_if \
      from any to $ext_ad
```

For completeness, there is also the `drop` keyword, which tell *pf(4)* to silently drop connections without sending any error messages. It is used when you override the default block policy (silently drop all blocked packets with the `set block-policy return` option (behavior identical to `return`).

```
############################################################
# options: set
#----------------------------------------------------------
# answer blocked TCP packets with TCP RSP and
# blocked UDP with ICMP destination-unreachable
set block-policy return
```

```
##########################################################
# packet filtering rules: "antispoof", "block", "pass"
#---------------------------------------------------------
# block and drop packets (override set block-policy
# return)
block drop in quick on $ext_if proto tcp \
      from any to $ext_ad port auth
```

Please note that the keyword described in this section are optional. Another important thing to remember is their incompatibility with *bridge(4)*.

8.1.3 Inbound or Outbound (in, out)?

The next *required* keyword that appears after either the `block` (followed by optional `drop`, `return-icmp`, `return-icmp6`, `return-rst`, or `return` keywords) or the `pass` keyword is the direction keyword. There are two direction keywords you can use: `in` or `out`. They are known to cause some confusion, especially when the firewall is equipped with more than one network interface, and when NAT rules are used along with filtering rules.

The key to understanding when a packet matches either the `in` or the `out` rule is remembering that these directions are relative to the firewall itself. If a packet is sent from an external host to the firewall, it matches the `in` rule on the firewall's external interface; when it is sent from the firewall itself, it matches the `out` on the external interface. Similarly, packets sent from internal hosts to the firewall and destined to external hosts will match `in` rules on the interface connecting your private network segment to the firewall and `out` rules on the firewall's external interface.

8.1.4 To Log or Not to Log (log, log-all)?

You can tell *pf(4)* to log packets matching certain rules to the `pflog0` interface. From there, they are picked up by *pflogd(8)* and stored in rotated log files located in */var/log*.

To start packet logging, use the `log` or the `log-all` keywords. The difference between them lies in the way they work with rules that contain either `keep state` or modulate state rules (more on these later); `log` logs only the state-making packets, while `log-all` logs all packets. If you use stateful filtering and want to capture all packets that match the `log` rule, use `log-all`, otherwise, use `log`.

Although the firewall does not need to be implemented on the latest, fastest machine you can get, the more traffic you log and the heavier the traffic that passes through the firewall's interface, the faster the hardware you use the better. This is especially true for the disks that must store the data. As you will learn later in this chapter, when we discuss the `dup-to` keyword, you can duplicate packets and send them to a different interface, where a dedicated packet logging machine can sit, listen, store, and analyze traffic. If you use `dup-to` for logging, then `log`, and `log-all` are redundant. Similarly, if you use span hosts on a bridge, the `log` or `log-all` keywords may not be necessary. See Chapter 11, *Logging and Log Analysis* for more information on this subject.

8.1.5 Finishing Early (quick)

Unlike NAT (`nat`, `binat`, `rdr`) rules, which are processed in the 'first matching rule wins' fashion, packet filtering is done in the 'last matching rule wins' way. While it is possible to carefully structure your ruleset in a way that avoids letting unwanted packets through, it is more convenient and simpler to put rules that you want to process faster (like very specific blocking rules) at the top of the packet filtering section of the ruleset and add the `quick` keyword to such rules. Whenever this keyword is used, *pf(4)* will execute the matching rule and will not try to match the packet against the rest of the ruleset. This saves some processing time, which quickly adds up on a busy link.

The `quick` keyword is added after the `log` or `log-all` keywords, or, in the absence of these keywords, after the `in` or `out` direction keywords:

```
pass in log-all quick on $ext_if proto tcp from any \
                          to $ext_ad port 80
```

or:

```
pass in quick on $ext_if proto tcp from any \
                      to $ext_ad port 80
```

Typical applications of `quick` rules include quickly blocking addresses of problematic sites and blocking packets with spoofed addresses.

> *Be careful when you are using* `quick` *in rulesets loaded*
> *with anchors. When used in an anchor ruleset, the*
> `quick` *keyword in the anchor finishes evaluation of both*
> *the named and the main ruleset.*

8.1.6 Network Interface Names (on)?

While the packet filtering rules grammar allows us to write general rules
that apply to all interfaces, we can seldom write a good ruleset without
adding rules for specific interfaces. The name of the interface is given after
the `on` keyword that appears after the `quick` keyword. The following examples show a few possible variations of keywords that appear *before* `on`:

```
block in on $ext_if
block in log-all on $ext_if
block in log-all quick on $ext_if
```

> *If you forgot the name of the interface, check the output of*
> `dmesg | less`*. When OpenBSD is not recognizing*
> *your network interface, read Chapter 4,* Configuring
> OpenBSD *for kernel modification tips. Note that if you*
> *are using a device connected to the serial interface (like a*
> *modem), such device may not be listed in* `dmesg` *output,*
> *but should still be recognized by the system. When you*
> *are not sure what name your network card falls under in*
> *OpenBSD, check the list displayed by the* `apropos`
> `driver` *command.*

8.1.7 Routing Options (fastroute, reply-to, route-to, dup-to)

Ordinarily, packets examined by *pf(4)* are routed according to the entries in
the firewall's routing table, which is what we want in most cases. You can
always check the routing table with:

```
$ route show
```

(The same command is used to modify the routing tables, see *route(4)*).

However, there might be times when you will want to bypass the routing table or to duplicate packets for intrusion detection or logging purposes. The following four keywords allow us to influence packet routing:

- fastroute — use the routing table.
- route-to — bypass the routing table and route matching packets through the interface whose name must be given after the route-to keyword. The name of the interface may be followed by the IP address of the host that should receive packets, when the IP address is used. The name and the address must be enclosed in parentheses, as in:

```
pass in on $ext_if route-to ($int_if $int_ad) all
pass in on $ext_if route-to $int_if all
```

- dup-to — create a copy of each matching packet, bypass the routing table and route the copied packet through the interface whose name must be given after the dup-to keyword. The name of the interface may be followed by the IP address of the host that is supposed to receive the copies, when the IP address is used. The name and the address must be enclosed in parentheses. The original packet is routed using entries in the routing table (as if fastroute was used).
- reply-to — routes replies to packet matching the rules that use this keyword through another interface. This lets you implement symmetric routing enforcement with state rules (keep state, modulate state), if you have two external interfaces.

The dup-to keyword is very useful for setting up a separate packet logging or intrusion detection system host. Simply add this rule to /etc/pf.conf on the firewall:

```
# ext_if -- external interface on the firewall
# log_if -- interface connecting the loging station
pass  in on $ext_if dup-to $log_if all
pass out on $ext_if dup-to $log_if all
```

Then, run *pf(4)* on the logging host with the following rule:

```
# ext_if -- external interface on the logging station
block in log on $ext_if all
```

How do you log on the logging host? Add a rule that allows connections to port SSH:

```
# ext_if -- external interface on the logging station
# log_keeper -- the address of the logging station
block in log on $ext_if all
block return-icmp in log quick on $ext_if proto tcp \
     from any to $log_keeper port auth
pass in log on $ext_if from any to $log_keeper port ssh
```

If you want to fine-tune logging parameters, read Chapter 11, *Logging and Log Analysis*.

Letting another host take care of logging or analysis of packets is a good thing, because it moves the additional load placed on the firewall's resources to another host. It makes logging complex setups like those described in Chapter 11, *Logging and Log Analysis*, unnecessary, while making the whole process of logging simpler and more stable. Of course, to create such setup you will need another machine and an additional network interface on the firewall (it's best to put the logging/analysis machine on a separate segment, or you will slow down the internal network by as much as 50%).

The dup-to, reply-to, and route-to keywords can be followed by *target address pools* (bitmask, random, round-robin, source-hash, static-port. You can read more about these options in Chapter 10, *Bandwidth Shaping and Load Balancing*.

8.1.8 IP Addressing Familes: IPv4 (inet) or IPv6 (inet6)

Pf(4) can filter packets with IPv4 (inet) and IPv6 (inet6) addresses. You select the addressing family with the inet (IPv4) or inet6 (IPv6) keywords. If you plan on dealing with IPv4 traffic only, add these rules for every interface on the firewall:

```
block in  quick inet6 all
block out quick inet6 all
```

or, you could write:

```
block in all
pass  in inet all
pass out inet all
```

8.1.9 Protocols (proto)

Another layer of filtering is filtering by protocol name or number. This is done with an addition of the `proto` keyword followed by the name(s) or number(s) of protocols that the packets are formed in accordance with. The list of protocols can be found in */etc/protocols*.

For example, if you want to let in only TCP packets, use this rule:

```
pass in quick on $ext_if proto tcp
```

> *Almost all popular services use TCP. You should block UDP packets sent to servers that only use TCP, because such packets are almost never legitimate traffic. If you do not know which protocol is used by which services, check* /etc/protocols. *The latest and the freshest listings are always in the IANA's online database:*
>
> *http://www.iana.org/assignments/protocol-numbers*

8.1.10 Source Address (from, any, all)

Source address filtering is typically used to stop two kinds of packets: those originating from hosts with legal IP addresses that we do not want to accept traffic from, and those that carry spoofed source addresses. In the first case, you will want to block packets from legal IP addresses if they're giving you so much trouble that you'd rather not accept traffic from them. In the second case, you ought to block packets with spoofed source addresses for your own safety as they will never be legitimate traffic. The following rule blocks packets with spoofed source addresses sent from external hosts and arriving on the firewall's external interface:

```
$block_ads = \
        {10.0.0.0/8, 172.16.0.0/12, 192.168.0.0/16, \
     224.0.0.0/4, 240.0.0.0/5, 127.0.0.0/8, 0.0.0.0}
block in quick on $ext_if from $block_ads
```

Conversely, we can specify addresses of hosts that we want to accept traffic from, as in:

```
block in quick on $ext_if from ! $allow_ads to any
```

> *Note the exclamation mark (!), which negates the value that follows it, so the rule above reads 'block incoming packets (and don't match them against other filtering rules) arriving on the external interface send from all IP addresses except $allow_ad and destined for any host.'*

There are two shortcuts that you can use to specify wider ranges of IP addresses. One is the `any` keyword, which when placed after `from` or `to`, matches any source (`from any`) or target (`to any`) address:

```
block in quick on $log_if from any to $log_ad
block in quick on $ext_if from $blockIPs to any
```

The second shortcut is the `all` keyword which replaces `from any to any`. The following two rules are synonymous:

```
block in on $ext_if from any to any
block in on $ext_if all
```

> *When you decide to use* `from` *you must also use* `to`, and vice versa.

Source address specification is a *required* part of any packet filtering rule, even if you use an all-encompassing `any` or `all` shortcuts.

8.1.11 Source Port (port)

For a finer degree of control, we can block or pass packets sent from a specific port on the interface from which the matching packets were sent. The port specification is listed after the source address specification and is marked with the `port` keyword, as in:

```
block in on $ext_if proto tcp from any port 80
```

The `port 80` notation is equivalent to `port = 80`. Other possible operators are <, >, <=, >=, ! =, <>, and ><:

```
# block packets destined for port 80
block in on $ext_if proto tcp from any to \
                    $dmz_www_ad port = 80


# block packets destined for all ports except port 80
block in on $ext_if proto tcp from any to \
                    $dmz_www_ad port != 80


# block packets destined for ports lower than port 80
block in on $ext_if proto tcp from any to \
                    $dmz_www_ad port < 80


# block packets destined for ports lower than and equal
# to port 80
block in on $ext_if proto tcp from any to \
                    $dmz_www_ad port <= 80


# block packets destined for ports higher than
block in on $ext_if proto tcp from any \
            to $dmz_www_ad port > 80


# block packets destined for ports higher than and equal
# to port 80
block in on $ext_if proto tcp from any to \
                    $dmz_www_ad port >= 80


# block packets destined for ports higher than port 80
# and lower than port 1024
block in on $ext_if proto tcp from any to \
                $dmz_www_ad port 80 >< 1024


# block packets destined for ports lower than port 80
# and higher than port 1024
block in on $ext_if proto tcp from any to \
                $dmz_www_ad port 80 <> 1024
```

Specifying port numbers makes sense only for those protocols that carry
source port information (like TCP or UDP). That is why you need to use
the proto keyword when you use the port keyword. Otherwise, *pfctl(8)*
will complain and refuse to load rules.

*Port numbers and the names of services that use them are
listed in /etc/services. The latest version of that list is
available from:*

http://www.iana.org/assignments/port-numbers

8.1.12 Sender's Operating System (os)

A new addition to *pf(4)* introduced in OpenBSD 3.4 is the ability to use the
operating system fingerprint database stored in */etc/pf.os*. That database is a
plain text file with one entry per line. You select fingerprints using three
fields: operating system name, operating system version, and sub-
type/patchlevel.

To use this feature add the os keyword followed by the fingerprint parameters after the source port number specification, or (when port number information is missing, right after the source address). For example, if you
wanted to match connections from Microsoft Windows, you would write:

```
pass in on $ext_if proto tcp from any os "Windows"
```

A more specific rule, matching connections from Microsoft Windows 2000
hosts, would be:

```
pass in on $ext_if proto tcp from any os "Windows 2000"
```

And, if you wanted to be even more specific, you could match packets from
Microsoft Windows 2002 Service Pack 4 (SP4):

```
pass in on $ext_if proto tcp from any os "Windows 2000 SP4"
```

What if you wanted to be 'creative' and used "Windows SP4?" It won't
match. Check it for yourself, write such rule and load it with:

```
# pfctl -f ./test-os
```

And check what *pfctl(8)* reports. When it finds a matching entry in
/etc/pf.os, you will see something like:

```
pass in on ne1 proto tcp from any os "Windows 2000 SP4"
```

If there is no matching entry, you will see:

```
pass in on ne1 proto tcp from any os "nomatch"
```

Always check if the os rules resolve to the signatures you specified, or you may be scratching your head wondering what is going on with them.

There are a few things you need to be aware of when you use this feature:

- operating system fingerprinting is not an exact science, and should not be though of as a security tool. It can be useful in fine-tuning rules that regulate the flow of packets (some hosts can connect to one host, while they cannot connect to another).
- it works for TCP connections only, so add the proto tcp keywords to such rules.
- the match is done on the TCP SYN packet (sent at teh time when the remote host attempts to establish a new connection). Therefore, when you load os rules into memory, they will do nothing to existing connections.
- when you add a on rule to your ruleset, *pf(4)* automatically loads */etc/pf.os* into memory. You can view its contents with:

  ```
  # pfctl -so
  ```

- for matching operating systems without entries in */etc/pf.os*, use the unknown string, e.g:

  ```
  pass in on ne1 proto tcp from any os "unknown"
  ```

Pf(4) expects to find the fingerprint database in */etc/pf.os*, but you can change it with the following option:

```
set fingerprints "/etc/pf.os-special-modifications"
```

8.1.13 Destination IP address (to, any, all)

Destination address filtering is typically used to pass only those packets that are destined to addresses where there are servers listening for connections, for example:

```
pass in on $ext_if from any to $dmz_www_ad
```

All syntax rules for source addresses discussed earlier are applicable to destination addresses. Destination address specification is a *required* part of any packet filtering rule, even if you use an all-encompassing any or all shortcuts.

8.1.14 Destination Port (port)

The destination port specification follows the destination address specification. All rules that apply to source ports, apply to destination ports. Of course, both are independent. You will probably use destination ports more often than source ports, as such rules are usually used to only let those packets through that are destined to ports where appropriate servers are listening, for example:

```
pass in on $ext_if proto tcp from any to \
        $ext_www_ad  port $ext_www_port
pass in on $ext_if proto tcp from any to \
        $ext_smtp_ad port $ext_smtp_port
pass in on $ext_if proto tcp from any to \
        $ext_ftp_ad  port $ext_ftp_port
```

Ports (source or target) only make sense for TCP or UDP protocols, so if *pfctl(8)* complains about your rules, check if you narrowed your rules to TCP or UDP.

8.1.15 User and Group Access Control (user, group)

One very handy feature of *pf(4)* is its ability to filter packets based on the names of the users and groups who own the sockets on which packets are sent or received. The user and group IDs can be given in form of names or numbers and it is possible to specify ranges and lists of IDs. When you list ranges, it is possible to construct them using the operators described earlier in the section on source ports:

```
pass out on $ext_if proto {tcp, udp} \
  from any to any user joe keep state

pass out on $ext_if proto {tcp, udp} \
  from any to any user > 10000 group users keep state
```

The user and group names are *effective* names, which may not be the same as the real name (as is the case with setuid and setgid processes). If you are having problems with these rules, remember that the user and group IDs are stored at the time a socket is created and they are not updated when the process creating a socket drops privileges (e.g., after a process binds to a privileged port as `root`, and then drops `root` privileges), so it may be that you need to use `root` ID in a rule instead of an unprivileged users's ID. Try this when you hit a stumbling block with rules user or group

In case of outgoing connections, the user IDs will match the user that opened the connection *from* the firewall itself. Similarly, for incoming connections, the user IDs will match the user that opened the socket for listening *on* the firewall. It is not possible to match usernames on connections forwarded with NAT rules. In case of forwarded connections, user or group IDs can match (or not match) a special username `unknown`. In this case, only two operators are allowed: = and !=.

> *User and group rules can only be used with TCP and UDP protocols.*

User and group names are used in *ftp-proxy(8)* setup described in Chapter 4, *Configuring OpenBSD*. Another application of user/group keywords is user authentication described in Chapter 12, *Using authpf*.

8.1.16 TCP Flags (flags)

TCP packet headers contain a flag field which plays an important role in the process of establishing, maintaining, and closing connections. Flags are important from the point of view of security, because some attackers abuse the three-way-handshake mechanism and other uses of TCP flags in denial of service (DOS) attacks (see CERT Advisories [CERT-1996.21] and [CERT-2000.21]) and other types of attacks aimed at hosts connected to the Internet.

As of OpenBSD 3.4, *pf(4)* recognizes the following TCP header flags:

- (S) YN: synchronize sequence numbers.
- (A) CK: acknowledge.
- (R) ST: reset.

- (F) IN: finish.
- (P)USH: push.
- (U)RG: urgent pointer.
- (E)CE: (ECN-Echo) explicit congestion notification echo.
- C(W)R: congestion window reduced.

The syntax for this portion of filtering rules is as follows: the flags keyword is followed by two lists of flags separated with a slash (/); the first is a list of flags from the second list that must be set. Those flags not on the first list must be unset. Flags not listed on the second list are ignored, and those flags from the second list missing from the first list may or may not be set:

```
# FIN must be set, ignore the rest
block in proto tcp all flags F/F
# FIN must be unset, ignore the rest
block in all flags /F
# FIN must be set, the rest must be unset
block in all flags F
# FIN must be set, ACK must be unset, ignore the rest
block in all flags F/FA
# FIN and ACK must be unset, ignore the rest
block in all flags /FA
```

TCP flags are described in [RFC 761] and [RFC 793]. A far more detailed discussion of TCP flags can be found in [Wright, Stevens 1994] Note that [Wright, Stevens 1994] does not describe the ECE and CWR flags, as these were added to the TCP header after it was published. For more information on ECE and CWR read [RFC 3168], [RFC 3168], and [RFC 3360].

The flags keyword makes sense only for TCP (proto tcp) packets.

8.1.17 ICMP Packets

Bogus ICMP packets are another way attackers can make your site inoperable, which is why *pf(4)* has special syntax for dealing with these useful, but potentially dangerous packets. For more information about the havoc ICMP packets can wreak read this paper:

http://www.giac.org/practical/gsec/DeokJo_Jeon_GSEC.pdf

Additional information on that subject can be found in [CERT-1996.26].

ICMPv4 packets are matched by the `icmp-type` keyword, while ICMP IPv6 are matched by the `ipv6-icmp-type` keyword. Both keywords are followed by the ICMP type number and the ICMP code number, separated with the `code` keyword.

For example, if you wanted the firewall to receive and reply to ping requests, you'd use the following rule:

```
pass in inet proto icmp icmp-type 8 code 0 keep state
```

The equivalent rule for IPv6 would be:

```
pass in inet6 proto icmpv6 icmpv6-icmp-type 8 code 0 keep state
```

Explanations of ICMPv4 message types and codes can be found in [RFC 792], while ICMPv6 message types and codes are discussed in [RFC 2463].

8.1.18 Stateful Filtering (keep state, modulate state, synproxy state)

Pf(4) is a *stateful* packet filter, which means that it is capable of keeping track of the state of connections. Stateful filtering has the following advantages:

- makes packet processing faster
- makes writing rulesets easier
- makes connections safer

The basic principle behind stateful filtering is simple. When the initial packet makes the connection on the firewall, the packet filter will create an entry in its state table for that connection. All subsequent packets that belong to the connection for which an entry in the state table exist will be let through without matching them against the whole ruleset. State tables are checked before the filter begins evaluating filtering rules.

The packet filter decides if a packet belongs to a connection for which a state exists by checking the packet's sequence number stored in the TCP header. When the sequence number falls out of a narrow window, the packet is dropped. This mechanism prevents spoofed packet injection into an established connection. Stateful inspection of packets is turned on with the `keep state` keywords placed near the end of a filtering rule (before queue lists, see Chapter 10, *Bandwidth Shaping and Load Balancing*):

```
pass out on $ext_if proto TCP all keep state
```

To keep memory usage under control, information about connections is removed from the state table after connections are closed or after they time out.

(By the way, when you use `nat/binat/rdr` rules, you are already using stateful filtering, as these rules create states automatically.)

There are two schools of thought about state creation. Some administrators insist that only packets with the `SYN` flag (i.e., the packets that initialize the connection) can create state. Others say that any packet ought to be able to create state, because such rules allow existing connections to create state and continue after the state tables are flushed with `pfctl -F state` or after the firewall is rebooted. Rules that create state only for packets with the `SYN` flag set will not be able to create state for existing connections.

The following rules allow all departing TCP packets to create state. As for inbound packets, only those sent to port 80 will be able to create state:

```
pass in   proto tcp all port 80 keep state
pass out proto tcp all keep state
```

If you want to limit packets that can create state to those that have the `SYN` flag set, add the `flags S/SA` condition, as in:

```
pass in proto tcp all port 80 flags S/SA keep state
pass out proto tcp all flags S/SA keep state
```

What about UDP or ICMP packets? Can *pf(4)* create state for these as well? Yes, it can. With UDP packets, which do not carry sequence numbers, the filter matches them to states using only address and port information.

As for ICMP, these are treated differently depending on their category. ICMP error messages that refer to TCP or UDP packets are matched against states for connections they refer to. As such they do not require separate rules, the packet filter will take care of this automatically. ICMP queries (like *ping(8)*) may need their own separate rules, like:

```
pass out inet proto icmp all icmp-type echoreq keep state
```

Initial sequence numbers, if chosen carelessly, can be used in dangerous attacks that exploit the fact that some TCP stacks use easily predictable values for initial sequence numbers. For more information about these attacks read [CERT VU#498440] or [Farrow 2003].

Pf(4) can prevent these attacks with the `modulate state` rule. To turn it on, use `modulate state` instead of `keep state`:

```
pass in  proto tcp all port 80 flags S/SA keep state
pass out proto tcp all flags S/SA keep state
```

becomes:

```
pass in  proto tcp all port 80 flags S/SA modulate state
pass out proto tcp all flags S/SA modulate state
```

The advantage of using `modulate state` is a higher level of security achieved by a more random initial sequence number chosen for connections that match such rules. Remember that `modulate state` can only be used with TCP connections. For other connections use `keep state`.

Another variant of stateful filtering is SYNPROXY. The idea behind this kind of state rule is to complete the TCP connection initialization handshake on behalf of both sides and once that is completed, pass packets back and forth. The `synproxy state` rules implement both `keep state` and `modulate state` features and only work with TCP connections:

```
pass in  proto tcp all port 80 flags S/SA synproxy state
```

SYNPROXY rules prevent SYN floods, a particularly nasty type of attack.

The behavior of the state engine can be controlled with global options applicable to all rules, and with local options specified on a per-rule basis. These options are: `limit states` and `timeout`.

The `limit states` *n* option set hard limits on the number of memory pools used by *pf(4)* to store state table entries. If you set this option, *pf(4)* will store only *n* state table entries. Administrators use this option to avoid performance hits and to prevent attacks from overwhelming the firewall's resources. This option must be listed in the options section of */etc/pf.conf*.

You can change these limits at will, but to reset them to their unlimited state, you have to comment out or remove `set limit states` rules in */etc/pf.conf*, and reboot your firewall machine.

The `timeout` option rule adjusts the expiration time of stateful connections. These rules only apply to packets matching stateful connections. The general syntax of this rule is `set timeout protocol.connectionstate timeout`, for example:

```
##########################################################
# options: "set"

# ex. 1 sets timeout of the stateful connection to 20
# seconds after receiving the first packet from the host
# initializing this connection.
set timeout tcp.first 20


# ex. 2 sets timeout of the stateful connection to 20
# seconds after receiving the first packet from the host
# initializing this connection, then, if the connection
# is established, every packet that matches the
# established state of a TCP connection resets the
# timeout of the TCP connection it is a part of to 10
# seconds.  This is very aggressive, and will result in
# a high percentage of lost valid connections on slow
# links.
set timeout tcp.first 20
set timeout tcp.established 10


# ex. 3 same as ex. 2, but both rules have been combined
# on a single line (the order of protocol.state rules is
# not relevant)
set timeout { tcp.first 20, tcp.established 10 }
```

Example 1 above sets a very aggressive rule. If the connection is not established in 20 seconds, it will be dropped. In example 2, the connection will be dropped if the firewall does not receive a packet that is a part of the established TCP connection in 10 seconds. This is a very aggressive setting.

The *protocol.connectionstate* pair can be one of these values:

- `tcp.first`
- `tcp.opening`
- `tcp.established`
- `tcp.closing`
- `tcp.finwait`
- `tcp.closed`

These settings are static (you need to reload the rules that use them to change their values), but you can make them *adaptive* with:

- `adaptive.start` — when the number of states exceeds this value, *pf(4)* begins linear scaling of all timeout values.
- `adaptive.end` — when the number of states exceeds this value, *pf(4)* sets all timeout values to 0, which expires them.

The formula used in linear scaling takes the following values: `adaptive.start`, `adaptive.end`, the current number of states stored in memory:

$$\frac{adaptive.\,end - number\ of\ states}{adaptive.\,end - adaptive.\,start} = scaling\ factor$$

So, if you set the following options (they can be set globally, in the options section, or on a per-rule basis):

```
set timeout {adaptive.start 5000, adaptive.end 20000}
```

and the number of states is 8500, the timeout values will be scaled down to the following fraction of their initial values:

$$\frac{20000 - 8500}{20000 - 5000} = \frac{11500}{15000} = 0.\,77\ (77\%)$$

To learn more about the TCP connection state transition cycle, consult
[RFC 761], and if you are still looking for more information, read [Stevens
1994, 1:240-242] and [Wright, Stevens 1994, 2:805-807].

It is possible to control other protocols, like UDP, or ICMP, but the number
of *protocol.state* matches is more limited:

- `udp.first`
- `udp.single`
- `udp.multiple`

- `icmp.first`
- `icmp.error`

- `other.first`
- `other.single`
- `other.multiple`

The `other` keyword is a catch-all category for protocols which are neither
TCP, UDP, nor ICMP.

The last timeout option, `interval` specifies the interval between flushing
expired states.

```
##########################################################
# options: "set"

set timeout interval 20
set timeout frags 20
```

> *Because* `optimization` *rules reset various global*
> `timeout` *settings, you should always list* `optimiza-`
> `tion` *rules before your* `timeout` settings.

Each `keep state` or `modulate state` can have its own set of options. These options are:

- `max` *n* — the maximum number (*n*) of concurrent states that can be created for this rule. See the earlier discussion of the `limit states` option

- `timeout`: timeout values for states created with this rule. See the earlier description of the `timeout` option.

A rule using state options could look like this:

```
pass in proto tcp all port 80 flags S/SA modulate \
state (max 1000, tcp.established 120, tcp.closing 10)
```

8.1.19 IP Options (allow-opts)

IP options are blocked by default, which is good from the point of view of security. If you want to allow them, you explicitly state your wish with the `allow-opts` keyword:

```
########################################################
# macro definitions
#-------------------------------------------------------
# ext_if -- the name of the firewall's external
#           interface
ext_if = "ne1"


########################################################
# packet filtering rules: "antispoof", "block", "pass"
#-------------------------------------------------------


pass in on $ext_if all allow-opts
```

In practice there is very little need for allowing these options, save for special application, as they may be used by attackers to mess with your network, or with other hosts on the Internet (in such cases, you might end up being accused of deliberate wrongdoing, if you enable these options and it results in problems for other hosts). IP options do have their legitimate uses, but if you don't explicitly need them, do not use `allow-opts`.

> *If you're curious, read [RFC 791] and [RFC 1108]. For a more detailed discussion, refer to [Wright, Stevens 1994] where you will find details of operation and implementation of IP options processing in BSD systems.*

The `allow-opts` keyword can only be used in `pass` rules.

8.1.20 Labels (label)

Labels are used to mark rules for which *pf(4)* will keep separate statistics. You can display these stats with *pfctl(1)*. A label is added with the `label` keyword followed by a text string. Labels are placed at the very end of rules:

```
pass in  on rl0 all label "incoming"
pass out on rl0 all label "departing"
```

To view statistics, use:

```
$ sudo pfctl -s labels
incoming 85 26 2024
departing 86 56 6960
```

When you add a lot of labels and want to see stats for just one label, use:

```
$ sudo pfctl -s labels | grep incoming
incoming 85 26 2024
```

The numbers that follow the labels are the number of positive rule matches, packets, and bytes.

Labels can contain pre-defined macros:

- `$srcaddr` — source IP address. This is the source IP address listed after the `from` keyword in the rule, not the packet's source address, so if you use `from any` and `label "from $srcaddr"` in the same rule you'll see a message similar to `from any 86 56 6960`.
- `$dstaddr`: destination IP address.
- `$srcport`: source port.
- `$dstport`: destination port.
- `$proto`: protocol name.
- `$if`: interface name.
- `$nr`: rule number.

8.2 Antispoof Rules

Source address spoofing is used to sneak packets past firewalls by setting their source addresses to the address assigned to one of the firewall's interfaces. Such packets ought to be dropped immediately, as they cannot be legitimate.

To help you quickly write secure anti-spoof rules, *pf(4)* defines a special `antispoof` keyword rule, that has the following syntax:

- The `antispoof` keyword. This part is required.
- The `log` keyword, if you want to log packets caught by this rule. This part is optional.
- The `quick` keyword, if you want to shorten the time taken to evaluate the whole ruleset. When you use that keyword, place `antispoof` rules at the beginning of the ruleset. This part is optional.
- The `for` keyword followed by the name of the interface for which *pf(4)* will generate anti-spoof rules. It is a common mistake to use `on` instead of `for`, so watch out for this. It is OK to list more than one interface in braces here, or to refer to a macro. This part is required.
- The addressing family, either `inet` for IPv4 or `inet6` for IPv6. This part is optional.

For example, if you wanted to write anti-spoof rules for interface ne1, you'd use:

```
antispoof for ne1
```

8.3 Filtering Rules for Redirected Packets

The problem of filtering redirected packets comes up over and over again in questions that the author receives from new users of *pf(4)*. How does one write rules that match redirected packets? Well, the main thing to remember when you are designing your ruleset and plan to use NAT or port/interface redirection, is to design your filtering rules to match packets *after* NATing and redirection, or you will waste a lot of time debugging the ruleset and scratching your head wondering what's wrong with your design and its implementation.

The rules of the road are quite simple (*inbound* and *outbound* qualifiers are relative to the firewall host):

- `rdr` rules. Packets sent by hosts other than the firewall itself, are matched by `block in` or `pass in` rules on the same interface you use in the `rdr` rule, e.g.:

```
# redirect all packets sent from the internal private
# network ($prv_ad) to port 80 on any address arriving
# at the interface connecting the private network with
# the firewall ($prv_if) to port 8080 on the cache
# server whose address is $ch_ad

rdr on $prv_if proto tcp from $prv_ad \
    to any port 80 -> $ch_ad port 8080

pass in on $prv_if proto tcp from $prv_ad \
                       to $ch_ad port 8080
```

- nat rules. Packets sent from NATed hosts appear as *outbound* packets on the firewall interface used in `nat` rules. Their source address and source port are changed to those of the firewall's interface. Therefore, they are matched by `block out` or `pass out` rules on that interface, e.g.:

```
# NAT hosts in the private network ($prv_ad) on the
# interface connecting the firewall to the Internet
# ($ext_if) using the firewall's external address
# ($ext_ad)

nat on $ext_if from $prv_ad to any -> $ext_ad

pass out on $ext_if proto tcp from $ext_ad to any
```

- binat rules. Packets sent from internal hosts appear as *outbound* packets on the interface used in `binat` rules. Their source address is changed to the external address used in the `binat` rule. Therefore, they are matched by `block out` or `pass out` rules on the interface used in the `binat` rule. Packets sent from external hosts appear as *inbound* packets on the interface used in `binat` rules. Their target address is changed to the internal address used in the `binat` rule. Therefore, they are matched by `block in` or `pass in` rules on the interface used in the `binat` rule.

```
#########################################################
# workstation_int -- the internal IP address of the
#                    binat-ed workstation
```

```
# workstation_ext -- the external IP address of the
#                     binat-ed workstation

binat on $ext_if from $workstation_int to any \
                         -> $workstation_ext

pass  in on $ext_if proto tcp from any \
                to $workstation_int
pass out on $ext_if proto tcp \
  from $workstation_ext to any
```

## Chapter 9

Dynamic Rulesets

In case you haven't noticed, the days of static network layout are over. The world around us is changing at an increasingly higher rate and so do the networks we manage. Our jobs are more and more similar to fixing planes while they are in the air. Fortunately, pf(4) is there to help us manage constant change.

One of the greatest challenges in network administration is managing and securing networks whose layout changes, often in an unorderly manner. Wireless Ethernet, telecommuting users, mergers and acquisitions, temporary alliances, etc. are all having a great impact on the networks we manage. It is very difficult to design and manage firewalls that can keep up with these changes. Fortunately, *pf(4)* is an advanced packet filter that can help administrators manage change and automate a lot of work. And because it runs of top of OpenBSD, it is possible to build advanced configurations that run on autopilot most of the time. Knowing how to build such systems requires knowledge of Unix, scripting, *pf(4)*, and other networking and security tools. In this chapter we will focus on those features of *pf(4)* that make it possible to build firewalls that adapt to change.

9.1 Designing an Automated Firewall

An automated firewall can adapt to changes in the local and the external environment. Changes to the firewall configuration can be periodic or dynamic, caused by unpredictable events.

Periodic changes are made with commands and scripts called from *cron(8)*, which can be configured to run *pfctl(8)* jobs like loading a different ruleset at different times of day (you can edit *cron(8)* jobs with *crontab(1)*). Such systems are not very flexible, but have their place. They are used to grant access to certain hosts at different times of day/night. Or they can be used to redirect connections from one host to another, while the first one is going through a backup routine. Such solutions are relatively rigid, with little space for the unpredictable.

More flexible solutions are those designed to react to dynamic, unpredictable events. These events can be friendly or unfriendly. A friendly event could be an attempt by one of the authorized users to log on the firewall to authenticate herself/himself. Such solutions are described in Chapter 12, *Using authpf*. An unfriendly event could be a port scan done on your firewall by the attacker looking for a way into your network. If such attempt was registered by your NIDS, the IP address of such host could be automatically added to the list of banned hosts, from which all connections are blocked. Such actions could be done automatically, without human intervention. One interesting project that lets *snort* (a very popular NIDS) automatically update *pf(4)* rulesets is *snort2pf*:

http://www.unix-geek.info/snort2pf.txt   *(snort2pf)*

Both kinds of automation require custom solutions as this territory is largely uncharted. Since each firewall is different, administrators write their own scripts that perform such tasks. Readers interested in building such solutions ought to have a good working knowledge of Unix and the following features of *pf(4)*:

- *The (interface) notation.* This simple notation solves the problem of not knowing the address assigned to the interface mentioned in a rule. Instead of giving an IP address, use something like (ne1), if the interface you will assign the IP address to is called ne1. When the name of the interface is stored in a macro, use the name of the macro in place of the name of the interface, e.g. ($ext_if). This particular feature is used in every ruleset where one or more addresses are assigned dynamically with DHCP. Of course, it can also be used when addresses are assigned statically. Remember to use the inet or inet6 keywords to specify which protocol should be filtered by your rules, as some interfaces resolve to more than one IP address class.
- *The hostname notation.* Similar to the (interface) notation, substitutes the hostname into address number. The inet or inet6 keywords might have to be used in such rules too.
- *The :broadcast notation.* Expands into the broadcast address, see Chapter 4, *Configuring OpenBSD*. The inet or inet6 keywords might have to be used in such rules too.

- *The* `:network` *notation.* Expands into the network addresses, see Chapter 4, *Configuring OpenBSD*. The `inet` or `inet6` keywords might have to be used in such rules too.
- *Macros.* As described in Chapter 5, */etc/pf.conf,* macros can be used to store names of interfaces, protocols, services, addresses and other bits of information that may be used in more than one rule and it is handy to be able to change all of them by editing the macro instead of editing the whole ruleset. You can change a macro definition in a ruleset loaded into memory with this command:

```
# pfctl -D macro=value
```

For example, if you wanted to write a script that automatically switches from one interface to another in the event of a failure of the first interface, your script could call *ping(1)* with the `-I` option to force pings through separate interfaces, and when the results are different than 0, your script would call *route(8)* to change the default route. Then, the script would call *pfctl(8)* to redefine the macro that stores the name of the external interface and the macro that stores the address of the interface, e.g.:

```
# pfctl -D ext_if=ne2
# pfctl -D 'ext_ad=192.168.25.34'
```

(Do not precede the macro name with $ when you redefine it.)
- *Tables.* Tables are special kinds of structures designed for more efficient storage of addresses, similar to macros in the way they are defined and used, but reserved for addresses only. They evaluate faster than equivalent macros or lists of addresses in braces. Tables can be empty at the time they are loaded into memory, and you can populate them later. Changes to tables can be done by hand or via scripts run by the user root, or by users who are given the permission to run *pfctl(8)* via *sudo(8).* It is possible to define more than one table, and they can be accessed separately (but they cannot have sections, like anchors). You can find out more about managing tables in Chapter 16, *Firewall Management.* A good example of using tables can be found in Chapter 13, *Using spamd.*
- *Anchors.* These structures allow us to write skeleton rulesets that change as we wish, without the need to reload the whole ruleset, or to restart *pf(4).* Need to change the NAT rules without changing packet filtering rules? No problem! Need to add or remove a filtering rule? Again, no problem!

What you need to do is quite simple. Just add one of the following commands at points where you would like to be able to insert additional rules:

- `nat-anchor` *anchorname*. Marks the place where you can insert `nat` rules. The *anchorname* parameter is used to identify the insertion point. There can be more than one `nat-anchor` in your ruleset and they will be evaluated in the order they appear in the main ruleset.
- `rdr-anchor` *anchorname*. Marks the place where you can insert `rdr` rules. The *anchorname* parameter is used to identify the insertion point. There can be more than one `rdr-anchor` in your ruleset and they will be evaluated in the order they appear in the main ruleset.
- `binat-anchor` *anchorname*. Marks the place where you can insert `binat` rules. The *anchorname* parameter is used to identify the insertion point. There can be more than one `binat-anchor` in your ruleset and they will be evaluated in the order they appear in the main ruleset.
- `anchor` *anchorname*. Marks the place where you can insert `block`, `pass`, and `antispoof` rules. The *anchorname* parameter is used to identify the insertion point. There can be more than one `anchor` in your ruleset and they will be evaluated in the order they appear in the main ruleset.

It is even possible to define a ruleset that consists of just four (or less) anchor points:

```
nat-anchor anchorname
rdr-anchor anchorname
binat-anchor anchorname
anchor anchorname
```

Then you could add, remove or modify named rulesets (lists of *pf(4)* rules) to these anchor points by hand, or with a script. Details can be found in Chapter 16, *Firewall Management*.

Anchors have two important features: they are not recursive, i.e. it is not allowed to have anchor definitions in named rulesets; and, they can have sections, which are evaluated in the alphabetic order (the anchors themselves are evaluated in the orders they appear in the ruleset), as in:

```
anchor ziggy
     ... section: ann
     ... section: dee
     ... section: zebedee
 ...
anchor john
     ... section: olo
     ... section: makumba
 ...
```

If you added a new section *ara* to anchor *john*, it would be evaluated before *olo*, but after evaluating the whole of *ziggy*.

Commands used to modify the named rulesets and anchors are described in Chapter 16, *Firewall Management*.

A very powerful feature of `anchor` anchors is pre-filtering, which controls when the rules loaded at anchor points will be evaluated. Allowed test are: direction (`in` or `out`), interface name (`on`), address family (`inet` or `inet6`), protocol names (`proto`), source/destination address/port (`from`, `to`, `port`), e.g.:

```
# anchor ziggy will be evaluated only when packets match
# the filtering conditions listed after anchor ziggy
anchor ziggy in on ne1 inet proto tcp \
  from any port 80 to any port > 1023
```

## Chapter 10

Bandwidth Shaping
and Load Balancing

Which packets are more important than others? How load balancing can help busy sites. How to keep your users from clogging your T1 link.

Load balancing and bandwidth shaping are two solutions for avoiding network congestion. *Pf(4)* implements them via 'pool options' enhancements to Network Address Translation (NAT) rules and via integration of the Alternative Queuing (ALTQ) mechanisms. Although similar in purpose, load balancing and bandwidth shaping are two different animals. The former is used mainly to evenly spread the load placed on busy hosts, such as HTTP servers, over multiple physical hosts, while the latter is used for shaping outbound traffic and limiting (in some way) inbound traffic.

10.1 Load Balancing

The purpose of load balancing is to more or less equally distribute packets among two or more hosts or links. While load balancing is a new addition to *pf(4)*, the concept itself is not new, certainly not to those readers who used the round robin load distribution offered by the *named(8)* DNS server:

```
www.example.com.     60    IN    A    a.a.a.a
www.example.com.     60    IN    A    a.a.a.b
www.example.com.     60    IN    A    a.a.a.c
www.example.com.     60    IN    A    a.a.a.d
```

When bind receives queries for *www.example.com*, it will return the following sets of addresses:

```
a.a.a.a a.a.a.b a.a.a.c a.a.a.d
```

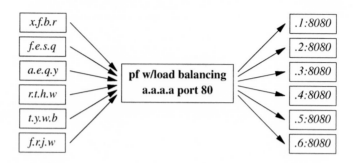

Figure 10.1: Load Balancing Implemented with *pf(4)*.

then:

```
a.a.a.b a.a.a.c a.a.a.d a.a.a.a
```

then:

```
a.a.a.c a.a.a.d a.a.a.a a.a.a.b
```

then:

```
a.a.a.d a.a.a.a a.a.a.b a.a.a.c
```

then:

```
a.a.a.a a.a.a.b a.a.a.c a.a.a.d
```

then:

```
a.a.a.a a.a.a.b a.a.a.c a.a.a.d
```

and so on ...

By serving a different reply each time it is asked for the address of *www.ex-ample.com*, *named* evenly distributes the load among four separate HTTP servers, all serving the same contents by sending clients to each one in turn. As the result of that, all servers should be receiving a quarter of the hits sent to *www.example.com* each.

Pf(4) load balancing works along similar principles to the DNS round robin method, but there are four main differences between them:

- *No need to edit the DNS records.* *Pf*-based load balancing is transparent.
- *More flexibility, better control.* In *pf(4)*, it is possible to use different load distribution algorithms for different classes of addresses, protocols, or ports.
- *Speed.* DNS round-robin is slower than *pf-based* load distribution.
- *Conservation of IP address space.* When you are running a publicly accessible web server and want to use round-robin DNS, you will have to use public IP addresses. No such need with *pf(4)*, just put as many web servers as you like in a DMZ (see Chapter 2, *Firewall Designs*) and they will all be accessible under the same single public IP address.

10.1.1 Implementing Load Balancing

Load balancing can be implemented with `nat` and `rdr` rules only (see Chapter 7, *Packet Redirection*); `binat` rules, due to their nature cannot be used in load balancing, because they bind exactly two IP addresses.

You can select the load balancing method that best matches your needs with these keywords:

- `round-robind` — used to implement the round-robin algorithm. It is the only algorithm allowed when more than one redirection target address is used, so we can write:

```
rdr on ne0 proto tcp from any to $ext_ad port 80 \
                -> { 10.1.1.1/24 } round-robin
```

and:

```
rdr on ne0 proto tcp from any to $ext_ad port 80 \
 -> { 10.1.1.1/24, 192.168.22.5/8, 10.34.2.76 } round-robin
```

and:

```
rdr on ne0 proto tcp from any to $ext_ad port 80 \
 -> { 10.1.1.45, 192.168.22.5, 10.34.2.76 } round-robin
```

- random — selects host addresses in a random fashion using the specified netblock instead of a list of different addresses like round-robin. A net-block is a network address written using the address/netmask notation described in Chapter 5, */etc/pf.conf*. For example, the following rule randomly redirects packets to 8 addresses in the 10.4.3.6/29 netblock:

```
rdr on ne0 proto tcp from any to $ext_ad port 80 \
                -> 10.4.3.6/29 random
```

What if you do not have 8 hosts in that network? You can assign more than one address to these host's interfaces bearing in mind that you cannot assign the same address to two interfaces. It is done with the *ifconfig(8)* alias option. When you do that, you will also have to configure the servers on these hosts to listen on additional addresses. That arrangement breaks the randomness of the solution, therefore, the hosts you add additional addresses to must be the ones that offer best performance.

- source-hash — when you use round-robin or random, *pf(4)* may redirect connections from the same source host to a different destination, which is not always desirable. If you wanted the same source host to connect to the same target host, use source-hash, which selects the destination address in a random way and associates it with the source address, all subsequent connections from the same source address will be redirected to the same target:

```
rdr on ne0 proto tcp from any to $ext_ad port 80 \
                -> 10.4.3.6/29 source-hash
```

Initial assignments are random, unless you specify a hash value:

```
rdr on ne0 proto tcp from any to $ext_ad port 80 \
  -> 10.4.3.6/29 source-hash hashstringcanbeanystring
```

- bitmask — not load balancing as such, maps addresses in nat on a one-to-one basis, but doesn't do bi-directional translation. Both netblocks must be of equal size:

```
# redirect connections:
# from 192.168.1.1 to 10.4.3.1
# from 192.168.1.2 to 10.4.3.2
# from 192.168.1.3 to 10.4.3.3
```

```
# and so on ...
nat on ne0 proto tcp from 192.168.1/24 to any \
                      -> 10.4.3/24 bitmask
```

> *Unfortunately,* `round-robin` *and* `random` *address as-
> signments break some protocols like SSL, which you may
> find unacceptable. The solution is to use* `source-hash`
> `bitmask` *translation.*

The `rdr` shown above are suitable for inbound connections or for redirecting ports on outbound connections to multiple proxies. What if you had
two links to the Internet and wanted them to be evenly utilized by internal
hosts for connections to the Internet? It is possible, but you will have to use
the `source-hash` option in `nat` rules. In this case, the addresses of the
external interfaces must belong to the same netblock, e.g.:

```
nat on $ext_if from 10.3.3.1/24 to any \
       -> 192.168.23.34/31 source-hash
```

Another possibility would be to use the `reply-to` routing option (see
Chapter 8, *Packet Filtering*) for sending replies through a different interface.

When you use pool options with `nat` rules, the `static-port` option will
let you turn off port reassignments done by these rules.

10.2 Bandwidth Shaping

Bandwidth shaping in OpenBSD is done with ALTQ, which is a part of the
KAME project.

http://www.kame.net   *(KAME, home of ALTQ)*

ALTQ is particularly effective when you want to ensure that certain packets
are more important than others and are processed faster. The solution used
by ALTQ to manage bandwidth is based on modifying the default 'first-in,
first-out' packet processing mechanism implemented in the BSD TCP/IP
stack, which processes packets in the order they arrive. In ALTQ, packets
are assigned to queues (lists of packets) with different priority. Packets in

queues with higher priority are processed before packets in queues with lower priority, which are held in memory until no packets are left in queues with higher priority.

Queues can be managed using several algorithms (schedulers) offered by ALTQ. OpenBSD 3.4 currently supports three schedulers: Priority Queuing (PRIQ), Class-Based Queuing (CBQ), and Hierarchical Fair Service Curve (HFSC). The main difference between them is the way they handle packets and bandwidth. PRIQ manages bandwidth by processing packets according to their priority levels. The higher the level, the faster such packets will be processed. CBQ allows queues to be arranged into complex trees of varying priority and bandwidth, as does HFSC, which gives the administrator an even finer degree of control over queue trees. In both cases, queue definitions start with a single scheduler rule and a list of queue definition rules.

10.2.1 The Anatomy of a Parent Rule

All queue definitions start with a single rule that defines the *parent* queue:

- *The* `altq` *keyword*. Marks the start of the parent queue definition. There can be only one parent queue assigned to any single interface. This part is required.
- *Interface specification.* The `on` keyword followed by the name of the interface to which you are assigning the parent queue. This part is required.
- *Scheduler.* Can be set to: `priq` (PRIQ), `cbq` (CBQ), or `hfsc` (HFSC). Selects the scheduler used on the parent queue. This part is required.
- *Maximum available bandwidth.* The `bandwidth` keyword followed by a number which ends with one of the following suffixes: b (bits per second), Kb (kilobits per second), Mb (megabits per second), or Gb (gigabits per second). This value is the maximum available bandwidth provided by the interface on which we are defining queues. It is OK to use a lower value (say, 10Mb instead of 100Mb,) but assigning a higher value will not help (you cannot make make the interface work faster than the hardware allows). This part is optional, if you omit it, *pfctl(8)* will try to automatically use the interface speed, if it can determine it, otherwise it will complain.
- *Queue length limit.* The `qlimit` keyword followed by an integer number. The value of this parameter tells ALTQ how many packets can be held in the queue. The default value is 50. You can increase it, if con-

nections are timing out too often (see also Chapter 14, *Ruleset Optimization* for information about state timeout values). This part is optional.
- *Token bucket regulator.* The tbrsize keyword followed by a number of bytes that tell ALTQ how quickly it should send packets. This part is optional and may be omitted, ALTQ will automatically adjust it to the optimal level.
- *The list of queues.* The queue keyword followed by a list of child queues in braces. Each queue name must be unique, but you do not need to list the default queue here (it is required anyway). The names of queues can be anything you want, as long as you do not use reserved *pf(4)* keywords. This part is required.

The following are examples of parent queue definitions:

```
# define a parent queue and give it a total of 45Mb of
# bandwidth to manage; define four child queues: ssh, www,
# other (default), ctrl (control); managed with PRIQ
altq on $ext_if priq bandwidth 45Mb \
 queue{ssh, www, other, ctrl}
```

```
# define a parent queue with a bandwidth of 45Mb and six child
# queues: accounting, developers, managers, users, other
# (default), ctrl (control); managed with CBQ
altq on $ext_if cbq bandwidth 45Mb \
 queue{accounting, developers, managers, users, other, ctrl}
```

```
# define a parent queue with a bandwidth of 45Mb and six child
# queues: accounting, developers, managers, users, other
# (default), ctrl (control); managed with HFSC
altq on $ext_if hfsc bandwidth 45Mb \
 queue{accounting, developers, managers, users, other, ctrl}
```

10.2.2 The Anatomy of a Queue Rule

Once you define the parent queues, it is time to define child queues attached to each parent queue:

- *The* queue *keyword.* Marks the start of a child queue definition. This part is required.
- *Queue bandwidth.* The bandwidth keyword followed by the maximum

bandwidth available to the child queue. It can be defined in bits (`b`), kilobits (`Kb`), megabits (`Mb`), gigabits (`Gb`), or percentage (`%`) of the immediate parent queue of the current queue. This part is required, but not available in PRIQ.

- *Queue priority.* The `priority` keyword followed by an integer number (0-15 in PRIQ queues, 0-7 in CBQ queues). The higher value of that argument, the higher the priority of the queue (15 is the highest priority in PRIQ, 7 in CBQ, 0 is the lowest priority in both). This part is required.
- *Scheduler options.* The name of the scheduler followed by a scheduler option in parentheses. These options can be one of the following:

  * `borrow` — (only in CBQ and HFSC) current queue can borrow bandwidth from its parent queue when the parent is not utilizing its own bandwidth in full.
  * `default` — every parent queue must have a single default child queue which manages packets that do not belong to other child queues.
  * `ecn` — packets in this queue are scheduled using Explicit Congestion Notification (ECN), described in [RFC 3168]. In short, ECN is an extension of RED, which enables routers to notify the client and the server that the network is slowing down due to congestion.
  * `red` — packets are scheduled using Random Early Detection (RED). When you use it, packets will be dropped proportionately to the length of the queue. Packets in longer queues are dropped earlier than packets in short queues. In practice, this means that communications like instant messaging, ssh, telnet, or HTTP will become more responsive, while long FTP or HTTP downloads will become even more slower.
  * `rio` — packets are scheduled using RED IN/OUT. To enable it, you must enable RIO and rebuild the kernel. To do this, you should the following line to your kernel configuration file:

```
option ALTQ_RIO
```

  For more information about rebuilding kernel, read *Upgrade-MiniFAQ*:

  http://www.openbsd.org/faq/upgrade-minifaq.html (Upgrade-MiniFAQ)

  This part is optional.

- *The list of child queues.* The list of child queues of the current queue, in braces. Each queue name must be unique. This part is optional in CBQ or HFSC, not allowed in PRIQ (there is only one level of child queues).

10.2.3 Assigning Queues to Packet Filtering Rules

Once you define the parent queue and its child queues, you will have to assign packets matched by various `pass` filtering rules. This is done with the `queue` keyword placed at the very end of a filtering rule, e.g.:

```
pass out quick on $ext_if from any to any queue users
```

It is allowed to list the names of two queues, e.g.:

```
pass out quick on $ext_if from any to any queue (users, admins)
```

When you list two queues, the second one will be used when:

- matching packets have their TOS set to lowdelay.
- matching TCP ACK packets with no data payload.

Packets not caught by rules assigning them to other queues will be automatically assigned to the default queue.

10.2.4 Priority Queuing (PRIQ)

The PRIQ scheduler uses a simple flat bandwidth division model, where you divide the bandwidth into smaller slices with different priority. It is an effective way to implement a simple queuing policy like 'ssh connections are more important than http and nttp connections,' or 'connections from the research department are more important than connections from the library, but both are less important than connections from the network administrators.'

Let's see how one could implement the following policy:

- DNS queries have the highest priority.
- connections to SSH and TELNET servers have lower priority than DNS queries.
- connections to various mail servers (SMTP, POP2, POP3, IMAP, IMAP3, POP3S) have lower priority than connections to SSH and TELNET servers.
- connections to WWW servers (HTTP, HTTPS) have lower priority than connections to Mail servers.

• all other connections have the lowest, default priority.

A sample ruleset based on the PRIQ scheduler giving different priorities to different types of services that users connect to is shown below:

```
# MACROS
# external interface
ext_if = "ne1"

# PARENT QUEUE DEFINITION
# define a PRIQ parent queue: bandwidth 45Mb, and
# five child queues: dns, ssh, www, mail, other (default)
altq on $ext_if priq bandwidth 45Mb \
 queue{dns, ssh, www, mail, other}

# CHILD QUEUE DEFINITIONS
# DNS lookups are given the highest priority, because we
# need them done asap
queue dns priority 14 priq(red)
# SSH connections are given one of the highest priorities,
# because they are often used for administrative purposes
queue ssh priority 13 priq(red)
# mail connections are given lower priority than SSH, but
# higher than HTTP/HTTPS, because we want to send/receive our
# mail as quickly as possible
queue mail priority 12 priq(red)
# HTTP/HTTPS connections are given lower priority, because they
# are not as time-sensitive as the other queues
queue www priority 11 priq(red)
# other connections are assigned to the default queue
queue other priority 10 priq(default)

# FILTERING RULES ASSIGNED TO QUEUES
# packets sent to port 53 (DNS) will be assigned to the dns
# queue, (note the use of keep state, instead of synproxy
# state or modulate state, as UDP packets can only be
# filtered with keep state
pass out quick on $ext_if inet proto udp \
 from any to any port 53 keep state queue dns
pass out quick on $ext_if inet proto tcp \
```

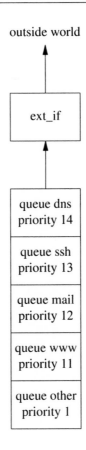

Figure 10.2: PRIQ-based ALTQ packet queuing setup for different external services.

```
from any to any port 53 synproxy state queue dns
# packets sent to port 22 (SSH), 23 (TELNET) will be assigned
# to the ssh queue
pass out quick on $ext_if inet proto tcp \
 from any to any port {22, 23} synproxy state queue ssh
# packets sent to port 25 (SMTP), 109 (POP2), 110 (POP3),
# 143 (IMAP), 220 (IMAP3), 995 (POP3S) will be assigned to
# the mail queue
pass out quick on $ext_if inet proto tcp \
 from any to any port {25, 109, 110, 143, 220, 995} \
 synproxy state queue mail
```

```
# packets sent to port 80 (HTTP), 443 (HTTPS) will be assigned
# to the www queue
pass out quick on $ext_if inet proto tcp \
 from any to any port {80, 443} synproxy state queue www
```

What if you wanted to give different priorities to connections initiated from different internal hosts?

- packets sent from hosts used by administrators have the highest priority.
- packets sent from hosts used by the accounts department have lower priority than packets sent from the hosts used by administrators.
- packets sent from hosts used by programmers have lower priority than packets sent from the hosts used by the accounts department.
- packets sent from hosts used by ordinary users have lower priority than packets sent from the hosts used by the programmers.
- all other connections have the lowest, default priority.

A sample ruleset based on the PRIQ scheduler giving different priorities to outbound connections from different internal hosts is shown on the next page:

```
# MACROS
# external interface
ext_if = "ne1"
# administrators' machines
admins_ad = "{a.a.a.a, a.a.a.b}"
# accounts' machines
accounts_ad = "{a.a.a.c, a.a.a.d, a.a.a.e}"
# coders' machines
coders_ad = "{a.a.a.f, a.a.a.g, a.a.a.h}"
# users' machines
users_ad = "{a.a.a.i, a.a.a.j, a.a.a.k}"


# PARENT QUEUE DEFINITION
# define a PRIQ parent queue: bandwidth 45Mb, and
# five child queues: admins, accounts, coders, users
# others (default)
altq on $ext_if priq bandwidth 45Mb \
 queue{admins, accounts, coders, users, others}
```

```
# CHILD QUEUE DEFINITIONS
# admins get the higest priority
queue admins priority 14 priq(red)
# the accounts department
queue accounts priority 13 priq(red)
# coders
queue coders priority 12 priq(red)
# ordinary users
queue users priority 11 priq(red)
# others
queue others priority 10 priq(default)


# FILTERING RULES ASSIGNED TO QUEUES
# admins
pass out quick on $ext_if inet proto tcp \
 from $admins_ad to any synproxy queue admins
pass out quick on $ext_if inet proto udp \
 from $admins_ad to any keep state queue admins
# accounts
pass out quick on $ext_if inet proto tcp \
 from $accounts_ad to any synproxy state queue accounts
pass out quick on $ext_if inet proto udp \
 from $accounts_ad to any keep state queue accounts
# coders
pass out quick on $ext_if inet proto tcp \
 from $coders_ad to any synproxy state queue coders
pass out quick on $ext_if inet proto udp \
 from $coders_ad to any keep state queue coders
# users
pass out quick on $ext_if inet proto tcp \
 from $users_ad to any synproxy state queue users
pass out quick on $ext_if inet proto udp \
 from $users_ad to any keep state queue users
```

The above ruleset assumes that internal hosts have routable public
addresses. What if you used NAT, which hides all hosts behind a single interface and sends all packets to the outside world with a source address of
the firewall's external interface? You can still differentiate between hosts, if
you define which ports can be used by each host:

```
# MACROS
# external interface
ext_if = "ne1"
# administrators' machines
admins_ad = "{a.a.a.a, a.a.a.b}"
# accounts' machines
accounts_ad = "{a.a.a.c, a.a.a.d, a.a.a.e}"
# coders' machines
coders_ad = "{a.a.a.f, a.a.a.g, a.a.a.h}"
# users' machines
users_ad = "{a.a.a.i, a.a.a.j, a.a.a.k}"


# PARENT QUEUE DEFINITION
# define a PRIQ parent queue: bandwidth 45Mb, and
# five child queues: admins, accounts, coders, users
# others (default)
altq on $ext_if priq bandwidth 45Mb \
 queue{admins, accounts, coders, users, others}


# CHILD QUEUE DEFINITIONS
# admins get the higest priority
queue admins priority 14 priq(red)
# the accounts department
queue accounts priority 13 priq(red)
# coders
queue coders priority 12 priq(red)
# ordinary users
queue users priority 11 priq(red)
# others
queue others priority 10 priq(default)


# NAT RULES
# admins
nat on $ext_if inet proto {tcp, udp} \
 from a.a.a.a to any -> ($ext_if) port 1024:6888
nat on $ext_if inet proto {tcp, udp} \
 from a.a.a.b to any -> ($ext_if) port 6889:12753
# accounts
nat on $ext_if inet proto {tcp, udp} \
 from a.a.a.c to any -> ($ext_if) port 12754:18618
```

```
nat on $ext_if inet proto {tcp, udp} \
 from a.a.a.d to any -> ($ext_if) port 18619:24483
nat on $ext_if inet proto {tcp, udp} \
 from a.a.a.e to any -> ($ext_if) port 24484:30348
# coders
nat on $ext_if inet proto {tcp, udp} \
 from a.a.a.f to any -> ($ext_if) port 30349:36213
nat on $ext_if inet proto {tcp, udp} \
 from a.a.a.g to any -> ($ext_if) port 36214:42078
nat on $ext_if inet proto {tcp, udp} \
 from a.a.a.h to any -> ($ext_if) port 42079:47943
# users
nat on $ext_if inet proto {tcp, udp} \
 from a.a.a.i to any -> ($ext_if) port 47944:53808
nat on $ext_if inet proto {tcp, udp} \
 from a.a.a.j to any -> ($ext_if) port 53809:59673
nat on $ext_if inet proto {tcp, udp} \
 from a.a.a.k to any -> ($ext_if) port 59674:65535


# FILTERING RULES ASSIGNED TO QUEUES
# admins
pass out quick on $ext_if inet proto {tcp, udp} \
 from ($ext_if) port 1024 >< 6888 to any queue admins
pass out quick on $ext_if inet proto {tcp, udp} \
 from ($ext_if) port 6889 >< 12753 to any queue admins
# accounts
pass out quick on $ext_if inet proto {tcp, udp} \
 from ($ext_if) port 12754 >< 18618 to any queue admins
pass out quick on $ext_if inet proto {tcp, udp} \
 from ($ext_if) port 18619 >< 24483 to any queue admins
pass out quick on $ext_if inet proto {tcp, udp} \
 from ($ext_if) port 24484 >< 30348 to any queue admins
# coders
pass out quick on $ext_if inet proto {tcp, udp} \
 from ($ext_if) port 30349 >< 36213 to any queue admins
pass out quick on $ext_if inet proto {tcp, udp} \
 from ($ext_if) port 36214 >< 42078 to any queue admins
pass out quick on $ext_if inet proto {tcp, udp} \
 from ($ext_if) port 42079 >< 47943 to any queue admins
# users
```

```
pass out quick on $ext_if inet proto {tcp, udp} \
  from ($ext_if) port 47944 >< 53808 to any queue admins
pass out quick on $ext_if inet proto {tcp, udp} \
  from ($ext_if) port 53809 >< 59673 to any queue admins
pass out quick on $ext_if inet proto {tcp, udp} \
  from ($ext_if) port 59674 >< 65535 to any queue admins
```

As you can see, PRIQ rules don't allow you to define how much bandwidth will be assigned to each child queue, it merely lets you control child queue priority. If you would like to have better control over bandwidth usage, use CBQ or HFSC.

10.2.5 Class-Based Queuing (CBQ)

The CBQ scheduler allows a finer degree of control over bandwidth. You can decide not only what priority each queue has, but also how much bandwidth can be used by each queue. Queues can be arranged in several levels of child queues. On top of that, it is possible to define queues that borrow bandwidth from parent queues. With these features, it becomes possible to implement policies like 'accounting must have at least 1Mb of bandwidth, developers may not use more than 2Mb, and managers may not use over 1Mb, but the boss must have at least 200Kb.'

The best way to learn CBQ is to start with a simple configuration. Suppose you want to share the bandwidth between two network segments connected to the firewall, and the firewall is doing NAT translation:

```
# MACROS
# external interface
ext_if = "ne1"
# DMZ interface
dmz_if = "ne2"
# private interface
prv_if = "ne3"


# PARENT QUEUE DEFINITION
# define a CBQ parent queue with 45Mb of the total bandwidth
# and three child queues: dmznet (hosts in the DMZ),
# prvnet (hosts in the private segment),
```

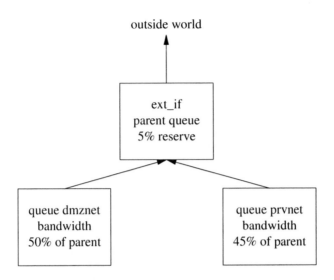

Figure 10.3: Dividing bandwidth between two internal network segments with CBQ.

```
# others (default, connections from the firewall itself)
altq on $ext_if cbq bandwidth 45Mb \
 queue{dmznet, prvnet, others}

# CHILD QUEUE DEFINITIONS
# give the outbound traffic from the DMZ 50% of parent
# bandwidth
queue dmznet bandwidth 50% priority 6 cbq(red)
# give the outbound traffic from the private network 49Mb of
# bandwidth
queue prvnet bandwidth 45% priority 6 cbq(red)
# give the outbound traffic from the firewall host itself
queue others bandwidth 5% priority 5 cbq(default)

# PACKET TRANSLATION
# Add NAT rules with clearly defined port ranges, so we know
# where the outbound packets are coming from (NAT will change
# their source address, and we'll need to use port numbers to
# know who's who
# Turn NAT off for connections between the private network
# and the DMZ segment
```

```
no nat on $ext_if inet proto {tcp, udp} \
  from $dmz_if:network to $prv_if:network
no nat on $ext_if inet proto {tcp, udp} \
  from $prv_if:network to $dmz_if:network
# do NAT between the DMZ network segment and the outside
# world
nat on $ext_if inet proto {tcp, udp} \
  from $dmz_if:network to any -> $ext_if port 1024:32255
# do NAT between the private network segment and the outside
# world
nat on $ext_if inet proto {tcp, udp} \
  from $prv_if:network to any -> $ext_if port 32256:65535


# PACKET FILTERING RULES BOUND TO QUEUES
pass out quick on $ext_if inet proto {tcp, udp} \
  from ($ext_if) port 1024 >< 32255 to any queue dmznet
pass out quick on $ext_if inet proto {tcp, udp} \
  from ($ext_if) port 32256 >< 65535 to any queue prvnet
```

The ruleset shown above shows a basic implementation of packet queuing that imposes bandwidth limits on outbound packets sent from the DMZ and the private network segments. No advanced packet queuing is done for these networks. Notice that the parent queue uses 50% of the interface bandwidth. This is to leave some bandwidth for the incoming connections, otherwise the users on the private network segment may use up all of the available bandwidth.

Let's see how that ruleset could be expanded into a more complex queue tree that implements the following packet queuing policy:

• the parent queue uses 50% of the total available bandwidth.
• the DMZ segment uses 50% of the parent queue bandwidth. Packets are queued using the CBQ scheduler without specifying bandwidth allocation, but with specified priority (like PRIQ, but we cannot use more than one scheduler, and the range of priority levels is smaller: 0 to 7).
• the private segment uses 49% of the parent queue bandwidth.
• each of the n private hosts gets $1/n$th of the parent queue's bandwidth (25% for each of the four hosts in this segment).
• packet queueing for each private host is done in a way similar to the queueing policy for DMZ hosts.

Here's a sample implementation of such policy:

```
# MACROS
# external interface
ext_if = "ne1"
# DMZ interface
dmz_if = "ne2"
# private interface
prv_if = "ne3"

# PARENT QUEUE DEFINITION
# define a CBQ parent queue: bandwidth 45Mb, and
# three child queues: dmznet (hosts in the DMZ),
# prvnet (hosts in the private segment),
# others (default)
altq on $ext_if cbq bandwidth 45Mb \
 queue{dmznet, prvnet, others}

# CHILD QUEUE DEFINITIONS
# give the outbound traffic from the DMZ 50% of bandwidth
queue dmznet bandwidth 50% priority 6 cbq(red) \
 queue(dns, ssh, www, mail)
# give the outbound traffic from the private network 49% of
# bandwidth
queue prvnet bandwidth 49% priority 5 cbq(red) \
 queue(host1, host2, host3, host4)
# give the outbound traffic from the firewall host itself
queue others bandwidth 1% priority 4 cbq(default)

# CHILD QUEUE DEFINITIONS: (for dmznet)
queue dns priority 6 cbq(red, borrow)
queue ssh priority 5 cbq(red, borrow)
queue mail priority 4 cbq(red, borrow)
queue www priority 3 priq(red, borrow)

# CHILD QUEUE DEFINITIONS: (for prvnet)
queue host1 bandwidth 25% priq(red) {dns1, ssh1, mail1, www1}
queue host2 bandwidth 25% priq(red) {dns2, ssh2, mail2, www2}
queue host3 bandwidth 25% priq(red) {dns3, ssh3, mail3, www3}
queue host4 bandwidth 25% priq(red) {dns4, ssh4, mail4, www4}
```

```
# CHILD QUEUE DEFINITIONS: (for host1)
queue dns1 priority 6 cbq(red, borrow)
queue ssh1 priority 5 cbq(red, borrow)
queue mail1 priority 4 cbq(red, borrow)
queue www1 priority 3 cbq(red, borrow)

# CHILD QUEUE DEFINITIONS: (for host2)
queue dns2 priority 6 cbq(red, borrow)
queue ssh2 priority 5 cbq(red, borrow)
queue mail2 priority 4 cbq(red, borrow)
queue www2 priority 3 cbq(red, borrow)

# CHILD QUEUE DEFINITIONS: (for host3)
queue dns3 priority 6 cbq(red, borrow)
queue ssh3 priority 5 cbq(red, borrow)
queue mail3 priority 4 cbq(red, borrow)
queue www3 priority 3 cbq(red, borrow)

# CHILD QUEUE DEFINITIONS: (for host4)
queue dns4 priority 6 cbq(red, borrow)
queue ssh4 priority 5 cbq(red, borrow)
queue mail4 priority 4 cbq(red, borrow)
queue www4 priority 3 cbq(red, borrow)

# NAT RULES
no nat on $ext_if from $dmz_if:network to $prv_if:network
no nat on $ext_if from $prv_if:network to $dmz_if:network
nat on $ext_if from $dmz_if:network to any \
 -> ($ext_if) port 1024:32255
nat on $ext_if from $prv_if:network to any \
 -> ($ext_if) port 32256:40574
nat on $ext_if from $prv_if:network to any \
 -> ($ext_if) port 40575:48893
nat on $ext_if from $prv_if:network to any \
 -> ($ext_if) port 48894:57212
nat on $ext_if from $prv_if:network to any \
 -> ($ext_if) port 57213:65535

# FILTERING RULES ASSIGNED TO QUEUES: (for dmznet)
pass out quick on $ext_if inet proto {tcp, udp} \
  from ($ext_if) port 1024 >< 32255 to any port 53 queue dns
```

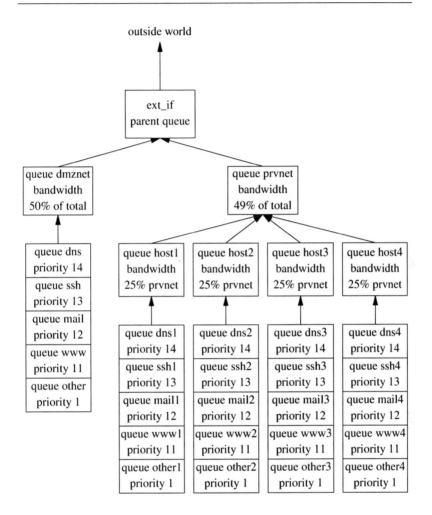

Figure 10.4: A more complex arrangement of queues.

```
pass out quick on $ext_if inet proto tcp \
 from ($ext_if) port 1024 >< 32255 to any port {22, 23} \
 queue ssh
pass out quick on $ext_if inet proto tcp \
 from ($ext_if) port 1024 >< 32255 to any \
 port {25, 109, 110, 143, 220, 995} queue mail
```

```
pass out quick on $ext_if inet proto tcp \
 from ($ext_if) port 1024 >< 32255 to any port {80, 443} \
 queue www

# FILTERING RULES ASSIGNED TO QUEUES: (for host1)
pass out quick on $ext_if inet proto {tcp, udp} \
 from ($ext_if) port 32256 >< 40574 to any port 53 queue dns1
pass out quick on $ext_if inet proto tcp \
 from ($ext_if) port 32256 >< 40574 to any port {22, 23} \
 queue ssh1
pass out quick on $ext_if inet proto tcp \
 from ($ext_if) port 32256 >< 40574 to any \
 port {25, 109, 110, 143, 220, 995} queue mail1
pass out quick on $ext_if inet proto tcp \
 from ($ext_if) port 32256 >< 40574 to any port {80, 443} \
 queue www1

# FILTERING RULES ASSIGNED TO QUEUES: (for host2)
pass out quick on $ext_if inet proto {tcp, udp} \
 from ($ext_if) port 40575 >< 48893 to any port 53 queue dns2
pass out quick on $ext_if inet proto tcp \
 from ($ext_if) port 40575 >< 48893 to any port {22, 23} \
 queue ssh2
pass out quick on $ext_if inet proto tcp \
 from ($ext_if) port 40575 >< 48893 to any \
 port {25, 109, 110, 143, 220, 995} queue mail2
pass out quick on $ext_if inet proto tcp \
 from ($ext_if) port 40575 >< 48893 to any port {80, 443} \
 queue www2

# FILTERING RULES ASSIGNED TO QUEUES: (for host3)
pass out quick on $ext_if inet proto {tcp, udp} \
 from ($ext_if) port 48894 >< 57212 to any port 53 queue dns3
pass out quick on $ext_if inet proto tcp \
 from ($ext_if) port 48894 >< 57212 to any port {22, 23} \
 queue ssh3
pass out quick on $ext_if inet proto tcp \
 from ($ext_if) port 48894 >< 57212 to any \
 port {25, 109, 110, 143, 220, 995} queue mail3
pass out quick on $ext_if inet proto tcp \
```

```
from ($ext_if) port 48894 >< 57212 to any port {80, 443} \
queue www3

# FILTERING RULES ASSIGNED TO QUEUES: (for host4)
pass out quick on $ext_if inet proto {tcp, udp} \
 from ($ext_if) port 57213 >< 65535 to any port 53 queue dns4
pass out quick on $ext_if inet proto tcp \
 from ($ext_if) port 57213 >< 65535 to any port {22, 23} \
 queue ssh4
pass out quick on $ext_if inet proto tcp \
 from ($ext_if) port 57213 >< 65535 to any \
 port {25, 109, 110, 143, 220, 995} queue mail4
pass out quick on $ext_if inet proto tcp \
 from ($ext_if) port 57213 >< 65535 to any port {80, 443} \
 queue www4
```

10.2.6 Hierarchical Fair Service Curve (HFSC)

The HFSC scheduler offers similar features to CBQ, but enhances the administrator's toolbox with the ability to define two types of packet schedulers: real-time and link-share. When real-time scheduling isn't used or no packets can be scheduled using this algorithm, link-share takes over. When more bandwidth is available, queues will use it, unless you place a cap on the bandwidth. The HFSC behavior is controlled with these parameters:

- realtime — controls the minimum bandwidth required for the queue. When more bandwidth is available, it will be used unless you use the upperlimit parameter. Packets are scheduled using the real-time scheduling algorithm first. When no packets are legible for real-time scheduling, or when you do not use real-time scheduling, HFSC will use link-share packet scheduling. This parameter is optional.
- linkshare — sets the minimum 'share' of the parent queue bandwidth for the current queue. When more bandwidth is available, it will be used unless you use the upperlimit parameter. If you also use the realtime parameter, it will take precedence over linkshare. This parameter must be used in HFSC queue definitions, or you must use the bandwidth keyword in the queue definition, before the hfsc() field, or *pfctl(8)* will complain. The simplest HFSC setup is shown later in this section.
- upperlimit — set the maximum bandwidth allowed for the queue.

HFSC will automatically apply this limit to whatever scheduler it is using. When you use this parameter in your queue definition, remember that it must be greater or equal to the limits defined in `realtime` and `linkshare`. This parameter is optional.

Each of these parameters can be followed by a single numeric value that defines the amount of bandwidth that the queue can use, or it can be followed by a triple of service curve parameters that define: (a) the initial level of bandwidth (*m1*), (b) time delay (*d*, measured in milliseconds), and (c) the level to which bandwidth will be adjusted after that time (*m2*). These parameters define the so-called *service curve*, which can be convex or concave, with the exception of the `realtime` parameter, which must be convex. A concave service curve is created, when the *m1* parameter is lower than *m2*. A convex curve is created when *m1* is higher than *m2*. It is also possible to define a flat service curve when *m1* is equal to *m2*. This can be replaced with a single value (*m1* and *d* are omitted).

Although it is possible to define priorities of queues with the `priority` keyword (see sections describing PRIQ and CBQ), just like CBQ, HFSC will not really make much use of it. The influence of that parameter over the final result is not huge and you can omit it to simplify your ruleset.

Another keyword that is largely redundant in queues that use HFSC, is `bandwidth`. There is really one case when it is handy, a simple HFSC queue configuration with a single level of queues, when `bandwidth` values are used as single-parameter `linkshare` settings:

```
altq on $ext_if hfsc bandwidth 45Mb \
 queue{dns, ssh, www, mail, other}

queue dns bandwidth 20%
queue ssh bandwidth 20%
queue mail bandwidth 20%
queue www bandwidth 20%
queue other hfsc(default)
```

is the equivalent of:

```
altq on $ext_if hfsc bandwidth 45Mb \
 queue{dns, ssh, www, mail, other}
```

```
queue dns hfsc(linkshare 20%)
queue ssh hfsc(linkshare 20%)
queue mail hfsc(linkshare 20%)
queue www hfsc(linkshare 20%)
queue other hfsc(default)
```

That was a simple example, let's see if we can come up with something more complex:

```
# PARENT QUEUE DEFINITION
altq on $ext_if hfsc bandwidth 45Mb \
 queue{dmznet, prvnet, others}


# CHILD QUEUE DEFINITIONS
# backlogs that last less than 10 seconds get 50% or more
# of the total available bandwidth, after 10 seconds, that lim-
it
# goes up to 65% of the total available bandwidth
queue dmznet hfsc(linkshare (50% 10000 65%))
# backlogs that last less than 5 seconds get 50% or more
# of the total available bandwidth, after 5 seconds, that limit
# goes down to 25% of the total available bandwidth
queue prvnet hfsc(linkshare (40% 5000 25%))
queue others hfsc(default)
```

The first important thing to remember is that the sum of the values of parameters of the same kind (e.g. the initial levels of bandwidth of the linkshare limit) must not exceed the total bandwidth available for the current level of queues. The default queue does not take part in this count. You can express these limits in the same units as those used with the bandwidth keyword (%, b, Kb, Mb, Gb).

In the previous example, the 45Mb of bandwidth assigned to the parent queue represents to 100% percent of the available bandwidth. It is divided into three queues: dmznet (takes at least 50% of the total), prvnet (takes at least 40% of bandwidth), and others (takes whatever's left). After the dmznet queue has been backlogged for more than 10 seconds, the HFSC scheduler will start increasing the amount of available bandwidth up to 65% of the total. When more bandwidth is available, it will be used, but that 65% is guaranteed (as is the initial 50%). When backlog disappears, the scheduler will slowly release the additional bandwidth and go back to 50%. Why increase bandwidth for this queue? To avoid backlogs and handle increased demand for bandwidth. Suppose there's a mail server, or an FTP server sitting in the DMZ and their patters on usage shown that there is an increase in demand near 10:00am and 4:00pm. A rule with two bandwidth levels will take care of this automatically, without tying up the additional bandwidth for the rest of the day. If you closely at the previous ruleset you will notice that the bandwidth allocated to that queue will be decreased after the backlog persists for 5 seconds. Why? To make room for the increased demand for bandwidth for the dmznet queue and to prevent users on the prvnet from hogging too much bandwidth.

As mentioned before, it is OK to use the linkshare parameter with the realtime parameter in the same queue, HFSC will automatically choose the one that will do a better job. You can use the same parameters for both, but some administrators differ them slightly. It's your choice, use whatever works best in your particular case, but remember that the service curve for realtime must be convex. In other words, when you use that parameter, you can only define a decrease the amount of available bandwidth over time. If you want to define an increase, use the linkshare parameter:

```
# PARENT QUEUE DEFINITION
altq on $ext_if hfsc bandwidth 45Mb \
 queue{dmznet, prvnet, others}


# CHILD QUEUE DEFINITIONS
# backlogs that last less than 10 seconds get 50% or more
# of the total available bandwidth, after 10 seconds, that
# limit goes up to 65% of the total available bandwidth
queue dmznet hfsc(linkshare (50% 10000 65%))
# backlogs that last less than 5 seconds get 50% or more
# of the total available bandwidth, after 5 seconds, that
# limit goes down to 25% of the total available bandwidth
queue prvnet \
 hfsc(realtime (40% 5000 25%) linkshare (40% 5000 25%))
queue others hfsc(default)
```

As was already mentioned, you can define a concave service curve for the linkshare parameter to decrease the amount of bandwidth available to some users and prevent thm hogging too much bandwidth. A much better

way is to place hard limits on the amount of bandwidth used by each queue,
use the `upperlimit` parameter:

```
# PARENT QUEUE DEFINITION
altq on $ext_if hfsc bandwidth 45Mb \
 queue{dmznet, prvnet, others}
```

```
# CHILD QUEUE DEFINITIONS
# backlogs that last less than 10 seconds get 50% or more
# of the total available bandwidth, after 10 seconds, that lim-
it
# goes up to 65% of the total available bandwidth
queue dmznet hfsc(linkshare (50% 10000 65%) \
 upperlimit (60% 10000 75%))
# backlogs that last less than 5 seconds get 50% or more
# of the total available bandwidth, after 5 seconds, that limit
# goes down to 25% of the total available bandwidth
queue prvnet hfsc(realtime (35% 5000 20%) \
 linkshare (35% 5000 20%) upperlimit (40% 5000 25%))
queue others hfsc(default)
```

Although you can define child queues of other queues in a way similar to
CBQ child queues, there is an important difference between them in the
way you specify the percentage of bandwidth available to the parent that a
child can use. While CBQ uses a 'proportional' method, HFSC uses a
'subtractive' method. To see how it works in practice, compare the following rules, which divide bandwidth in the same way, yet the percentage
notation is different:

```
# CBQ
altq on $ext_if cbq bandwidth 20Mb \
 queue{dmznet, prvnet, others}
```

```
# prvnet gets 8Mb
queue prvnet bandwidth 40% queue{host1, host2}
# host1 gets 4Mb
queue host1 bandwidth 50%
# host2 gets 4Mb
queue host2 bandwidth 50%
```

```
# HFSC
altq on $ext_if hfsc bandwidth 20Mb \
 queue{dmznet, prvnet, others}

# prvnet gets 8Mb
queue prvnet hfsc(linkshare 40%) queue{host1, host2}
# host1 gets 4Mb
queue host1 hfsc(linkshare 20%)
# host2 gets 4Mb
queue host2 hfsc(linkshare 20%)
```

10.2.7 Queuing Incoming Packets

ALTQ does a very good job of queuing outbound packets, but what about inbound packets? Although it is possible to create queues for inbound connections, they will be truly helpful when they are matched by bandwidth limits imposed before packets reach your network. This can be done by your ISP, who must configure their routers to limit the incoming traffic to a preset level. Otherwise, ALTQ will not be of much help, because once the packets arrive on the external interface, it is already too late to stop them as they already used the bandwidth.

What you can do, is add ALTQ queues and pass out rules for interfaces connection the firewall host to the internal network segments. However, these limits will only work for connections initiated by external hosts. Connections initiated by inside hosts and NAT-ed will not match those pass out rules, because they will be passed without checking thanks to the state mechanism invoked by the NAT rules (nat, binat, or rdr). This is why some users will be able to use all of the available bandwidth even if you set hard limits, these limits apply to outbound packets, not inbound ones. The solution is to put a router before the firewall, it can be an OpenBSD box configured as a bridge (see Chapter 4, *Configuring OpenBSD*) and implement ALTQ/filtering rules on the inerface connecting the bridge to the firewall.

10.2.8 Which Scheduler Is Best?

There is no easy answer, but you can use the following guide to decide which ALTQ scheduler is more appropriate in your particular case:

- when all you need is set up queue priorities (some services, users, or hosts are more important than others), use PRIQ.
- when you want to divide bandwidth into smaller slices, with guaranteed minimum levels, use CBQ.
- when you want to do everythig you can do with CBQ, but also want the queues to be able to adjust to changes in traffic patterns, use HFSC.
- when you want to place upper limits on bandwidth usage, use HFSC.

> *Do not expect ALTQ to be 100% accurate. It does a splendid job of queuing packets, but you must remember that TCP traffic does not flow like water from a tap, nor it is a easily divisible. Also, ALTQ works best when there is a backlog, for situations of interface underutilization, ALTQ does not have much to do. When you run into problems, always try to simplify your queue layout. Too much complexity is always bad for performance. Sometimes the solution will be a change of hardware (mainboard, processor, or network card); other times it will be fine-tuning of the TBR parameter. Experiment, but not too much, remember that ALTQ is not a cure for a clogged network severely lacking bandwidth.*

## Chapter 11

Logging and Log Analysis

In this chapter we will discus using pf(4) *for packet logging, archiving, and analysis.*

Although it may not seem as exciting as packet redirection or filtering, one of the most important features of *pf(4)* is its ability to log packets passing in and out of the firewall's interfaces. While many do not see this as especially interesting, it has become one of the essential features that firewalls are judged on and approved for use. Because of the rise in break-in attempts and various clandestine activities on the Internet, logs have become crucial pieces of evidence in trails, detective work, and active defense.

Many organizations, military and government agencies being among the most obvious and earliest users of this functionality, already log all traffic as a part of their active monitoring, evidence gathering, and analysis activities. Banks, large corporations, even universities use it as well. Even research departments at large corporations doing cutting-edge work are often monitored to prevent or detect information leakage.

It may not be long before all networks connected to the Internet will actually be required to keep logs of all traffic passing through their external interfaces. People have already been charged on the evidence found in firewall logs, so it is important to learn how to use them.

There is another side to recording, analysis, and archiving of firewall logs—they will inevitably contain a mixture of private data that belongs to employees with more or less classified company data. This is a potential legal trap. Once you touch private data (and it is very hard to tell when you do without examining it), you will enter a very dangerous area with plenty of potential for getting sued for invasion of privacy. You must therefore have clear and consequently enforced policy for log

*gathering, storage, and removal. Such policy must be
both a set of written procedures for the security personnel
who have access to firewall logs as well as in the form of
a legal document. Do not rely on your own judgment in
these matters and hire a lawyer who will draft a policy
according to your organization's policies, requirements,
and the laws under which you operate.*

In the rest of this chapter we will focus on technical details, leaving the
legal issues to the lawyers.

11.1 Enabling Packet Logging

Packet logging is always on, but packets are only sent to logs, when they
match a rule with the `log` keyword (see Chapter 8, *Packet Filtering*).
Therefore, all we have to do to capture some packets is to edit */etc/pf.conf*
and put the `log` keyword after either the `in` or `out` keywords in `block`,
`pass`, or `anitspoof` rules. For example:

```
# block all incoming packets
block in on $ext_if all
```

becomes:

```
# block and log all incoming packets
block in log on $ext_if all
```

> *You can add the* `log` *or* `log-all` *keywords to any
> packet filtering rule.*

11.2 Log Analysis

Packet logging is a good network administration practice, because it lets us
spot problems with communication and early signs of break-in attempts. Of
course, logging packets alone won't help; we need to learn how to analyze
and manage log files generated by *pf(4)*.

Because *pf(4)* log files are stored in a binary format unfit for viewing with
human eyes, we need a tool that will translate them into plain text. That

tool is the venerable *tcpdump(8)* utility, one of the essential network monitoring programs. We can use it to watch *pf(4)* logs in real time with:

```
# tcpdump  -n -e -ttt -i pflog0
```

The system should reply with:

```
tcpdump: WARNING: pflog0: no IPv4 address assigned
tcpdump: listening on pflog0
```

You can ignore the warning, *tcpdump(8)* prints it, because the `pflog0` interface does not have an IP address, which it doesn't need, and wait for packets to fall into your carefully planted honey pot. It is quite likely that you will not see any packets at all, for a long time. What went wrong? Nothing, actually. You are lucky and your firewall is not a target of a port scan or a cracking attempt. A series of repeated attempts to connect to unavailable ports is a sign that somebody might be trying to probe your machine for open ports. They are not necessarily trying to break in (they may be network researchers, or even your ISP), but you should be alert and if such attempts occur frequently, you might need to investigate them more closely. However, before you raise an alarm and call the authorities, make sure that these attempted connections are not responses to your own connection attempts!

It's a good feeling to know that all is quiet on the blocked ports, but you'd probably like to see some action, if only to check that everything is working as it should. All right, open */etc/pf.conf* again and add the `log` keyword to the `pass out` rules for the external interface. For example:

```
# allow TCP IPv4 connections to the outside world,
# keep state
pass out on $ext_if inet proto tcp all flags S/SA \
                                     synproxy state
pass out on $ext_if inet proto { udp, icmp } all \
                                     keep state
```

becomes:

```
# allow and log TCP IPv4 connections to the outside
# world, keep state
```

```
pass out log on $ext_if inet proto tcp all flags S/SA \
                                        synproxy state
pass out log on $ext_if inet proto { udp, icmp } all \
                                        keep state
```

Save the changes and replace the old *pf(4)* ruleset with the new one:

```
# pfctl -F all ; pfctl -f /etc/pf.conf
```

Then, run *tcpdump(8)* again, and point your web browser to any external page. Now you should see a stream of packets.

11.3 Which Packets Do You Want to Capture?

Why do some packets get written to */var/log/pflog* and some do not? It all boils down to the way *pf(4)* works.

Packets are written to */var/log/pflog*, when the last rule they match includes the `log` keyword. Packets not caught by rules with the `log` keyword won't be logged. Therefore, if you want to capture all traffic, you need to add the `log` keyword to all `block`, `pass`, `antispoof`, `in` and `out` rules in your */etc/pf.conf*, save for the `lo0` loopback device. On the flip side, if you want to limit logging to a smaller group of packets, add the `log` or `log-all` keywords only to those rules that catch the packets you want to log. For example, to log all inbound packets sent to your networks from the outside, add the `log` keyword to all `antispoof, pass  in` and `block  in` rules for the external interface.

Three special cases we have not discussed yet are the `keep  state`, `modulate  state`, and `synproxy  state` rules. We have a choice of using either of the `log` or `log-all` keywords here, depending on which packets we want to log. The `log` keyword will only log those packets that make state, while `log-all` will log all packets.

But if we are really concerned about security, shouldn't we be logging all packets arriving and leaving on all interfaces on the firewall? Ideally, yes, because that is the only way to ensure that you know what goes on over the boundary between your network and the rest of the world. But in such cases, you need to construct an efficient system for automated log analysis and management. Log files grow fast and take up a lot of storage space; there is little point in gathering more data than you can analyze.

OK, suppose that you decide to log all traffic on all interfaces. The first thing you need to do is turn global logging on by adding the `log` or `log-all` keywords (where appropriate) to every rule for every interface on the firewall (`ne0`, `ne1`, `tun0`, or whatever the names of the interfaces that you are telling *pf(4)* to monitor are). Load those new rules into *pf(4)*, as described earlier in this chapter, and check that the packets are being logged into */var/log/pflog* with:

```
# /usr/sbin/tcpdump -r /var/log/pflog
```

If all goes well, you are now monitoring all traffic passing, and attempting to pass, through the firewall. There is a lot of data to munch through, and if you are to manage it, you need to learn how to use *tcpdump(8)*. The man page for *tcpdump* provides plenty of information, so instead of repeating it all, we're going to mention only a few tricks.

Probably the greatest feature of *tcpdump(8)* are its rich options and expressions. For example, to display packets stored in a file in a more compact way, use:

```
# tcpdump -q -r /var/log/pflog
```

or, if you wanted to read packets straight from an interface, use:

```
# tcpdump -q -i ne0
```

To display only packets related to a specific port, use:

```
# tcpdump -r /var/log/pflog port 80
```

To display only packets related to a specific host, use:

```
# tcpdump -r /var/log/pflog host chumbawamba
```

To display only packets related to a specific network (or network segment), use:

```
# tcpdump -r /var/log/pflog net xxx.xxx.xxx.xxx
```

Additional expressions allow us to filter packets by their destination and protocol (see man tcpdump for details). An even more elaborate filtering can be achieved by combining *tcpdump(8)* expressions, e.g.:

```
# tcpdump -r /var/log/pflog "host chumbawamba and port 80"
```

or:

```
# tcpdump -q -1 ne0 "host chumbawamba and port 80"
```

Remember that you can safely experiment with filtering expressions, because they do not affect the contents of */var/log/pflog*. Try different *tcpdump(8)* options and expressions and try to make sense of them with the help of the man page.

So, if all went well, you should have now a steady flow of packet data to plow through. OK, but how do you manage that flood of information? The answer to that is automation. Watching *pf(4)* logs can be exciting for the first few hours, but it soon becomes a boring activity best left to the machines. But first we need to know how OpenBSD manages *pf(4)* logs.

11.4 The Secret Life of Logs

The *pf(4)* packet logging mechanism uses the standard system logger daemon *syslogd(8)* to store packet information in */var/log/pflog*. The */var/log* directory is the place where the system stores most of the important system logs: *authlog*, *daemon*, *maillog*, *messages*, *secure*, or *wtmp*.

Just like *maillog* or *messages*, *pflog* is rotated to make sure that the logs don't bring the system to its knees by filling the filesystem. Log rotation is the job of the *newsyslog(8)* command that runs every hour as a *cron(8)* job.

You can check this with crontab -1 -u root, which should display the *crontab(1)* entry for the user root (you need to be logged in as root, or the system won't let you do this). Somewhere at the top of the list you should see these lines:

```
# rotate log files every hour, if necessary
0 * * * * /usr/bin/newsyslog
```

When *newsyslog* is run it will check the size of */var/log/pflog* and, if necessary, rename it, create an empty /var/log/pflog, and compress the old /var/log/pflog with gzip(1). The name of the archived log begins with the original log filename and ends with the 0.gz suffix. So, /var/log/pflog becomes /var/log/pflog.0.gz and syslogd(8) can begin filling up /var/log/pflog again. The whole cycle repeats every hour, and when newsyslog(8) decides that /var/log/pflog is ready to be archived again, it will rename /var/log/pflog.0.gz to /var/log/pflog.1.gz and repeat the steps described earlier.

At any given point in time, your firewall will store up to four *pflog* archives. When a new archive is created, the archive with the highest number (*pflog.3.gz*) is overwritten with the younger archive, (*pflog.2.gz*). You can check the times when they were created in the following way:

```
# ls -l /var/log/pflog*
-rw------- 1 root wheel 268582 May 27 11:37 pflog
-rw------- 1 root wheel 1993502 May 27 10:59 pflog.0.gz
-rw------- 1 root wheel 1220902 May 27 10:00 pflog.1.gz
-rw------- 1 root wheel 1625010 May 27 08:58 pflog.2.gz
-rw------- 1 root wheel 1334018 May 27 08:00 pflog.3.gz
```

On firewalls servicing busy networks, the best we can hope for is a four-hour snapshot of the traffic. If we want to extend that time, we have two choices: either modify the *newsyslog* entry in *crontab*, or edit the /etc/newsyslog.conf entry for *pflog*.

Editing *crontab* allows us to only change the delay between consecutive *newsyslog* runs; the longer the delay, the larger the logs and their archives will be. The procedure is quite simple. Do (as root):

```
# crontab -e -u root
```

and change:

```
# rotate log files every hour, if necessary
0 * * * * /usr/bin/newsyslog
```

to:

```
# rotate log files every two hours, if necessary
0-23/2 * * * /usr/bin/newsyslog
```

Then press Esc and type :x followed by a hit on the **Enter/Return** key on your keyboard. *Cron(8)* will run *newsyslog(8)* every two hours, keeping an eight-hour snapshot of the traffic. (Changing the value of the hour field to 0-23/6 would give us a 24-hour snapshot of the traffic. For additional information on cron read man cron, man crontab, and man 5 crontab.) The files will be larger, but there will still be a limit on the number of *pflog* archives kept in */var/log*.

If you want to change the number of archives newsyslog keeps in */var/log*, or increase their size without affecting all other logs, you need to get familiar with */etc/newsyslog.conf*, the configuration file for *newsyslog(8)*. Open */etc/newsyslog.conf* in a text editor (*vi(1)* will do nicely) and locate the following lines:

```
# logfilename owner.group mode ngen size time [ZB]
/var/log/pflog 600 3 250 * ZB /var/run/pflogd.pid
```

As you can see, the owner.group field is empty, which means that the archives of *pflog* will be owned by the user running *newsyslog(8)* (typically root). You could consider changing the owner and the group to a different user, if you have plans to automate the downloading of *pflogs* to another workstation for later analysis. Why not just log in as root and download the archives? Because you cannot be sure that your network is internally secure unless you have control over all machines on it. And even then, there is (however remote) a possibility that you may download rogue code that snoops on your network. But it is better to leave that setting alone and write a script that copies the archives to another place, changing its owner and permissions.

The mode field specifies the write, read, and execute privileges. The default 600 (owner can read and write) is a good choice and should be left alone. The highest number a log archive can have is set in the ngen field. The default value is 3, which tells *newsyslog(8)* to keep at most 4 (0 - 3) *pflog* archives. If you wanted to keep more, say 24 archives, you'd need to set it to 23. This increases the time required to complete the whole procedure of log rotation, so do not go overboard.

The size field defines the minimum size (in kilobytes) of the log file that qualifies it for archiving. The default setting is 250 kilobytes. Increasing its value will result in longer delays between log rotations; decreasing it will result in more frequent rotation of logs, quite possibly at every *newsyslog(8)* run. Next we encounter the time field, set by default to *, which tells *newsyslog(8)* to ignore it. Should you set it to 1, it will rotate *pflog*, if the last log rotation was done one or more hours ago. This setting overrides the values in the *size* field. The [ZB] flags field and the pid file options should be left alone (you can learn more about them from man newsyslog).

OK. So now you know how the operating system keeps an eye on the logs so they don't cause trouble. What if you want to archive them for longer than *newsyslog(8)* settings allow? There are two solutions: one is to write a script that runs 10-15 minutes after *newsyslog(8)* and checks to see if the scripts have been rotated, then stores them in a safe place (possibly on another machine); the other is to set up a log monitoring station on a separate local network segment (not the one used by ordinary users, nor the DMZ segment). Such station ought to have two Ethernet cards: one for receiving packets sent to it by rules that use the dup-to keywords (see Chapter 8, *Packet Filtering*); another for the system administrator to log on the logging station. The logging station ought to be running *pf(4)* with a ruleset that blocks and logs all inbound packets. A script running at regular intervals can check for new archived logs, mark them with a time stamp and move to another location on the logging station or write them to a CD-R, tape, or another external storage device.

Why go to such lengths? Well, if you are running a network where you store or process highly valuable information, or you run a site that may become a target of an attack because of the content it serves, you should not take chances. If you store logs on the firewall or on another machine on the network protected by that firewall and your defenses are compromised, malicious hackers will want to cover their steps and remove the information about their visit from the system and *pf(4)* logs.

11.5 Bandwidth and Disk Space Requirements

How big a log partition or disk should be? That largely depends on the amount of data you want to store. The upper limit can be computed using this formula:

$$\frac{max.\ speed\ of\ the\ interface\ (Mbps) \times 24 \times 3600}{8}$$

So, if you wanted to compute the amount of space needed to store logs arriving on a 100Mbps interface on the monitoring station over a period of 24 hours, you'd need a rather large partition or disk (note that 1MB is assumed to be 1024KB, not 1000KB):

$$\frac{100 \times 24 \times 3600}{8} = 1080000MB = 1055GB = 1.1TB$$

Wow! That's a lot of data to play with! You might have a problem, because you cannot buy a 1.1 TB disk today although there are news of 200GB disks, so that day may be nearer than one might think. But don't worry. If you absolutely need that kind of capacity, you can build or buy a RAID array to handle it. Another problem is disk subsystem bandwidth. If your disk cannot write information fast enough, the performance of the firewall and the network connection suffers. Suddenly, the performance of the I/O subsystem begins to affect the performance of an otherwise very capable firewall machine.

In practice, you are unlikely to saturate such link, at least on a small or medium sized network, because (a) the firewall machine probably cannot send data fast enough, (b) the monitoring station cannot receive data at that rate, and (c) the traffic on your network does not reach the 100Mbps limit.

But even if it was nearer 600GB, we'd still have a problem. We can solve it in several ways:

- *Use a RAID array to store data.* A pure brute force hardware/software solution. May be necessary on high-risk sites or when logs are monitored in real-time by NIDS software, which can take some automated actions.
- *Keep less data on the disk by moving it to a tape, CD-R or CD-RW.* Requires fast and automated backup hardware. Expensive.
- *Log less data.* Not possible in all cases.
- *Use separate logging stations for each subnet.* Spreads the load, increases complexity.

The first solution is based on a hardware, simply buy enough disks to hold as much data as you need and configure them in a way that suits your needs (man raidctl for more information or look it up in [Artymiak, 2000]).

The second solution still requires a large disk, but not as large as 1.1TB. If your firewall was really receiving 1.1TB of data in a day, it would require a modest 44GB of data in an hour. A 100GB disk could, therefore, hold the current log plus data from the last hour. That old log ought to be written to an external storage device before the current log closes and is rotated. That should not be a problem, if you own a fast tape streamer capable of recording up to 44GB of data per hour. Other storage media, such as CD-R, CD-RW, DVD-R, or optical disks are just not fast enough or cannot hold enough data. But this is theory and one cannot realistically expect a small or medium sized network to have such resources. And they probably do not have to, because the amount of traffic logged will be much lower. How much? Well, the answer to that question has to be found by the administrator who will watch the amount of traffic on the monitoring station's interface over a period of a few weeks.

A far less expensive, and much saner, solution for those networks that do not need to log all traffic, is optimization of the *pf(4)* logging setup. Instead of logging all traffic on all interfaces, you can only log traffic entering and leaving the external interface. That should be good enough for catching most of the interesting traffic and will make log analysis and storage more manageable.

To see how much storage space we'll need this time, we'll use our magic formula again, using a fast ADSL modem as an example. Suppose it is a 7 (downlink) / 3 (uplink) Mbps model:

$$\frac{7 \times 24 \times 3600}{8} = 75600MB = 74GB$$

Now, 74GB of data per day is certainly more manageable than 1.1TB. Furthermore, the external interface is never working at 100% of its maximum transfer rate, and we can safely assume that we need a paltry 40GB (or less) of space to store uncompressed traffic logged over a period of 24 hours. A 100GB disk will hold two days worth of data plus enough space for another 12 hours. That is enough data to get a very good view of suspicious activities. Also, 40GB is well within capacity of inexpensive modern DDS/DAT streamers.

What's more, if we tell *pf(4)* to log only incoming packets, we further decrease the amount of space needed to log traffic. Just how much of a saving it will be depends on the patterns of usage of our network. If the amount of outbound traffic passing though the external interface is a significant portion of the overall traffic on that interface, the savings might be substantial; otherwise, they might not be noticeable.

1.6 Logging on a Bridge (Span Ports)

When you run your OpenBSD box, you can easily log traffic passing through it to an external machine with *span ports*, a feature of *bridge(4)*, which lets you configure one of the interfaces to transmit a copy of every packet received by the bridge.

You can configure an interface as a span port with the following command added to the appropriate */etc/bridgename.if* file:

```
addspan rl2
```

For more information, consult *brconfig(8)* and *bridgename.if(5)*, and Chapter 4, *Configuring OpenBSD*.

## Chapter 12

Using authpf

In this chapter we'll discuss authpf(8), *the authenticating gateway shell that offers an elegant solution to the problem of making sure that the users behind the firewall really are who say they are.*

The problem of user authentication is a complex one, not only because it is a technological challenge, but also because it must be done in a way that will cause the least user rebellion against the system.

One-time user authentication on the computer he or she is working at is not good enough, especially when users are mobile and often disable password protection or use weak passwords. If you write a ruleset that is based solely on IP addresses or port numbers, your firewall may fail quickly when one of the machines it is protecting falls into wrong hands or is otherwise broken into. One of the methods for making sure this doesn't happen is user authentication done on the firewall implemented with *pf(4)* and *authpf(8)*. It is quite simple, each user who wants to connect to the firewall, must log on the firewall via *ssh(1)*. When the authentication is successful, the firewall loads a ruleset (via anchors) that allows that user access to the network. Every user can have a separate ruleset, limiting them in what they can do. This solution is used to secure wireless networks, which are particularly vulnerable to host identity theft, but it is also being used increasingly often on 'wired' networks to add another layer of defense.

Every user whom you want to authenticate must have an account on the firewall and a copy of an SSH client on its computer before they can log on.

12.1 Configuring authpf

- */etc/authpf/authpf.conf* — the *authpf(8)* configuration file. Contains the name of the anchors where redirection and filtering rules are loaded into.

The default name is `authpf`, but you can change it to something else:

```
anchor=userrules
```

If you want to leave the default setting, use:

```
# touch /etc/authpf/authpf.conf
```

- */etc/authpf/authpf.allow* — contains the list of user names allowed to authenticate on the firewall, one name per line.
- */etc/authpf/banned/* — not a file but a directory, which contain the list of user who are banned from accessing the firewall. To ban user `joe`, use:

```
# touch /etc/authpf/banned/joe
```

To let him use the firewall again, use:

```
# rm /etc/authpf/banned/joe
```

- */etc/authpf/authpf.message* — the message displayed upon successful authentication.
- */etc/authpf/authpf.problem* — the message displayed upon authentication failure.

12.2 Configuring sshd

Add the following lines to */etc/ssh/sshd_config*:

```
Protocol 2
ClientAliveInterval 15
ClientAliveCountMax 3
```

This will make sure that users are logged off the firewall after 60 seconds of inactivity.

12.3 Configuring Login Shell

To successfully authenticate a user on the firewall, you must change her/his shell to *authpf(8)*. Do it with *vipw(8)*:

```
# vipw
```

and change the last field from something like /bin/sh to /usr/sbin/authpf.

If you want to limit access to system resources, read *loging.conf(5)*.

12.4 Writing pf Rules for authpf

Rules for authenticating users reside in */etc/authpf/users/*, e.g. rules for joe reside in */etc/authpf/users/joe/authpf.rules*. Users for whom such rulesets do not exist have their rules set to those from */etc/authpf/authpf.rules*.

To load those rulesets into the main ruleset, */etc/pf.conf* must contain the following anchors placed in relevant places:

```
nat-anchor authpf
rdr-anchor authpf
binat-anchor authpf
anchor authpf
```

Writing rulesets for authenticating users is like writing other named rulesets, but there are two important additions, in the form of the $user_ip macro, which expands to the IP address of the host that the user authenticated from, and the $user_id macro that expands to the name of the user authenticating on the firewall (see Chapter 8, *Packet Filtering* for more information about filtering with user names. This allows us to write rules that are bound to users, not hosts.

12.5 Authenticating User Joe

Let's walk through a simple example, in which we'll create an authentication setup for use joe who will be allowed to connect to external HTTP servers. We assume that user joe already has an ordinary user account. If you do not kow how to do it, read Chapter 4, *Configuring OpenBSD*.

Create */etc/authpf/authpf.conf*:

```
# touch /etc/authpf/authpf.conf
```

Add user joe to */etc/authpf/authpf.allow*:

```
# echo "joe" >> /etc/authpf/authpf.allow
```

Create a welcome message:

```
# echo "Where are you going with that NIC in your hand?" >
/etc/authpf/authpf.message
```

Create a message displayed when there are problems with authentication:

```
# echo "I'm sorry Dave ..." > /etc/authpf/authpf.problem
```

Configure *sshd(8)* (see section 12.2).

Configure login shell (see section 12.3).

Clear *pf(4)* ruleset:

```
# pftcl -F all
```

Create a directory for joe's ruleset:

```
# mkdir -p /etc/authpf/users/joe
```

Create a new ruleset for *joe*. We add only add a filtering rule, you can create as many rules as you like, just remember to not use the quick keyword. Read Chapter 5, */etc/pf.conf* and Chapter 9, *Dynamic Rulesets* for more information about limits of anchor rulesets:

The */etc/pf.conf* ruleset will contain the following rules:

```
ext_if = "ne1"
int_if = "ne2"

nat-anchor authpf
rdr-anchor authpf
binat-anchor authpf
block in on $ext_if all
block out on $ext_if all
```

```
# allow connections to SSH on the internal interface (otherwise
# joe, residing in the private network segment will not be able
# to connect and authenticate.
pass in on $int_if inet proto tcp \
 from any to ($int_if) port 22 flags S/SA synproxy state
anchor authpf
```

Make a copy of */etc/pf.conf*:

```
# cp /etc/pf.conf /etc/pf.conf.old
```

Open */etc/pf.conf* and edit it, so it contains rules similar to those shown earlier.

Save */etc/pf.conf* (press **Esc**, type : x and hit the **Enter/Return** key).

Reload the ruleset (this is best done from the console and not over the network, if you make a mistake you might cut yourself off the line):

```
# pftcl -F all ; pfctl -f /etc/pf.conf
```

Create a ruleset for joe:

```
# vi /etc/authpf/users/joe/authpf.rules
```

And type this:

```
# MACROS
ext_if = "ne1"

# allow user joe to connect to HTTP servers
pass out on $ext_if inet proto tcp \
 from $user_ip to any port 80 flags S/SA synproxy state
```

Save joe's ruleset (press **Esc**, type : x and hit the **Enter/Return** key).

Use an SSH client (command-line or window-based) to connect to the firewall from one of the machines on the private network. You should see the following message:

```
Hello, joe, You are authenticated from host "192.168.32.12"
Where are you going with that NIC in your hand?
```

That's it! You can now repeat this process for other users.

Later on, when you want to see who's authenticating on your firewall, use:

```
# ps -ax | grep authpf
25487 p1  Is+     0:00:04 -authpf: joe@192.168.32.12 (authpf)
```

## Chapter 13

Using spamd

In this chapter we get to know one particularly interesting anti-spam tool, spamd(8).

There are two ways to fight spam: passive and active. The passive way is to accept all mail and then filter it to remove spam. While you can certainly achieve good results with modern Bayesian spam filters, this method does not do much to deter spammers and will cost you more and more in the long run. When spammers look at logs, they will see that their mail was accepted by your host and they will assume that it is OK with you to send more spam your way. More spam means more work for filters, which will use more CPU cycles, further slowing down your communication with the outside world.

The active way of fighting spam involves keeping a list of IP addresses of hosts known to send spam and reject connections from these hosts to port 25. While very efficient, this method has one tiny fault, it is a quick way to inform spammers that your host won't accept connections from their servers and can be removed from their list. They will try to deliver their payload from a different IP, or go after other hosts (or both).

An even better way to deter spammers is to make it expensive for them to deliver mail by slowing down their mail delivery software. This is exactly what *spamd(8)* does. It uses the SMTP specification [RFC 2821] to inject spam back into the sender's mail queue by sending the `450 Requested mail action not taken: mailbox unavailable` error message. This method is very effective as it uses standard communication protocol, to which all mailers must adhere.

13.1 Configuring spamd

Spamd(8) is designed to co-exist with all mail daemons, and to cause the least trouble to the system administrator. Because it never accepts mail from spammers, the load it places on the system is negligible and because it's job is very well-defined, configuring it is a breeze.

Out of all options listed in *spamd(8)*, the two that are most important are:

- `-p port` — specifies which port should *spamd(8)* listen for connections on. This cannot be port 25, since that is where the real *sendmail(8)* or other MTA is listening on. Choose one on of the higher ports that are not used for anything else, like 8025, 8125, etc.
- `-c connections` — the maximum number of concurrent connections accepted by *spamd(8)*. The default is 200, but you can adjust it up or down, as you wish.

Other options are explained in *spamd(8)* and we are not going to dwell on them here. If you are not sure which ones you need, let *spamd(8)* use the defaults.

You can start *spamd(8)* from the command line:

```
# spamd -p 8025 -c 200
```

Or, to start *spamd(8)* automatically at system startup add the following line to */etc/rc.local*:

```
spamd -p 8025 -c 200
```

Because *spamd(8)* is not listening on port 25, *pf(4)* must redirect connections from spammers' hosts to the port defined with the `-p` option (in our case, 8025). The list of spammer's addresses will be held in the `<spamd>` table, that can be updated while *pf(4)* and *spamd(8)* are running.

The contents of */etc/pf.conf* will differ depending on where the MTA is running. If you are new to *pf(4)* and *spamd(8)* start with these simple rulesets. First, we assume that the MTA is running on the firewall host. It listens on port 25, as all MTAs do:

```
# MACROS
ext_if = "ne1"

# Tables
table <spamd> persist
```

```
# NAT rules
# redirect connections from spammers to spamd, all legitimate
# connections will not be redirected
rdr on $ext_if inet proto tcp \
 from <spamd> to ($ext_if) port 25 -> 127.0.0.1 port 8025
# block all incoming connections
block in on $ext_if all
# pass redirected connections to spamd listening on the local
# loop interface (lo0)
pass in on lo0 inet proto tcp \
 from <spamd> to 127.0.0.1 port 8025
# pass legitimate connections to port 25 on the
# external interface
pass in on $ext_if inet proto tcp \
 from any to ($ext_if) port 25 flags S/SA synproxy state
```

The ruleset will look differently if you want to redirect connections to port 25 to the MTA running on another host.

```
# MACROS
ext_if = "ne1"
# here, we assume that the MTA is running on a machine
# located in the DMZ and connected to the DMZ interface
$dmz_if = "ne2"
mta_ad = "192.168.24.63"
mta_pt = "1025"

# Tables
table <spamd> persist

# NAT rules
# redirect connections from spammers to spamd
rdr on $ext_if inet proto tcp \
 from <spamd> to ($ext_if) port 25 -> 127.0.0.1 port 8025
# redirect all legitimate connections to the real MTA
rdr on $ext_if inet proto tcp \
 from any to ($ext_if) port 25 -> $mta_ad port $mta_pt
# block all incoming connections
block in on $ext_if all
# pass redirected connections to spamd listening on the local
```

```
# loop interface (lo0)
pass in on lo0 inet proto tcp \
  from <spamd> to 127.0.0.1 port 8025
pass out on $dmz_if inet proto tcp \
  from any to $mta_ad port $mta_pt flags S/SA synproxy state
```

Copy one of the above rulesets and make modifications necessary to make it work on your machine (change addresses, port numbers, interface names, etc.), save it and reload with:

```
# pfctl -F all ; pfctl -f /etc/pf.conf
```

You are now set and can begin populating the spamd table, either by hand, or via a script: To test the new setup, run *spamd(8)*:

```
# spamd -p 8025 -c 200
```

Next, add the address of the host from which you will try to connect to port 25 on the firewall:

```
# pfctl -t spamd -T add 192.168.23.11
```

Then, try to connect from that host (it's address will be different from the one given above, and the address of the firewall will be different from the one given below):

```
# telnet 192.168.2.1 25
```

You should see a message appearing very slowly in the terminal window. That is a sign that *spamd(8)* is working.

Next, remove the address of the test host from <spamd>:

```
# pfctl -t spamd -T delete 192.168.23.11
```

Then, try to connect from that host (it's address will be different from the one given above, and the address of the firewall will be different from the one given below):

```
# telnet 192.168.2.1 25
```

You should now see a banner of the MTA waiting for delivery of mail.

Once it is running, *spamd(8)* is designed to be configurable in-flight, and comes with a configuration utility, *spamd-setup(8)* which sends config-uration directives and makes changes to the spamd table automatically. It does its magic by parsing the *spamd.conf(5)* configuration file located in */etc/spamd.conf*, retrieving blacklists (lists of addresses known to send spam), and removing addresses from whitelists (addresses that we never want to put on a blacklist, even if they manage to get on some blacklist). Then, it sends the data in the format understood by *spamd(8)* to the port that the daemon is listening on.

Spamd-setup(8) must be run from root account or form another user's account as long as it has access to run it via *sudo(8)*. It's best to run *spamd-setup* at regular intervals from *cron(8)*.

## Chapter 14

Ruleset Optimization

Every CPU cycle counts. Here are a few ideas on how to save them.

The job of a firewall administrator does not stop once the rules are working and the firewall is doing its job. Another, quite often forgotten step, is the optimization of firewall rules.

The aim of optimization is to make your firewall do its job in shorter time and using less CPU time and memory. While such problems may seem distant to small network administrator, they are very familiar to administrators of busy networks where every delay is magnified and perceived by the users as a slow or unreliable connection.

14.1 The pf Optimization Checklist

Pf(4) does a very good job of automatically optimizing rulesets, but you can help it in various ways:

- *Write clean rules*. It's as obvious as that, but often forgotten. Simple, short rules are not only easier to understand, but also easier for *pf(4)* to optimize and more efficient.
- *Learn to use the* `quick` *keyword*. This little keyword can greatly speed up the process of ruleset evaluation. Think about it, if your packet filtering section contains 100 rules, but most of the traffic is matched by the first rule and not the other 99 rules, then the time required to parse these rules is wasted. If you add the `quick` keyword to the first rule, then you will save a lot of CPU time and speed up your firewall at no cost. For more information see Chapter 8, *Packet Filtering*.
- *Learn to use the* `pass` *keyword in NAT rules*. Its' job is similar to the `quick` keyword in packet filtering rules. It skips the packet filtering section and passes packets directly to the destination address.
- *Change the order of rules*. Another trick, related to the previous idea is

changing the order of the rules in the packet filtering section. If you use rules with the `quick` keyword, put them before those without the `quick` keyword.

- *Use tables instead of lists of addresses.* Tables are more efficient than lists of addresses. Read Chapter 5, */etc/pf.conf* and Chapter 9, *Dynamic Rulesets.*

- *Do not use ppp packet filtering.* Although *ppp* comes with its own packet filter, which you can use for filtering dial-up connections (that includes various DSL devices as well as analog modems, or digital ISDN modems), *pf(4)* will be a much safer solution.

- *Use bridge packet filtering.* If possible, configure your firewall as an invisible filtering bridge. It is a very secure solution. Consult Chapter 4, *Configuring OpenBSD.*

- *Outsource logging.* Send logs to another machine. Read Chapter 11, *Logging and Log Analysis.*

- *Upgrade your network hardware.* Yup, faster cards, hubs, switches, and better cabling might help.

- *Use bandwidth shaping.* This might require a faster machine with more RAM, but with ALTQ you will be able to control patterns of usage of your network. More information in Chapter 10, *Bandwidth Shaping and Load Balancing.*

- *Re-design your network.* When your firewall cannot keep up with the growth of your network, it doesn't necessarily mean that it's the fault of *pf(4)*. For example, when a NAT-ing firewall starts to clog the network, you might be running out of ports on the external interface (for a solution, read Chapter 7, *Packet Redirection.* On other times, visitors to your web site might be getting too many 'server busy' responses. If that is the case, you might want to consider adding another HTTP server and implementing load balancing.

- *Upgrade your hardware.* When all else fails, upgrade the machine you run OpenBSD and *pf(4)* on. Pay careful attention to the efficiency of all subsystems: disks, system bus, memory, and network cards. The processor speed is not the only, and not the most important parameter here.

14.2 Pf Optimization Options

The `optimization` rule controls the packet filter engine optimization options. The old optimization options `-O` found in earlier version of have been replaced with the `optimization` *algorithm* rule. There are six values of the *algorithm* argument:

- `default` — as its name says, it's the default optimization algorithm.
- `normal` — same as `default`.
- `high-latency` — used for high-latency links, such as satellite links. Expires idle connections later than `default`.
- `satellite` same as `high-latency`.
- `aggressive` — expires idle connections earlier than `default`; using less memory and CPU time while possibly dropping some legitimate connections.
- `conservative` — tries to avoid dropping any legitimate connections at the expense of increased memory usage and CPU utilization.

> *Don't forget to reload the new options after changing the optimization algorithm.*

Before you rush to enable these optimization rules, you should know that these algorithms make a difference in special cases like high-latency connections, or very busy corporate, government, or education networks. Small networks and networks with low traffic will see no noticeable performance improvements.

The `optimization` rule is a shortcut for quickly setting a bunch of `timeout` rules. If none of them seem to work in your particular setup, consider adjusting the `timeout` values yourself, as described in Chapter 8, *Packet Filtering*.

## Chapter 15

Testing Your Firewall

Is you firewall working as it should, or are there some strange communication problems? Why that small change you made suddenly cut you off? In this chapter we'll learn how to test the firewall, how to monitor it, and where to look for information.

Testing your ruleset is a multi-stage process. It is never too early to begin testing your firewall, and it certainly is not a good idea to put an untested firewall straight into production use.

15.1 Pencil Test

The first test of your firewall must be done before you start mucking around with hardware and *pf(4)*. It should be done with a pen or a pencil and a piece of paper. Simply draw boxes (hosts) and connect them with arrows, each marked with service and protocol names or port numbers that are allowed to pass through the firewall, and think what rules need to be used. The picture doesn't have to be pretty, but it ought to be clear enough to be understood without ripping your head apart. Once you have your firewall diagram, write filtering/NAT/ALTQ and other rules down on another piece of paper. You do not need to use *pf(4)* syntax, plain English will work just fine. After you're done, try to read these rules and follow the paths on the diagram, checking if the rules you are using will actually work in your mind. It is even better to ask a colleague to do it for you, because he or she will have a fresh mind and will be able to spot design flaws quicker than yourself. When you find something that doesn't quite work, revise your rules and repeat the process again. If you don't understand something, refer to other parts of this book, the *pf.conf(5)* man page, and the reference material listed in *Bibliography*.

After you are confident you know what you want *pf(4)* to do, begin writing the ruleset, one rule at a time. Start with general rules with the broadest scope and add more specific ones after you get the general setup working.

Every time you want to make a change, make a copy of the old ruleset:

```
# cp /etc/pf.conf /etc/pf.conf.old
```

Make changes to *etc/pf.conf* and save them. Then, flush the old ruleset from memory and reload the new one. To make sure that you don't get cut off, when you are testing your new ruleset without physical access to the firewall machine, use the following command:

```
# pfctl -F all
# pfctl -f /etc/pf.conf ; sleep 10 ; pfctl -f /etc/pf.conf-old
```

Then, check if the new rules are working fine. When they are, add a new rule and repeat that procedure again. (If you need more time to perform checks, increase the value of the *sleep(1)* argument from 10 seconds to 20 or 30.) Should things go wrong, the previously working version of the ruleset will be loaded automatically and you will be saved the inconvenience of having to walk or drive to the machine to make changes from the console.

When all is working fine, commit the new ruleset to CVS (for a short course in CVS, see Chapter 5, *etc/pf.conf*):

```
# cvs ci -m 'Added spamd rules' /etc/pf.conf
```

OK, but how do you know that the rules are working as they should? Read on.

15.2 Checking Host Availability

The simplest, yet one of the more effective testing tools is the humble *ping(8)*. Provided you configured *pf(4)* to pass ping requests and replies (see Appendix B), you should be able to use *ping(8)* to perform the following checks:

• *Is the firewall host up and running?* Simply ping the firewall, e.g. when the firewall is located at 192.168.15.7 (the address assigned to the interface it connects to the LAN segment you are sending pings with), do:

```
$ ping 192.168.15.7
```

If you want to send tst packets through a specific interface, give *ping(8)*
the address of that interface:

```
$ ping -I 192.168.15.1 192.168.15.7
```

Let it run for a few seconds, press **Ctrl+C**, and read statistics printed on
screen, have a look at the percentage of packet loss. When that value is
0%, you have a perfect connection, when it is equal to 100% there is no
connection to the firewall or all packets are being dropped. Values in-be-
tween indicate that the network or the firewall is heavily loaded and some
packets are being lost, but the firewall is up and running.

- *Are hosts on the other side of the firewall running?* When the firewall is
  configured to let responses to ping datagrams pass back to the sender, you
  can send pings to check other hosts, on other LAN segments, in the DMZ,
  or on the outside of the firewall. Results are interpreted in the same way
  as the results of sending pings to the firewall, but a 100% loss of packets
  does not necessarily indicate that the firewall is down. It may be dropping
  packets because that's how the *pf(4)* is configured. Therefore, another
  check is required in such cases, because the firewall may pass responses
  to pings sent from the firewall itself, but not from the hosts protected by
  that firewall. To do it, log on the firewall and ping the same hosts again.
  The interpretation of results is the same as for the firewall test, but again,
  a 100% packet loss may be simply a confirmation that pings are not being
  let through the firewall, because that's how *pf(4)* has been configured and
  it's just doing its job. Yet another possibility could be that the hosts you
  are trying to ping is dropping the packets you send it on purpose, to
  prevent DoS attacks. In such case, you need to check if other hosts on the
  outside respond to pings. When they don't there may be a problem with
  your connection to the Internet.

  > *Be careful with sending pings to external hosts. If you
  > swamp them with requests, you may trigger their NIDS
  > and someone might be thinking they caught a dangerous
  > villain. A couple of pings sent their way will not get you
  > in trouble, but if you start* ping(8) *and go to make a
  > coffee, don't be surprised to get a call from the other
  > side's administrator. Should you have really bad luck,
  > you might get legal action started against you, so use*

ping(8) *sparingly.* *(The same goes for* traceroute(8), mtr(8), *or other similar tools.)*

15.2.1 When Ping Cannot Help

When *ping(8)* says that the host you are trying to reach is down, there is a possibility that it is configured to ignore your pings. In such case, try connecting to one of the ports on that server with *telnet(1)*.

For example, to check if the remote server is up and running, try:

```
$ telnet www.example.com 80
```

You can replace the hostname with an IP address and you can replace the port number with the service name (see */etc/services*):

```
$ telnet 10.5.45.2 http
```

When these attempts are unsuccessful, you may assume that:

- *Pf(4) may be blocking packets.* Try connecting to other hosts with *pf(4)* turned off. When that helps, check */etc/pf.conf* for offending rules.
- *The routing is not set up properly.* Assuming that *pf(4)* is configured to let all packets pass and that NAT is configured correctly, if used at all, it is possible that the routing information is not correct. Check if the gateway address on the local hosts points to the internal interface on the firewall, or when the firewall is working as an invisible filtering bridge—to the host that acts as the gateway for the local LAN segment. Another thing to check is the gateway address on the firewall or the gateway host. See Chapter 4, *Configuring OpenBSD* for more information.
- *The target host is down.* In that case, restart the host, if you have the right to do so and can do it, or wait until its administrators do it. Depending on your circumstances, it may be appropriate to let them know there is trouble.
- *You are blocked by a firewall on the other side.* Do they have a reason to block you? Get in touch with their administrator and ask.
- *There is a problem with the network equipment.* Check cables, hubs, switches, routers, power plugs.

15.3 Discovering Open Ports on Remote Hosts

When you are at a loss and cannot connect to a server over a network, there is a tool that can help, but you need to be very careful with it. It is called *nmap*, and can be found in OpenBSD packages.

Nmap is, among other things, a port scanner. It uses clever tricks to discover which ports are open on a target machine, does fingerprinting (discovers which version and which operating system the remote host is running) and can be your last chance of finding out, if the host you are trying to check does allow some kind of connections, without going there and checking it yourself.

> *Do not forget that it is possible to have more than one IP address assigned to a single interface (with the ifconfig(8)* alias *option). In that case, run nmap on every IP address you are interested in!*

Because *nmap* is so powerful, it is an ideal tool for network administrators and security specialists. Unfortunately, it is also used by people with less friendly intentions, who use it to learn about remote hosts they wish to break into. Therefore, it is very important that you do not scan hosts that you do not manage or do not have the permission to scan. If you let *nmap* loose on other people's hosts you will get yourself in serious legal trouble.

15.4 Testing Network Performance

When the network is slowing down, the reasons for that could be numerous and you will have to do some detective work to get to the source of the problem.

- *The local network is overloaded.* To test that hypothesis, ping various hosts on the local network and see what time values they return. If they are in hundreds of milliseconds, you may have a problem with your local network segment. Somewhere, something's wrong. The target hosts could be overloaded, the cabling may be damaged, someone might be downloading huge files (put them on a diet, use ALTQ to limit bandwidth). Or, someone might be messing with your network. Monitor the situation, and if the problems don't disappear, get to work.

Be careful, when you decide that the solution is an upgrade of network cards to something more speedy, you might suddenly overload the firewall host or the external link, or both. Often an upgrade in one LAN segment causes a trickle-down effect and requires un-planned upgrades to the rest of the infrastructure.

- *The firewall host is overloaded.* The machine that worked fine two months ago might suddenly slow down. Why? You are probably asking too much from it. Did you switch on packet logging? Did you add more hosts behind the firewall? Did you start serving WWW from the DMZ? Did you start using ALTQ for bandwidth shaping? Did you install *snort* on the firewall host? Positive answers to these questions mean that you get what you deserve for putting additional load on the firewall host without checking if it can handle it. Periodic slowdowns usually mean that the firewall does not have enough CPU power, memory (most likely), or that there is a problem with the I/O subsystem. So, which one is it, Doc? For a quick diagnosis of how the processor is coping, use *uptime(1)*:

```
$ uptime
```

Check the load averages reported by *uptime(1)*. When they are equal to 1 or higher, either the processor is overloaded or there is a shortage of memory, or both.

Uptime(1) also reports the time that elapsed since the last system restart. If you notice that it is constantly low, it may be a sign that you are having problems with the system or the hardware that cause frequent reboots. It is something you should investigate.

For a more accurate information about the processor and the memory, use *vmstat(8)*:

```
$ vmstat -c 10
```

The first three columns (r, b, w) ought to be 0, they may be temporarily greater than 0, but if such situations persist they are a sign of trouble. When column r is greater than 0, the processor is overloaded; when column b is greater than 0, there is probably a problem with the I/O sub-system (the disk are too slow, happens when you do extensive logging); and when w is greater than 0 your machine is short of memory and has to swap to disk. In all cases, the network connections will be affected. Pay particular attention to swapping, as it severely degrades the firewall performance. Often adding more memory will have a much better effect than a faster processor, disk, RAID, or a faster network card.

Yet another performance indicator reported by *vmstat(8)* is the amount of time the processor is idle (`cpu id`). The higher that value, the better, but it cannot be 100% idle all the time, of course. There are two schools of thinking about that indicator. Some say that a 10%–20% reserve is OK, while others say that it ought to be at most 50%. When the load is applied evenly, it is OK for the processor to be quite busy (10% idle), but when the load is bursty, the CPU ought to be idle at 50% or more. Another popular system performance measuring tool is *top(1)*, which has its critics, who claim that it places additional load on the system and blurs the overall picture of system performance. While it is true, it displays a lot of useful information about the system. It can be run in interactive mode:

```
$ top
```

or in batch mode:

```
$ top -b
```

(If you long for a simple, visual interface in text mode, try *systat(1)*.)

Another important tool for monitoring performance is *netstat(1)*, used to check parameters of the network connections, interfaces, and so on. To use it, type:

```
$ netstat
```

Watch out for high values of the `Recv-Q` queue and the `Send-Q` queue. When `Recv-Q` is constantly high, your host may be having problems with processing packets it receives. High values of `Send-Q` may indicate that the external hosts may be having problems processing packets fast enough. To make *netstat(1)* work faster disable name lookups, with:

```
$ netstat -n
```

To check the status of a particular network interface, use:

```
$ netstat -n -I rl0
```

The most important information, from the point of view of performance are values of `Ierrs` (inbound packet errors), `Oerrs` (outbound packet errors), and `Colls` (collisions, low values are OK, values above 15% indicate that there may be a need to split the busy segment into a smaller one.

- *The external link or the internal link on the firewall is overloaded.* Run *netstat(8)* on the firewall, check stats for interfaces and see if you can spot the source of the problem.
- *The external networks are overloaded.* When the local network and the firewall are not overtaxed, the problem may lie on the outside. Run *traceroute(8)*, *traceroute6(8)*, or *mrtg* (must be installed from packages, see Chapter 4, *Configuring OpenBSD*) and see what they report. *Pf(4)* must be configured to let *traceroute(8)* work (see Appendix B). When problems persist, it may be time to change your ISP to someone with better links or to buy more bandwidth.
- *The external hosts are overloaded.* Try to connect to a remote host using *telnet(1)*, your browser, or other clients that the remote machine serves and compare response times with other similar hosts. When problems persist, get in touch with the administrator of the remote system.

15.5 Are packets passing through PF?

How do you know if packets are passing through the firewall? *Ping(8)*, *traceroute(8)*, *telnet(1)*, or other simple tools might not always help. When you encounter such problems, try *tcpdump(8)*. You can use it to display packets arriving at a selected interface, to write packets to a file, and to filter packets.

For example, the following command displays all packets arriving and leaving the `ne0` interface:

```
# tcpdump -i ne0
```

If you wanted to write them to a file, you'd use:

```
# tcpdump -i ne0 -w ne0-capture
```

And if you wanted to read them later on, you'd use:

```
# tcpdump -r ne0-capture
```

Depending on your preferences, *tcpdump(8)* output can be made less verbose (-q) or more verbose (-vv). For faster operation, you might want to turn IP address to name translation with -n.

The real fun begins, when you use *tcpdump(8) expressions.* Expressions are used to filter packets and display only those that we are interested in, e.g. (displays packets sent from host whose address is 10.3.4.6):

```
# tcpdump -i ne0 src host 10.3.4.6
```

(displays packets sent to or from port 25):

```
# tcpdump -i ne0 port 25
```

You can run tcpdump on the firewall and the hosts surrounding it and watch the output of *tcpdump(8)* for specific information. For example, if you wanted to know if your ruleset is letting packets from a certain host pass, use src host. similarly, the same parameter can help when you want to make sure that packets from a certain host do not pass through the firewall, when you see them, it is a sign that the ruleset ought to be adjusted.

When problems you are experiencing are difficult to spot, you might use *ethereal* (found in ports and packages), which makes *tcpdump*'s output easier to understand. Should that fail, you may need to do some detective work, and for that you will use the -w option, which writes packets to a file. Later, with the help of *tcpreplay* That technique will be used in many cases, but *tcpdump(8)* can also help measure network performance Another useful debugging technique is turning packet filtering off and replacing it with packet logging.

Then, after you captured some traffic, use *tcpreplay* (it's in the ports and packages) to send that traffic again. The captured packets can be sliced and pasted with *tcpslice* (also in packages). Other tools of interest are: *tcptrace*, *tcpstat*, and *tcpshow*.

15.6 Additional tools

It is impossible to list and describe all network and security tools that OpenBSD comes with. The following list ought to direct you in your search, and help you quickly find the tool you are looking for. Please note that even if some tool you are looking for is not available in the ports or packages collection, it is probably available in source form on the Internet and can be built using the OpenBSD compiler tools. Be careful with code downloaded from the Internet and always download it from trusted sites.

- *Scanning, fingerprinting tools:* angst, arirang, cgichk, ettercap, firewalk, ndiff, nmap, p0f, portscanner, queso, scanssh, siphon, sniffit, smbsniff, strobe, whisker, xprobe.
- *Scanning, fingerprinting detection tools:* aide, courtney, portsentry, smurflog, snort, scanlogd, task.
- *Network Intrusion Detection Systems (NIDS):* libnids, snort.
- *Protocol analysis tools:* arpwatch, ethereal, parse, pcapmerge, ssldump, tcpdump.
- *Network utilities:* aggregate, arping, ctrace, dlint, fping, hping, libnet, nemesis, netpipes, ngrep, socket, tcpcat , tcpflow, tcplist, tcpreen.
- *Network performance monitoring tools:* http_load, http_ping, iperf, ipfm, mtr, mrtg, netperf, netpipe, oproute, top, tcpbalst, trafd, trafshow, ttcp.

## Chapter 16

Firewall Management

Firewalls built with OpenBSD and *pf* are specialized Unix systems and as such they are managed just like any other Unix-class system. A lot of concepts are similar, but there are a few differences, due to the fact that *pf(4)* is a complex piece of software and has its own management tool, *pfctl(8)*.

16.1 General Operations

- *Enable pf(4)*:

  ```
  # pfctl -e
  ```

- *Disable pf(4)*:

  ```
  # pfctl -d
  ```

- *Enable pf(4) and load the ruleset stored in /etc/pf.conf*:

  ```
  # pfctl -e -f /etc/pf.conf
  ```

16.2 Pfctl Output Control Options

- *Suppress informational messages.* Display error and warning messages only. Option -q. Can be used with other options.

- *Be more verbose.* Display additional information. Option -v. Can be used with other options.

- *Be even more verbose.* Display more information. Option -vv. Can be used with other options.

16.3 Managing Rulesets

• *Load the whole ruleset from a file*:

```
# pfctl -f /etc/pf.conf
```

• *Parse the ruleset stored in a file but don't load it.* Good for ruleset debugging purposes:

```
# pfctl -n -f /etc/pf.conf
```

• *Load rules, or the whole ruleset from standard input (STDIN).* Replace the name of the file with –, e.g.:

```
# echo "block in all" | pfctl -f -
```

• *Flush everything*:

```
# pfctl -F all
```

16.4 Managing Macros

• *Define (or override) a macro*:

```
# pfctl -D macro=value
```

e.g.:

```
# pfctl -D ext_if=ne0
```

When the value of the macro contains characters that may be interpreted by the shell, enclose everything after –D in single quotes:

```
# pfctl -D 'locals={192.168.22.32, 192.168.22.33}'
```

16.5 Managing Tables

• *Load only table definitions for a file*:

```
# pfctl -T load -f /etc/pf.conf
```

- *Create an empty table*. Works like adding an address to an existing table:

  ```
  # pfctl -t sometable -T add 192.168.23.2
  ```

- *Add a new address to a table*:

  ```
  # pfctl -t sometable -T add 192.168.23.3
  ```

- *Delete an address from a table*:

  ```
  # pfctl -t sometable -T delete 192.168.23.3
  ```

- *Replace addresses from a table with address list loaded from a file*:

  ```
  # pfctl -t sometable -T replace -f addresses
  ```

- *Display the list of all tables*:

  ```
  # pfctl -s Tables
  ```

- *Display addresses in a table*:

  ```
  # pfctl -t sometable -T show
  ```

- *Check if the given address matches a table*:

  ```
  # pfctl -t sometable -T test 192.168.23.3
  ```

- *Check if the given addresses match a table*:

  ```
  # pfctl -t sometable -T test -f addresses
  ```

- *Clear all statistics for a table*:

  ```
  # pfctl -t sometable -T zero
  ```

- *Kill a table*:

  ```
  # pfctl -t sometable -T kill
  ```

- *Flush all addresses from a table*:

  ```
  # pfctl -t sometable -T flush
  ```

16.6 Managing pf Options

- *Load only options from a file*:

  ```
  # pfctl -O -f /etc/pf.conf
  ```

16.7 Managing Queues

- *Load only queue definitions from a file*:

  ```
  # pfctl -A -f /etc/pf.conf
  ```

- *Display queue definitions*:

  ```
  # pfctl -s queue
  ```

- *Display queue definitions and per-queue statistics*:

  ```
  # pfctl -v -s queue
  ```

- *Display and update queue definitions and per-queue statistics*. Updates are displayed every 5 seconds:

  ```
  # pfctl -vv -s queue
  ```

- *Flush queue definitions*:

  ```
  # pfctl -F queue
  ```

16.8 Managing Packet Redirection Rules

- *Load only packet redirection rules from a file*:

  ```
  # pfctl -N -f /etc/pf.conf
  ```

- *Display currently loaded packet redirection rules*:

  ```
  # pfctl -s nat
  ```

- *Flush packet redirection rule definitions*:

  ```
  # pfctl -F nat
  ```

16.9 Managing Packet Filtering Rules

- *Load only filter rules from a file*:

  ```
  # pfctl -R -f /etc/pf.conf
  ```

- *Display filtering rule definitions*:

  ```
  # pfctl -s rules
  ```

- *Display filtering rule definitions and per-rule statistics*:

  ```
  # pfctl -v -s rules
  ```

- *Flush filtering rule definitions*:

  ```
  # pfctl -F rules
  ```

16.10 Managing Anchors

- *Load rules into anchor xyz*:

  ```
  # pfctl -a xyz -f somerules
  ```

- *Load rules into named ruleset abc of anchor xyz*:

  ```
  # pfctl -a xyz:abc -f somerules
  ```

- *Display NAT rules form named ruleset abc of anchor xyz*:

  ```
  # pfctl -s nat -a xyz:abc
  ```

Other modifiers allowed in `-F` are: `all`, `queue`, `rules`, `state`, `info`, and `tables`.

- *Display currently loaded anchors*:

  ```
  # pfctl -s Anchors
  ```

- *Display currently loaded named rulesets in an anchor*:

  ```
  # pfctl -s Anchors -a someanchor
  ```

- *Flush all rules from anchor xyz*:

  ```
  # pfctl -F all -a xyz
  ```

  Other modifiers allowed in `-F` are: `nat`, `queue`, `rules`, `state`, `info`, and `tables`.

- *Flush all rules from ruleset abc of anchor xyz*:

  ```
  # pfctl -F all -a xyz:abc
  ```

  Other modifiers allowed in `-F` are: `nat`, `queue`, `rules`, `state`, `info`, and `tables`.

16.11 Managing States

- *Display all states*:

  ```
  # pfctl -s state
  ```

- *Perform DNS lookups on displayed states*. Add the `-r` option when you are using the `-s state` option.

- *Kill all states originating from host abc*:

  ```
  # pfctl -k abc
  ```

- *Kill all states originating from host abc to host xyz*:

```
# pfctl -k abc -k xyz
```

- *Flush states*:

```
# pfctl -F states
```

- *Display changes to the state table via* pfsync(4):

```
# ifconfig pfsync0 up
# tcpdump -s1500 -evtni pfsync0
```

16.12 Managing Operating System Fingerprints

- *Display all loaded operating system fingerprints*:

```
# pfctl -s osfp
```

- *Flush all loaded operating system fingerprints*:

```
# pfctl -F osfp
```

16.13 Statistics

- *Display all stats*:

```
# pfctl -s all
```

- *Display filter information (statistics and counters)*:

```
# pfctl -s info
```

- *Display current pool memory hard limits*:

```
# pfctl -s memory
```

- *Display global timeouts*:

```
# pfctl -s timeouts
```

• *Display statistics for rules with labels*:

```
# pfctl -s labels
```

16.14 Additional Tools for Managing pf

Although *pfctl(8)* is the best tool for managing *pf(4)*, there are a few additional items you should know about, because they can greatly help you in you everyday work:

• *pfstat* — collects and plots *pf(4)* statistics.

  http://benzedrine.cx/pfstat.html   *(pfstat)*

• *pftop* — similar to *top(1)* or *ntop*, displays basic *pf(4)* stats.

  http://www.eee.metu.edu.fr/~canacar/pftop/   *(pftop)*

• *fwanalog* — parses *pf(4)* logs and translates them into *Analog* format.

  http://www.tud.at/programm/fwanalog   *(fwanalog)*

Manual Pages

Unlike online help distributed with other operating systems, the OpenBSD manual pages truly are the best source of information related to almost every component of this fine piece of software.

A.1 Using the OpenBSD Manual

The OpenBSD system manual is available from the command line, all you have to do is type the man command followed by the name of man page:

```
$ man dhcp
```

As you might have noticed, this book contains names of many manual pages that end with a number enclosed in parentheses. That number indicates the section number the page in question belongs to, e.g. *ls(1)* is a reference to the manual page for the *ls* command stored in section 1. Such notation is used, because there may exist more than one page with the same name. To specify which page you want to see, precede the name of the page with the section number:

```
$ man 1 ls
```

What if you don't know which page contains the information you are looking for, let alone the section number? Use the *apropos(1)* command:

```
$ apropos dhcp
dhclient(8) - Dynamic Host Configuration Protocol
☞ (DHCP) Client
dhclient-script(8) - DHCP client network configuration
☞ script
dhclient.conf(5) - DHCP client configuration file
dhclient.leases(5) - DHCP client lease database
```

```
dhcp(8) - configuring OpenBSD for DHCP
dhcp-options(5) - Dynamic Host Configuration Protocol
☞ options
dhcpd(8) - Dynamic Host Configuration Protocol Server
dhcpd.conf(5) - dhcpd configuration file
dhcpd.leases(5) - DHCP client lease database
```

When *apropos(1)* returns more results that can fit on a single screen, use this set of commands:

```
$ apropos dhcp | less
```

What if the page you read did not answer your questions? Have a look at the pages in the *SEE ALSO* section found near the end of almost every manual page and at the pages referred to in the main text of the page you are reading.

The truly determined can use the following command to dig deeper into the bowels of the manual:

```
$ grep -r bridge /usr/share/man/
```

What you'll see is a list of lines showing the names of files where the `bridge` keyword was found. The numbers at the end of the file names shown in the output are the manual section numbers.

A.1.1 Reading the OpenBSD Manual Pages on the Web

It is possible to read the OpenBSD manual pages online with your browser, which is very handy when you don't have OpenBSD up and running, or when you saved disk space and did not install the *man34.tgz*. They are available on the following page:

http://www.openbsd.org/cgi-bin/man.cgi   *(OpenBSD Manual)*

A.2 Pages Related to PF

There are several manual pages describing *pf* and its components:

• *authpf(8)* — the authenticating gateway user shell. Discussed in Chapter 12, *Using authpf*.

- *pf(4)* — Daniel Hertmeier's Packet Filter.
- *pf.conf(5)* — a long description of the *pf* configuration file.
- *pf.os(5)* — description of the format of the operating systems' fingerprint database.
- *pfctl(8)* — the *pf* management tool. Discussed in Chapter 16, *Firewall Management*.
- *pflogd(8)* — the *pf* logging daemon. Discussed in Chapter 11, *Logging and Log Analysis*.
- *pfsync(4)* — the *pf* states table logging interface. Discussed in Chapter 15, *Testing Your Firewall*.
- *spamd(8)* — the anti-spam daemon. Discussed in Chapter 13, *Using spamd*.
- *spamd-setup(8)* — the tool for parsing and loading spammer's addresses. Discussed in Chapter 13, *Using spamd*.
- *spamd.conf(5)* — *spamd(8)* configuration file syntax. Discussed in Chapter 13, *Using spamd*.

A.3 Other Pages of Interest

The following pages are good starting points when you are learning the OpenBSD operating system or the *pf* packet filter:

- *afterboot(8)* — things you need to do after installing OpenBSD.
- *bpf(4)* — the Berkeley Packet Filter.
- *intro(4)* — a concise introduction to special files and devices.
- *intro(7)* — a list of most important pages in section 7 (miscellaneous).
- *intro(8)* — a short description of the contents of section 8 (system management).
- *networking(8)* — a concise introduction to the OpenBSD networking facilities. Since the topic is huge, it is only a general overview, but nonetheless useful. If you are looking for specific answers, read other pages related to devices, protocols, services, and tools. Still lost? Read [Stevens 1994].

Rules for Popular (and Less Popular) Services

So, you want to know how to write a rule for service x*? Is there a table of rules you can use? The answers are here.*

Writing a rule for a service begins with a look at the contents of */etc/services*. When you find a name and a matching port number, you have most of the information you need to write your rule. If the service is not listed in */etc/services*, it may be listed in this file:

http://www.iana.org/assignments/port-numbers

When you find them there, use the port number, not the name of the service. Note that the port numbers are not guaranteed to be what you expect them to be, because administrators are free to configure them as they wish, although ports lower than 1024 tend to be quite stable.

Another important piece of information is the transport protocol used, which often is TCP or UDP. UDP-based services are often problematic and care must be taken when you are dealing with them. The rule here is to use TCP unless you explicitly need UDP.

- *I want to block connections from external hosts to a specific port on the host running* pf(4). Start with (remember to use the `proto` keyword followed by `tcp`, or `udp`, or both). This is important, because ports are Only defined in TCP and UDP protocols; ICMP, RSVP, and others that do not use TCP or UDP for transport do not use ports:

```
# if -- the interface on which packets arrive
# block both TCP and UDP IPv4
block in on $if inet proto {tcp, udp} \
 from any to ($if) port $blocked_port
# block both TCP and UDP IPv6
block in on $if inet6 proto {tcp, udp} \
 from any to ($if) port $blocked_port
```

- *I want to pass connections from certain external hosts to a specific port on the firewall, but block them from other hosts.* Start with:

```
# if -- the interface on which packets arrive
# block both TCP and UDP IPv4
block in on $if inet proto {tcp, udp} \
 from any to ($if) port $blocked_port
pass in on $if inet proto {tcp, udp} from $OK_address \
    to ($if) port $blocked_port
# block both TCP and UDP IPv6
block in on $if inet6 proto {tcp, udp} \
 from any to ($if) port $blocked_port
pass in on $if inet6 proto {tcp, udp} from $OK_address \
    to ($if) port $blocked_port
```

When you only want to pass IPv4 packets, remove the
pass ... inet6 rule.

- *I want to redirect connections from external hosts from one port to another.*

```
# ext_if -- the external interface
rdr in on $ext_if inet \
 from any to ($ext_if) port $target_ports \
 -> $target_host $redirected_port
rdr in on $ext_if inet6 \
 from any to ($ext_if) port $target_ports \
 -> $target_host $redirected_port
```

- *I want to redirect connections from internal hosts to proxy.*

```
# ext_if -- the external interface
```

```
# int_if -- the internal interface
rdr in on $int_if \
  from any to any port $target_port \
  -> $proxy_host $redirected_port
```

- *How do find out which ports are opened by a particular piece of software?* Consult the relevant documentation, but if that doesn't help, do some detective work. Run the software, then run *nmap* on the hosts running that software. Also, run *tcpdump(8)* on the firewall host and filter out traffic to and from the host running that software.

- *Why some protocols need two or more ports?* Some protocols are just designed that way, for better or worse. They usually open two connections at different ports, one for data and one for control. In such cases, it is difficult to write filtering rules for them, unless you can know the numbers of these ports beforehand. What you can do is proxy them like you proxy the FTP described in Chapter 4, *Configuring OpenBSD*

- *What's the difference between* nat *and* rdr *proxy?* The main difference is the fact that rdr rules do not change the source address of a packet.

- *I tried everything, and still don't get it.* Read the protocol specification. Use *nmap* and *tcpdump(8)*. Ask around, no shame in learning.

B.1 Dealing with ICMP

The Internet Control Message Protocol (ICMP) is a very important tool for IP network diagnostics. Tools like *ping(8)* use it to find out whether the host you are trying to ping is running, down, or rejecting connections; routers use it to perform some automatic administrative tasks, etc. Unfortunately, ICMP is being abused by hackers, and it is often advised to block it, which makes tools like *ping(8)* inoperable.

Rather than completely block it, you could let some types of ICMP responses pass through your firewall, with some caution. The following rules are for a screened network firewall configuration.

- *Echo Request & Echo Reply* — let administrators ping (send Echo Request and accept Echo Reply) external hosts:

```
# prv_if -- the interface that private hosts connect
#           to the firewall
pass in on $prv_if inet proto icmp \
 from $admin_hosts \
 to any icmp-type 8 code 0 keep state
```

- *Echo Request & Echo Reply* — let private hosts ping (send Echo Request and accept Echo Reply) the firewall host:

```
# prv_if -- the interface that private hosts connect
#           to the firewall
pass in on $prv_if inet proto icmp \
 from $prv_if:network \
 to ($prv_if) icmp-type 8 code 0 keep state
```

- *Echo Request & Echo Reply* — let your ISP network ping (send Echo Request and accept Echo Reply) the firewall host:

```
# ext_if -- the interface that firewall host connects
#           to the outside world
pass in on $ext_if inet proto icmp \
 from $ISP_net_address \
 to ($ext_if) icmp-type 8 code 0 keep state
```

- *Destination Unreachable* — block outbound Destination Unreachable messages except for Fragmentation Needed, pass inbound Destination Unreachable messages:

```
# ext_if -- the interface that firewall host connects
#           to the outside world
# prv_if -- the interface that private hosts connect
#           to the firewall
pass in on $ext_if inet proto icmp \
 from any \
 to any icmp-type 3
pass out on $ext_if inet proto icmp \
 from any \
 to any icmp-type 3 code 4 keep state
pass in on $prv_if inet proto icmp \
 from prv_if:network \
 to any icmp-type 3
```

```
pass out on $prv_if inet proto icmp \
 from any \
 to prv_if:network icmp-type 3 code 4 keep state
```

- *Source Quench* — pass inbound and outbound packets:

```
# ext_if -- the interface that the firewall host connects
#            to the outside world
# prv_if -- the interface that private hosts connect
#            to the firewall host
pass in on $ext_if inet proto icmp \
 all \
 icmp-type 4 keep state
pass in on $prv_if inet proto icmp \
 all \
 icmp-type 4 keep state
```

- *Time Exceeded* — pass inbound and outbound packets:

```
# ext_if -- the interface that the firewall host connects
#            to the outside world
# prv_if -- the interface that private hosts connect
#            to the firewall host
pass in on $ext_if inet proto icmp \
 all \
 icmp-type 11 keep state
pass in on $prv_if inet proto icmp \
 all \
 icmp-type 11 keep state
```

- *Parameter Problem* — pass inbound and outbound packets:

```
# ext_if -- the interface that the firewall host connects
#            to the outside world
# prv_if -- the interface that private hosts connect
#            to the firewall host
pass in on $ext_if inet proto icmp \
 all \
 icmp-type 12 keep state
```

```
pass in on $prv_if inet proto icmp \
  all \
  icmp-type 12 keep state
```

B.2 Fixing FTP

FTP and other protocols that open two or more connections are always problematic, because they need proxy software to operate correctly through the firewall.

A solution to FTP client access to external servers is shown in Chapter 4, *Configuring OpenBSD*. What about FTP servers? You need to know which ports does the server open for connections besides port 21. In case of *ftpd(8)* the are in range 49152 through 65535, while the Windows 2000 FTP server opens ports 5000 through 65534. When the server is running on the same host as *pf(4)*, use:

```
pass in on $ext_if proto tcp from any \
  to any port 21 keep state
pass in on $ext_if proto tcp from any \
  to any port > 49151 keep state
```

When the FTP server is running in a DMZ, use the *reverse ftp-proxy* solution described in Chapter 4, *Configuring OpenBSD*.

B.3 Template Rules for Services Using TCP and UDP

The long ruleset presented later in this chapter contains examples of rules for passing or blocking certain services based on TCP. It is also very easy to adapt them to filter services using UDP, although we generally block it when it is not absolutely necessary, for safety. These example were written for a few typical firewall configurations described in Chapter 2, *Firewall Designs*. The service filtered in these rules is the Secure Shell (SSH). SSH servers are listening on port 22,and that's the assumption the ruleset is based on.

> *Adapting rules for other TCP services is very easy and often involves a mere change of the target port number. More information about doing this can be found in the next section of this appendix.*

A word of warning. Do not apply the examples blindly, but choose only those rules that you need. For example, if you block all incoming connections, but want to pass connections to port 22 originating on the outside of the firewall, choose the **pass** rule for the screened host/LAN or the one for the bastion host.

All of these rules fit nicely into the more general rulesets presented in Appendix C.

```
#### Bastion Host ####
# a lone host connected directly to the Internet or LAN
# macros for the bastion host:
# ext_if -- the name of the interface connecting the bastion
#           host to other (external) hosts
ext_if = "ne1"
# filtering rules for the bastion host:
# -- allow connections from the bastion host to external hosts
#    on port 22 (SSH)
# note: to let IPv6 packets pass, copy the following rule and
#       change inet to inet6
pass out on $ext_if inet proto tcp \
 from ($ext_if) port > 1023 \
 to any port 22 \
 flags S/SA modulate state
# -- allow connections from external hosts to the bastion host
#    on port 22 (SSH)
# note: to let IPv6 packets pass, copy the following rule and
#       change inet to inet6
pass in on $ext_if inet proto tcp \
 from any port > 1023 \
 to ($ext_if) port 22 \
 flags S/SA modulate state
# -- block connections from the bastion host to external hosts
#    on port 22 (SSH)
# note: you need two rules to block IPv4 and IPv6 packets, if
#       you use the ($ext_if) notation instead of the numeric
#       address, and the $ext_if interface has both IPv4 and
#       IPv6 addresses.
block out on $ext_if inet proto {tcp, udp} \
 from ($ext_if) \
 to any port 22
```

```
block out on $ext_if inet6 proto {tcp, udp} \
 from ($ext_if) \
 to any port 22
# -- block connections from external hosts to the bastion host
#     on port 22 (SSH)
# note: you need two rules to block IPv4 and IPv6 packets, if
#        you use the ($ext_if) notation instead of the numeric
#        address, and the $ext_if interface has both IPv4 and
#        IPv6 addresses.
block in on $ext_if inet proto {tcp, udp} \
 from any \
 to ($ext_if) port 22
block in on $ext_if inet6 proto {tcp, udp} \
 from any \
 to ($ext_if) port 22


#### Screened Host/LAN ####
# the firewall has public IP addresses assigned to its
# interfaces, the private hosts also have public IP addresses
# macros for the screened host/LAN:
# ext_if -- the name of the interface connecting the firewall
#            to external hosts, the Internet, the outside world
ext_if = "ne1"
# prv_if -- the name of the interface connecting the firewall
#            to the private (internal) host(s)
prv_if = "ne1"
# filtering rules for the screeened host(s):
# -- allow connections from the private host(s) to external
#     hosts on port 22 (SSH)
#     note: private hosts can connect to the firewall's port 22
#            too
pass in on $prv_if inet proto tcp \
 from $prv_if:network port > 1023 \
 to any port 22
pass out on $ext_if inet proto tcp \
 from $prv_if:network port > 1023 \
 to any port 22 \
 flags S/SA modulate state
# -- allow connections from external hosts to the private
```

```
#    host(s) on port 22 (SSH)
pass in on $ext_if inet proto tcp \
 from any port > 1023 \
 to $prv_if:network port 22
 flags S/SA modulate state
pass out on $prv_if inet proto tcp \
 from any port > 1023 \
 to $prv_if:network port 22
# -- block connections from the private host(s) to external
#    hosts on port 22 (SSH), also block connections to port 22
#    on the firewall host
# note: you need two rules to block IPv4 and IPv6 packets, if
#       you use the :network notation instead of the numeric
#       address, and the $ext_if interface has both IPv4 and
#       IPv6 addresses.
block in on $prv_if inet proto {tcp, udp} \
 from $prv_if:network \
 to any port 22
block in on $prv_if inet6 proto {tcp, udp} \
 from $prv_if:network \
 to any port 22
# -- block connections from external hosts to the private
#    host(s) on port 22 (SSH)
# note: you need two rules to block IPv4 and IPv6 packets, if
#       you use the :network notation instead of the numeric
#       address, and the $ext_if interface has both IPv4 and
#       IPv6 addresses.
block in on $ext_if inet proto {tcp, udp} \
 from any \
 to $prv_if:network port 22
block in on $ext_if inet6 proto {tcp, udp} \
 from any \
 to $prv_if:network port 22
# -- allow connections from external hosts to the firewall
#    on port 22 (SSH)
pass in on $ext_if inet proto tcp \
 from any port > 1023 \
 to ($ext_if) port 22
 flags S/SA modulate state
```

```
pass out on $prv_if inet proto tcp \
 from any port > 1023 \
 to ($ext_if) port 22
# -- block connections from external hosts to the firewall
#     on port 22 (SSH)
# note: you need two rules to block IPv4 and IPv6 packets, if
#       you use the ($ext_if) notation instead of the numeric
#       address, and the $ext_if interface has both IPv4 and
#       IPv6 addresses.
block in on $ext_if inet proto {tcp, udp} \
 from any \
 to ($ext_if) port 22
block in on $ext_if inet6 proto {tcp, udp} \
 from any \
 to ($ext_if) port 22
# -- allow connections from the private hosts to the firewall
#     on port 22 (SSH)
pass in on $prv_if inet proto tcp \
 from $prv_if:network port > 1023 \
 to ($prv_if) port 22
 flags S/SA modulate state
# -- block connections from private hosts to the firewall
#     on port 22 (SSH)
# note: you need two rules to block IPv4 and IPv6 packets, if
#       you use the ($ext_if) notation instead of the numeric
#       address, and the $ext_if interface has both IPv4 and
#       IPv6 addresses.
block in on $prv_if inet proto {tcp, udp} \
 from $prv_if:network \
 to ($prv_if) port 22
block in on $prv_if inet6 proto {tcp, udp} \
 from $prv_if:network \
 to ($prv_if) port 22


#### Invisible Bridge ####
# the firewall has no IP addresses assigned to its
# interfaces, the private hosts have public IP addresses
# macros for the screened host/LAN:
```

```
# ext_if -- the name of the interface connecting the firewall
#          to external hosts, the Internet, the outside world
ext_if = "ne1"
# prv_if -- the name of the interface connecting the firewall
#          to the private (internal) host(s)
prv_if = "ne1"
# prv_ad -- the addresses of the private hosts
prv_ad = "{x.x.x.a, x.x.x.b, ...}"
# filtering rules for the screeened host(s):
# -- allow connections from the private host(s) to external
#    hosts on port 22 (SSH)
pass out on $ext_if inet proto tcp \
 from $prv_ad port > 1023 \
 to any port 22 \
 flags S/SA modulate state
# -- allow connections from external hosts to the private
#    host(s) on port 22 (SSH)
pass in on $ext_if inet proto tcp \
 from any port > 1023 \
 to $prv_ad port 22 \
 flags S/SA modulate state
# -- block connections from the private host(s) to external
#    hosts on port 22 (SSH)
# note: you need two rules to block IPv4 and IPv6 packets, if
#       you use the :network notation instead of the numeric
#       address, and the $ext_if interface has both IPv4 and
#       IPv6 addresses.
block out on $ext_if inet proto {tcp, udp} \
 from $prv_ad \
 to any port 22
block out on $ext_if inet6 proto {tcp, udp} \
 from $prv_ad \
 to any port 22
# -- block connections from external hosts to the private
#    host(s) on port 22 (SSH)
# note: you need two rules to block IPv4 and IPv6 packets, if
#       you use the :network notation instead of the numeric
#       address, and the $ext_if interface has both IPv4 and
```

```
#       IPv6 addresses.
block in on $ext_if inet proto {tcp, udp} \
 from any \
 to $prv_ad port 22
block in on $ext_if inet6 proto {tcp, udp} \
 from any \
 to $prv_ad port 22



#### NAT + Screened Host/LAN ####
# the firewall has public a IP addresse assigned to its
# external interface, the private hosts also have no public IP
addresses
# macros for the screened host/LAN:
# ext_if -- the name of the interface connecting the firewall
#           to external hosts, the Internet, the outside world
ext_if = "ne1"
# prv_if -- the name of the interface connecting the firewall
#           to the private (internal) host(s)
prv_if = "ne1"
# NAT rules for the NAT + Screened Host/LAN setup:
# -- NAT connections from the private host(s) to external
#    hosts on port 22 (SSH)
nat on $ext_if inet proto tcp \
 from $prv:network port > 1023 \
 to any port 22 \
 -> ($ext_if)
# filtering rules for the NAT + Screened Host/LAN setup:
# -- allow connections from the private host(s) to external
#    hosts on port 22 (SSH)
pass out on $ext_if inet proto tcp \
 from $prv_if:network port > 1023 \
 to any port 22 \
 flags S/SA modulate state
# -- allow connections from external hosts to the firewall
#    on port 22 (SSH)
pass in on $ext_if inet proto tcp \
 from any port > 1023 \
 to ($ext_if) port 22 \
 flags S/SA modulate state
```

```
# -- block connections from external hosts to the firewall
#     on port 22 (SSH)
# note: you need two rules to block IPv4 and IPv6 packets, if
#       you use the ($ext_if) notation instead of the numeric
#       address, and the $ext_if interface has both IPv4 and
#       IPv6 addresses.
block in on $ext_if inet proto {tcp, udp} \
 from any \
 to ($ext_if) port 22
block in on $ext_if inet6 proto {tcp, udp} \
 from any \
 to ($ext_if) port 22
# -- allow connections from the private hosts to the firewall
#     on port 22 (SSH)
pass in on $prv_if inet proto tcp \
 from $prv_if:network port > 1023 \
 to ($prv_if) port 22
 flags S/SA modulate state
# -- block connections from private hosts to the firewall
#     on port 22 (SSH)
# note: you need two rules to block IPv4 and IPv6 packets, if
#       you use the ($ext_if) notation instead of the numeric
#       address, and the $ext_if interface has both IPv4 and
#       IPv6 addresses.
block in on $prv_if inet proto {tcp, udp} \
 from $prv_if:network \
 to ($prv_if) port 22
block in on $prv_if inet6 proto {tcp, udp} \
 from $prv_if:network \
 to ($prv_if) port 22
```

B.4 Adapting the Template for Other Services

You can use the rules presented in the previous section for other TCP-based protocols. In most cases, all you have to so is change the port number from 22 to something else:

- Auth (auth, port 113)
- HyperText Transfer Protocol (www port 80)
- HyperText Transfer Protocol Proxy (no single name or port, typically

8008, 8080)
- Internet Message Access Protocol, v2 (imap, port 143)
- Internet Message Access Protocol, v3 (imap3, port 220)
- Lightweight Directory Access Protocol (ldap3, port 389)
- Lightweight Directory Access Protocol over SSL (ldap3, port 636)
- Line Printer Spooler (LPD) (printer, port 515)
- IMAP over TLS/SSL (imaps, 993)
- Microsoft Global Catalog (msft-gc, port 3268)
- Microsoft Global Catalog with LDAP/SSL (msft-gc-ssl, port 3269)
- MySQL (mysql, port 3306)
- IMAP over TLS/SSL (imaps, 993)
- IRC Server (irc-serv, 529)
- PostgreSQL (postgresql, port 5432)
- Post Office Protocol, v2 (pop2, port 109)
- Post Office Protocol, v3 (pop3, port 110)
- Post Office Protocol, v3 over TLS/SSL (pop3s, port 995)
- QuickTime (rtsp port 554, 7070)
- RealAudio (rtsp port 554, 7070)
- Secure HyperText Transfer Protocol (https port 443)
- Simple Mail Transfer Protocol (smtp, port 25)
- Usenet News Transfer Protocol (nntp, port 119)
- WHOIS (whois, port 43) — allow only connections to external hosts, do not run whois services on your network.
- X Font Service (font-service, port 7100)
- X Window Server (x11, port 6000-6063) — use tunnellng to secure this service.

All rules are for IPv4 traffic (inet), if you want to adapt them to IPv6 traffic, either change inet to inet6 (if you don't want to pass/block IPv4 packets), or duplicate them changing inet to inet6.

When you want to adapt these rules to services that use TCP and UDP, simply copy the relevant pass rule and change proto tcp to proto udp and change modulate state to keep state. This will be needed in the case of Domain Name System (domain, port 53), which uses both TCP and UDP.

Should you want to adapt these rules to services that use UDP and not TCP, change proto tcp to proto udp and change modulate state to keep state in the. the relevant pass rule. This trick will work for the

Network Time Protocol (`ntp`, port 123), Trivial FTP (`tftp`, port 69), Simple Network Management Protocol (`snmp` port 161, `snmp-trap` port 162), and the X Display Management Control Protocol (`xdmcp` port 177).

Block rules can remain unchanged, unless you want to make them more specific, in which case you need to delete either `tcp` or `udp` as needed.

Rule Templates
for
Typical Firewall Configurations

The following are starting points for firewall rulesets implementing firewall designs described in Chapter 2, *Firewall Designs*.

C.1 Bastion Host

A bastion host is a lone host connected to the Internet or a LAN. It is running *pf(4)* for protection from the external threats and does not allow any inbound connections unless they are in response to its own outbound connections. An example of a bastion host would be a machine connected to the Internet via a xDSL modem.

```
# Macros
# ext_if -- the interface to the outside world
ext_if="ne0"

# Options
set require-order yes
set block-policy drop
set optimization normal
set loginterface none

# Normalize packets
scrub in all
scrub out all

# Filter packets
# block all incoming connections sent from the outside
```

```
# log all blocked packets
block in log all
# pass all connections originating from the screened
# host
pass out quick on $ext_if inet \
 from ($ext_if) to any flags S/SA keep state

# anitspoof rule on the external interface
antispoof for $ext_if
```

C.2 Bastion Host II (Some Access Allowed)

A bastion host in this example is a lone host connected to the Internet or a LAN. It is running *pf(4)* for protection from the external threats and does allow some inbound connections. An example of this kind of a bastion host would be a WWW and mail server connected to the Internet via an xDSL modem. SSH connections are allowed for administrative purposes.

```
# Macros
# ext_if -- the interface to the outside world
ext_if="ne0"

# Options
set require-order yes
set block-policy drop
set optimization normal
set loginterface none

# Normalize packets
scrub in all
scrub out all

# Filter packets
# block all incoming connections sent from the outside
# log all blocked packets
block in log all
# pass all connections originating from the bastion
# host
pass out quick on $ext_if inet \
 from ($ext_if) to any flags S/SA keep state
```

```
# pass all connections originating from external hosts to
  port 80 (WWW) on the bastion host
pass in quick on $ext_if inet proto tcp \
  from ($ext_if) \
  to ($ext_if) port 80 \
  flags S/SA synproxy state
# pass all connections originating from external hosts to
  port 22 (SSH) on the bastion host
pass in quick on $ext_if inet proto tcp \
  from ($ext_if) \
  to ($ext_if) port 22 \
  flags S/SA synproxy state
# pass all connections originating from external hosts to
  port 25 (SMTP) on the bastion host
pass in quick on $ext_if inet proto tcp \
  from ($ext_if) \
  to ($ext_if) port 25 \
  flags S/SA synproxy state

# anitspoof rule on the external interface
antispoof for $ext_if
```

C.3 Screened Host/LAN (Public IP Addresses)

A screened host or LAN is a setup with the firewall host (the machine running *pf(4)*) sitting between the outside world and the screened hosts. In this example, the firewall's external and private interfaces are assumed to have public IP addresses. The private hosts are also assumed to have public IP addresses. No inbound connections are allowed unless they are in response to the outbound connections from the screened LAN or the firewall itself. The firewall doubles as a router. An example of such setup would be a private network with no external access allowed.

```
# Macros
# ext_if -- the interface to the outside world
ext_if="ne0"
# prv_if -- the interface to the private hosts
prv_if="ne1"
# prv_hosts -- the list of addresses of hosts on the
#              screened LAN
```

```
prv_hosts = "{x.x.x.1, x.x.x.10, x.x.x.5}"

# Options
set require-order yes
set block-policy drop
set optimization normal
set loginterface none

# Normalize packets
scrub in all
scrub out all

# Filter packets
# block all incoming connections sent from the outside
# log all blocked packets
block in log all
# pass all connections originating from the firewall and
# the screened LAN
pass out quick on $ext_if inet \
 from ($ext_if) to any flags S/SA modulate state
# pass all connections originating from the screened LAN
pass in quick on $prv_if inet from $prv_hosts to any flags S/SA

# anitspoof rule on the external interface
antispoof for $ext_if
# anitspoof rule on the private interface
antispoof for $prv_if
```

C.4 Screened LAN (Some Access Allowed)

A screened host or LAN is a setup with the firewall host (the machine running *pf(4)*) sitting between the outside world and the screened hosts. In this example, the firewall's external and private interfaces are assumed to have public IP addresses. The private hosts are also assumed to have public IP addresses. Some inbound connections are allowed. The firewall doubles as a router. An example of such network would be a company network with a WWW and mail servers opened to the world and external SSH connections allowed for administrative purposes.

```
# Macros
```

```
# ext_if -- the interface to the outside world
ext_if="ne0"
# prv_if -- the interface to the private hosts
prv_if="ne1"
# prv_hosts -- the list of addresses of hosts on the
#               screened LAN
prv_hosts = "{x.x.x.1, x.x.x.10, x.x.x.5}"
# prv_www -- the address of host running the HTTP server
prv_www = "x.x.x.1"
# prv_smtp -- the address of host running the SMTP server
prv_smtp = "x.x.x.10"

# Options
set require-order yes
set block-policy drop
set optimization normal
set loginterface none

# Normalize packets
scrub in all
scrub out all

# block all incoming connections sent from the outside
# log all blocked packets
block in log all
# pass all connections originating from the firewall
# and the screened LAN
pass out quick on $ext_if inet \
 from ($ext_if) to any flags S/SA modulate state
# pass all connections originating from the screened LAN
pass in quick on $prv_if inet from $prv_hosts to any flags S/SA

# pass all connections originating from external hosts to
 port 80 (WWW) on one of the internat hosts
pass in quick on $ext_if inet proto tcp \
 from ($ext_if) \
 to $prv_www port 80 \
 flags S/SA synproxy state
# pass all connections originating from external hosts to
 port 22 (SSH) on all internal hosts
```

```
pass in quick on $ext_if inet proto tcp \
  from ($ext_if) \
  to $prv_ad port 22 \
  flags S/SA synproxy state
# pass all connections originating from external hosts to
  port 25 (SMTP) on one of the internal hosts
pass in quick on $ext_if inet proto tcp \
  from ($ext_if) \
  to $prv_smtp port 25 \
  flags S/SA synproxy state

# anitspoof rule on the external interface
antispoof for $ext_if
# anitspoof rule on the private interface
antispoof for $prv_if
```

C.5 NAT + Screened LAN

This configuration is similar to a screened LAN with public IP addresses, but only the external interface on the firewall has a public IP address. Private hosts have private IP addresses. No inbound connections are passed unless they are in response to outbound connections from the firewall or the screened LAN. The firewall doubles as a router. An example of such configuration would be a private network hidden behind a single IP address.

```
# Macros
# ext_if -- the interface to the outside world
ext_if="ne0"
# prv_if -- the interface to the private hosts
prv_if="ne1"
# prv_hosts -- the list of addresses of hosts on the
#                 screened LAN
prv_hosts = "{192.168.1.1, 192.168.1.10, 10.3.1.5}"

# Options
set require-order yes
set block-policy drop
set optimization normal
set loginterface none
```

```
# Normalize packets
scrub in all
scrub out all

# Translate packets
nat on $ext_if inet proto {tcp, udp} \
 from $prv_hosts to any -> ($ext_if)

# Filter packets
# block all incoming connections sent from the outside
# log all blocked packets
block in log all
# pass all connections originating from the firewall
pass out quick on $ext_if \
 from ($ext_if) to any flags S/SA modulate state
# pass all connections originating from the screened LAN
pass in quick on $prv_if from $prv_hosts to any flags S/SA

# anitspoof rule on the external interface
antispoof for $ext_if
# anitspoof rule on the private interface
antispoof for $prv_if
```

C.6 NAT + Screened LAN + DMZ

An extension of NAT + Screened LAN, this configuration allows external connections to be passed into a separate DMZ segment where publicly accessibile servers reside.

```
# Macros
# ext_if -- the interface to the outside world
ext_if="ne0"
# prv_if -- the interface to the private hosts
prv_if="ne1"
# dmz_if -- the interface to the DMZ
dmz_if="ne2"
# prv_hosts -- the list of addresses of hosts on the
#              screened LAN
prv_hosts = "{192.168.1.1, 192.168.1.10, 10.3.1.5}"
```

```
# dmz_hosts -- the list of addresses of hosts in the
#               DMZ
dmz_hosts = "{192.168.2.1/32, 192.168.2.2/32, 192.168.2.3}"
# dmz_www -- the address of the WWW server in the DMZ
dmz_www = "192.168.2.1/32"
# dmz_smtp -- the address of the SMTP server in the DMZ
dmz_smtp = "192.168.2.2/32"
# dmz_dns -- the address of the DNS server in the DMZ
dmz_dns = "192.168.2.3/32"

# Options
set require-order yes
set block-policy drop
set optimization normal
set loginterface none

# Normalize packets
scrub in all
scrub out all

# Translate packets
# nat for the private hosts
nat on $ext_if inet from $prv_hosts to any -> ($ext_if)
# nat for the DMZ hosts
nat on $ext_if inet from $dmz_hosts to any -> ($ext_if)
# redirect connections to port 80 (HTTP) to DMZ
rdr on $ext_if inet proto tcp \
 from any to ($ext_if) port 80 -> $dmz_www
# redirect connections to port 25 (SMTP) to DMZ
rdr on $ext_if inet proto tcp \
 from any to ($ext_if) port 25 -> $dmz_smtp
# redirect connections to port 53 (DNS) to DMZ
rdr on $ext_if inet proto {tcp, udp} \
 from any to ($ext_if) port 53 (DNS) -> $dmz_dns

# Filter packets
# block all incoming connections sent from the outside
# log all blocked packets
block in log all
# pass all connections originating from the firewall
```

```
pass out quick on $ext_if inet \
 from ($ext_if) to any flags S/SA modulate state
# pass all connections originating from the screened LAN
pass in quick on $prv_if from $prv_hosts to any flags S/SA
# pass all connections originating from the DMZ
pass in quick on $dmz_if from $dmz_hosts to any flags S/SA
# pass all connections to the WWW host in the DMZ
pass in on $ext_if from any to $dmz_www \
            port 80 flags S/SA synproxy state
# pass all connections to the SMTP host in the DMZ
pass in on $ext_if from any to $dmz_smtp \
            port 25 flags S/SA synproxy state
# pass all connections to the DNS host in the DMZ
pass in on $ext_if from any to $dmz_dns \
            port 53 flags S/SA keep state


# anitspoof rule on the external interface
antispoof for $ext_if
# anitspoof rule on the private interface
antispoof for $prv_if
```

C.7 Invisible Bridge

An invisible bridge is a host with no IP addresses assigned to it. Its general configuration is similar to the screened host/LAN setup, but the invisibility means that it cannot be easily hacked (there's no address to send malicious packets to).

```
# Macros
# ext_if -- the interface to the outside world
ext_if="ne0"
# prv_if -- the interface to the private hosts
prv_if="ne1"
# prv_hosts -- the list of addresses of hosts on the
#              screened LAN
prv_hosts = "{x.x.x.1, x.x.x.10, x.x.x.5}"

# Options
set require-order yes
set block-policy drop
```

```
set optimization normal
set loginterface none

# Normalize packets
scrub in all
scrub out all

# Filter packets
# block all incoming connections sent from the outside
# log all blocked packets
block in log on $ext_if all
# pass all connections originating from the screened LAN
pass out quick on $ext_if inet \
 from $prv_hosts to any flags S/SA modulate state

# anitspoof rule on the external interface
antispoof for $ext_if
# anitspoof rule on the private interface
antispoof for $prv_if
```

Helping OpenBSD and PF

Although OpenBSD and *pf* are free software, the world around us is a place where most things need to be paid for. Just like everyone else, developers working on OpenBSD and *pf* must pay for their food, hardware, electricity, Internet access, and many other goods and services they use in everyday life. They are people like you and me, and like all of us they will continue working on their projects for as long as long as they feel an incentive to do so. And there is really no better incentive than a fistful of green ones. What these guys need is financial security and a steady flow of cash, because the human mind works best when it does not have to think of earning money to keep itself alive and warm. So, by helping the OpenBSD project, you are helping developers focus on improving the quality of their code instead of chasing jobs and worrying about paying bills. This is good for all users of OpenBSD.

If you are still not convinced that paying developers of free software is something you should do, think about it in a slightly different way. A more selfish way. When you pay these bright people you are, in a way, securing your own future, because by giving them money you are making sure they will keep on improving the tools you get for free. The long term effects of your donations will be better tools for you, and better tools translate into serious saving and increases in revenue to your business. The good news is that you do not need to donate outrageously large amounts of money and you can do it online, with a credit card or from your PayPal account.

D.1 Buy Official CD-ROMs, T-Shirts, and Posters

There are several ways you can donate money to the OpenBSD project. One of the most popular ways to do it are purchases of the official Open-BSD CD-ROM sets published twice a year at the time of release of each new version of the OpenBSD operating system, in May and October (of course, there is nothing wrong with purchases made at other times). Apart from the official CD-ROM sets, the OpenBSD project sells t-shirts and other collectible items that help fund it. To make a purchase, visit the *Ordering* page, where you will be able to place your order online, or find addresses of your official local distributors:

http://www.openbsd.org/orders.html   *(the official OpenBSD online store)*
http://www.kd85.com   *(kd85.com, the official European distributor)*

> *Beware of freeloaders who will sell you OpenBSD on*
> *CD-ROM for very low prices. They sell what everyone*
> *can download for free from* ftp.openbsd.org *and do not*
> *donate any money to the project. This hurts the whole*
> *OpenBSD ecosystem and takes money away from the*
> *developers.*

A purchase of the official OpenBSD CD-ROM set can help you in dealings with tax authorities and software auditors. They always ask for invoices and licenses, which you can provide, if you buy OpenBSD directly from the OpenBSD project or its official distributors.

D.2 Make Small, but Regular Donations

If you cannot afford the official CD-ROM set, then by all means download the latest release for free, but remember to make a donation to the project. You can do it online with a credit card or via PayPal, the instructions are on the *Donations* page:

http://www.openbsd.org/donations.html   *(OpenBSD Donations)*

A particularly cost-effective way of helping the project without you budget even noticing it is making small, but regular contributions. Let's do some simple math. Suppose you make a monthly donation of $5. It is not a particularly huge amount of money, but if you multiply it by the number of months in a year, it translates into $60—still not a huge pile of cash. However, if only 1,000 people make such small, but regular contributions, the project will suddenly have an additional $60,000 to distribute to developers. Of course, you can choose to contribute more, as long as you can afford it. Remember that the point here is not to spend your life's savings, but to choose an amount that you will be able to contribute regularly without even noticing.

> *An added bonus of making donations to the OpenBSD*
> *project is the fact that, apart from funding the devel-*
> *opment of your favorite software, you can also make*
> *yourself famous. After you make a donation, your name*
> *goes on the list on the* Donations *page and the whole*
> *world knows that you are one of the good guys who*
> *support OpenBSD. If good karma is not enough, you can*
> *add a link to your page and get free advertising. Of*
> *course, if you prefer to remain anonymous, that can be*
> *arranged too.*

If you would like to send a check or arrange other forms of funding, you should get in touch with Theo de Raadt (the leader of the OpenBSD project). You will find the necessary details on the *Project Goals* page:

http://www.openbsd.org/goals.html   *(OpenBSD Project Goals)*

The donations you make to the OpenBSD project may not be tax deductible, but they could be written off as business costs. When in doubt, consult you accountant or tax advisor.

D.3 Hire Developers of OpenBSD and PF

If you are looking for people with deep knowledge of Unix, OpenBSD, SSH, *pf*, or network security, consider hiring developers of OpenBSD, OpenSSH, or *pf*. These people have a very intimate knowledge of the system and the Open Source software tools, and they may save you a lot of time and money. The developers of OpenBSD and *pf* are scattered around the world, and they may be living near you, or willing to relocate. Some of them may be willing to telecommute, if traveling or relocation are not possible.

How do you find them? There are several ways, depending on how open you want to be about it. The most obvious way is to check the CVS repository of the OpenBSD project and see who's working on which part of the system. Or, you could join the *misc* or *tech* mailing lists. To join, visit the *Mailing lists* page:

http://www.openbsd.org/mail.html

Note that not all people who post to *misc* are OpenBSD developers, but you will be able to find pointers to the right people, if you ask. The *tech* mailing list is reserved for technical discussion, which means that the signal-to-noise ratio is higher and it is easier to find the people you are looking for there. Should you prefer to keep a low profile, you can always write to Theo de Raadt to direct you to the right person. His address can be found on the *Project Goals* page:

http://www.openbsd.org/goals.html   *(OpenBSD Project Goals)*

If you prefer to go straight to the people you want to reach, you can always find them on the Web. For example, Daniel Hartmeier's site would be the best place to look for information about getting in touch with him:

http://www.benzedrine.cx   *(Daniel Hartmeier, developer of* pf*)*

Links to other developers' and consultants' sites can be found at dmoz.org:

http://dmoz.org/Computers/Software/Operating_Systems/Unix/BSD/
☞ *OpenBSD/Personalities/*

Others can be found with Google, simply search for: *openbsd developer*

http://www.google.com   *(Google)*

D.4 Donate Hardware

Another way to help the OpenBSD project is through donations or leases of hardware. The benefits are obvious—the more silicon to test OpenBSD on, the better. However, before you send your old server farm north to Canada, check what the project needs first. The list of current hardware requests is published on the *Hardware wanted* page:

http://www.openbsd.org/want.html   *(OpenBSD Hardware Wanted)*

D.5 Spare Some of Your Precious Time

If you are an able C programmer, you can help by pitching in and giving a hand with maintenance of existing code or by contributing your own code.

Remember though that this is a long-term commitment and requires regular participation in the core development activities.

D.6 Spread the Word

Yet another way to help OpenBSD is by spreading the word about it. As long as you don't do it like a zealot, you will find plenty of ears willing to hear the gospel. Be polite, patient, and open to questions. Learn to accept criticism. Remember that you only have one chance to make a good first impression and whatever memories you leave in the minds of the people you speak to will likely be generalized and applied to the OpenBSD community as a whole.

If you want to have something to give away at user meetings, to your friends, or to your clients, print this appendix and and pass it on to your friends and clients. To help you preserve your copy of this book, the whole appendix is available in PDF format at:

http://www.devguide.net/books/openbsdfw-02-ed/

Feel free to link to this document from your sites or pages. The more people learn how to help the OpenBSD project, the better.

D.7 Attend Training Seminars

The author of this book organizes *pf* training seminars in Europe. If you are interested in attending or would like him to do a training session in your offices, write to *jacek@devguide.net*.

A percentage of the income derived from these seminars goes straight to the OpenBSD project.

D.8 Encourage People to Buy this Book

You may not know it, but you already helped the OpenBSD project when you bought this book. The author donates at least 1 USD to the project from the sale of every copy of this book. If you like this book, recommend it to your friends.

This and other OpenBSD books written by Jacek Artymiak are available from devGuide.net and the following distributors and bookstores:

http://www.devguide.net   *(devGuide.net)*
http://www.openbsd.org/orders.html   *(the official OpenBSD online store)*
http://www.kd85.com   *(kd85.com, the official European distributor)*
http://www.lehmanns.de   *(Lehmanns Fachbuchhandlung GmbH)*
http://www.lmz.at   *(Lehrmittelzentrum Technik GmbH-LMZ)*

Bibliography

The RFC documents mentioned in this book are not listed here to save space. They are available at the *RFC-Editor* webpage:

http://www.rfc-editor.org

CERT Vulnerability notes and Advisories are available at:

http://www.cert.org

Artymiak 2003.
Jacek Artymiak. *The OpenBSD Gazetteer*. Lublin: devGuide.net, 2003.

Cheswick, Bellovin, Rubin 2003.
William R. Cheswick, Steven M. Bellovin, and Aviel D. Rubin. *Firewalls and Internet Security*. Boston: Addison-Wesley, 2003.

Dooley 2002.
Kevin Dooley. *Designing Large-Scale LANs*. Sebastopol: O'Reilly & Associates, 2002.

Farrow 2003.
Rik Farrow. *Sequence Number Attacks*. Downloaded from: *http://www.networkcomputing.com/unixworld/security/001.txt.html*, *2003.*

Frisch 2002.
Æleen Frisch. *Essential System Administration*. Sebastopol: O'Reilly & Associates, 2002.

Gast 2002.
Matthew Gast. *802.11 Wireless Networks: The Definitive Guide*. Sebastopol: O'Reilly & Associates, 2002.

Handley, Paxson, Kreibich 2001.
Mark Handley, Vern Paxson, and Christian Kreibich. *Network Intrusion Detection: Evasion, Traffic Normalization, and End-to-End Protocol Semantics.* Downloaded from:
http://www.icir.org/vern/papers/norm-usenix-sec-01-html/, 2001.

Lamb, Robbins 1998.
Linda Lamb and Arnold Robbins. *Learning the vi Editor.* Sebastopol: O'Reilly & Associates, 1998.

Limoncelli, Hogan 2002.
Thomas A. Limoncelli and Christine Hogan 2002. *The Practice of System and Network Administration.* Boston: Addison-Wesley, 2002.

Malan, Watson, Jahanian, Howell 2000.
G. Robert Malan, David Watson, Farnam Jahanian and Paul Howell. *Transport and Application Protocol Scrubbing.* Tel Aviv: IEEE Infocom, 2002. Downloaded from:
http://www.ieee-infocom.org/2000/papers/340.ps

Potter, Fleck 2002.
Bruce Potter and Bob Fleck. *802.11 Security.* Sebastopol: O'Reilly & Associates, 2002.

Rosenthal 2003.
Morris Rosenthal. *Computer Repair with Diagnostic Flowcharts.* 2003

Wessels 2001.
Duane Wessels. *Web Caching.* Sebastopol: O'Reilly & Associates, 2001.

Wright, Stevens 1994.
Gary R. Wright and W. Richard Stevens. *TCP/IP Illustrated, Volume 2: The Implementation.* Boston: Addison-Wesley, 1994.

Spurgeon 2000.
Charles E. Spurgeon. *Ethernet: The Definitive Guide.* Sebastopol: O'Reilly & Associates, 2000.

Stevens 1994.
W. Richard Stevens. *TCP/IP Illustrated, Volume 1: The Protocols.* Boston: Addison-Wesley, 1994.

Stevens 1994a.
W. Richard Stevens. *TCP/IP Illustrated, Volume 3: TCP for Transactions, HTTP, NNTP, and the UNIX® Domain Protocols.* Boston: Addison-Wesley, 1994.

Vesperman 2003.
Jennifer Vesperman 2003. *Essential CVS.* Sebastopol: O'Reilly & Associates, 2003.

Yuan, Strayer 2001.
Ruixi Yuan and W. Timothy Strayer. *Virtual Private Networks: technologies and solutions.* Boston: Addison-Wesley, 2001.

Zwicky, Cooper, Chapman 2000.
Elizabeth D. Zwicky, Simon Cooper, and D. Brent Chapman. *Building Internet Firewalls.* Sebastopol: O'Reilly & Associates, 2000.

Index

About this Book

Like many other books about Unix systems, this one too was created using standard open source tools born in the Unix environment and available for many popular commercial and free implementations of Unix.

The manuscript was created on a variety of computers running OpenBSD and Mac OS X. As he always does, the author used the *vi(1)* text editor to create and edit the manuscript. Every source file that this book was created from is stored in a CVS repository. Spelling was (hopefully) improved with the help of the immortal *ispell(1)*.

The layout of this book was implemented in *groff(1)*, a free implementation of *troff* (originally by Joseph F. Ossanna) written by James Clark and currently maintained by Werner Lemberg. Fonts used in this book are as standard as they get and come from the default set of fonts found in every implementation of *groff(1)*. All line art was created using *gpic(1)*, while tables and equations were typeset with *tbl(1)* and *eqn(1)*. Final PostScript and PDF files were generated with *groff(1)*, *gs(1)*, and *gv(1)*.

The 'packet storm' cover image was generated using Caligari trueSpace, a commercial 3d graphics and animation package. The source 3d objects used to render the final image were generated by an obscenely short Python script running in the Python interpreter built into Caligari trueSpace. After rendering, the image was transfered to Adobe Photoshop and incorporated into the final cover design.